Undergraduate Topics in C

M000165761

'Undergraduate Topics in Computer Science' (UTiCS) delivers high-quality instructional content for undergraduates studying in all areas of computing and information science. From core foundational and theoretical material to final-year topics and applications, UTiCS books take a fresh, concise, and modern approach and are ideal for self-study or for a one- or two-semester course. The texts are all authored by established experts in their fields, reviewed by an international advisory board, and contain numerous examples and problems, many of which include fully worked solutions.

The UTiCS concept relies on high-quality, concise books in softback format, and generally a maximum of 275-300 pages. For undergraduate textbooks that are likely to be longer, more expository, Springer continues to offer the highly regarded Texts in Computer Science series, to which we refer potential authors.

More information about this series at http://www.springer.com/series/7592

John Hunt

A Beginners Guide to Python 3 Programming

 Springer

John Hunt
Midmarsh Technology Ltd
Chippenham, Wiltshire, UK

ISSN 1863-7310   ISSN 2197-1781   (electronic)
Undergraduate Topics in Computer Science
ISBN 978-3-030-20289-7   ISBN 978-3-030-20290-3   (eBook)
https://doi.org/10.1007/978-3-030-20290-3

This Springer imprint is published by the registered company Springer Nature Switzerland AG
The registered company address is: Gewerbestrasse 11, 6330 Cham, Switzerland

This book was written for, and is dedicated to, my daughter Phoebe and son Adam; I could not be prouder of either of you.

Preface

There is currently huge interest in the Python programming language. This is driven by several factors; its use in schools with the Raspberry Pi platform, its ability to be used for DevOps scripts, its use in data science and machine learning and of course the language itself.

There are many books on Python, however, most assume previous programming experience or are focussed on particular aspects of Python use such as data science or machine learning or have a scientific flavor.

The aim of this book is to introduce Python to those with little or very little programming knowledge, and then to take them through to become an experienced Python developer.

As such the earlier parts of the book introduce fundamental concepts such as what a *variable* is and how a *for loop* works. In contrast, the later chapters introduce advanced concepts such as functional programming, object orientation, and exception handling.

In between a wide range of topics are introduced and discussed from a Python point of view including functions, recursion, operators, Python properties, modules and packages, protocols and monkey patching, etc.

After the core elements of Python are established, each new subject area is introduced by way of an introductory chapter presenting the topic in general, providing background on that subject, why it is of importance, etc. These introductions cover Structured Analysis, functional programming, and object orientation.

Some of the key aspects of this book are:

1. It assumes very little knowledge or experience of Python or programming.
2. It provides a basic introduction to Python as well as advanced topics such as generators and coroutines.
3. This book provides extensive coverage of object orientation and the features in Python 3 supporting classes, inheritance, and protocols.
4. Pythons' support for functional programming is also presented.

5. Following on from introducing the basic ideas behind functional programming, the book presents how advanced functional concepts such as closures, currying, and higher-order functions work in Python.
6. The book includes exercises at the end of most chapters with online solutions.
7. There are several case studies spread through the book that broaden understanding of preceding topics.
8. All code examples (and exercise solutions) are provided online in a GitHub repository.

Chapter Organization

Each chapter has a brief introduction, the main body of the chapter, followed by a list of (typically) online references that can be used for further reading.

Following this, there is typically an *Exercises* section that lists one or more exercises that build on the skills you will have learned in that chapter.

Sample solutions to the exercises are available in a GitHub online repository that supports this book.

What You Need

You can of course just read this book; however, following the examples in this book will ensure that you get as much as possible out of the content.

For this, you will need a computer.

Python is a cross-platform programming language and as such you can use Python on a Windows PC, a Linux box or an Apple Mac, etc. So you are not tied to a particular type of operating system; you can use whatever you have available.

However, you will need to install some software on that computer. At a minimum, you will need Python.

This book focusses on Python 3, so you will need that. Some guidance on this is provided in Chap. 2 on setting up your environment.

You will also need some form of editor in which to write your programs. There are numerous generic programming editors available for different operating systems with Vim on Linux, Notepad++ on Windows and Sublime Text on Windows, and Macs being popular choices.

However, using an integrated development environment (IDE) editor such as PyCharm will make writing and running your programs much easier.

Using an IDE

The IDE I prefer for Python is PyCharm, although it is not the only IDE for Python by any means, but it is a very widely used one.

Other IDEs available for Python include:

- Rodeo which is a lightweight, open source, IDE see https://rodeo.yhat.com.
- Jupyter Notebook which is a web-based IDE and is particularly good for data scientists https://jupyter.org.
- Visual Studio Code. This is a very good free editor from Microsoft that has really useful features https://code.visualstudio.com.
- Sublime Text is more of a text editor that color codes Python; however, for a simple project it may be all you need https://www.sublimetext.com.

Downloading the PyCharm IDE

PyCharm is provided by JetBrains who make tools for a variety of different languages. The PyCharm IDE can be downloaded from their site—see https://www.jetbrains.com/. Look for the menu heading 'Tools' and select that. You will see a long list of tools, which should include PyCharm.

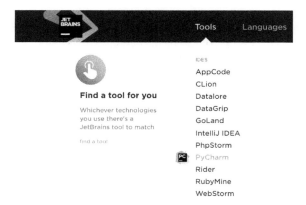

Select this option. The resulting page has a lot of information on it; however, you only need to select the 'DOWNLOAD NOW'. Make sure that you select the operating system you use (there are options for Windows, Mac OS, and Linux).

There are then two download options available: Professional and Community. The Professional version is the charged for option, while the Community version is free. For most of the work I do in Python, the Community version is more than adequate and it is therefore the version you can download and install (note with the Professional version you do get a free trial but will need to either pay for the full version at the end of the trial or reinstall the Community version at that point).

Assuming you selected the Community edition the installer will now download, and you will be prompted to run it. Note you can ignore the request to subscribe if you want.

You can now run the installer and follow the instructions provided.

Setting Up the IDE

You need to first start the PyCharm IDE. Once started, the first dialog shown to you asks if you want to import any settings you may have had for another version of PyCharm. At this point, select 'Do not import settings'.

Step through the next set of dialogs selecting the look and feel (I like the light version of the IDE), whether you want to share data with JetBrains, etc. Once you have completed this, click the 'Start PyCharm' option.

You should now be presented with the landing screen for PyCharm:

We will now create a project for you to work in. A project in PyCharm is where you write your programs and how you config what version of Python you are using and any libraries that you might need (such as graphics libraries, etc.).

Click on the 'Create New Project' option in the landing dialog.

You will now be asked where you want to create this new project. Again you can use the default location, but you will need to give it a name, I will call my project `python-intro`.

It is also worth making sure that the Python interpreter you installed has been picked up by the IDE. You can do this by opening the 'Project Interpreter: New Virtualenv environment' option and making sure that the base interpreter field is populated appropriately. This is shown below:

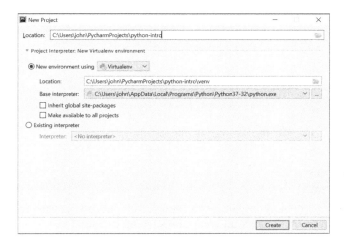

If all is OK, then select 'Create'; if the base interpreter is not specified or is incorrect, then click on the '…' button to the right of the field and browse to the appropriate location.

On opening the PyCharm project, you should see a Welcome message; click 'Close' and the project will be set up for you.

When you open the project, you will be shown at least two views. The left-hand view is the 'Project' view which shows you all the directories and files in your project. The right-hand area is where the editor is presented that allows you to type in your program. For example,

Project tree showing files and directories in the project

Editor window for writing programs in

The third area that may be shown represents the output from your program. If this is the first time you have opened the project, then it may not yet be visible. However, if you run a program, it will be shown at the bottom of the IDE. For example:

Console window for helloworld program

Conventions

Throughout this book, you will find a number of conventions used for text styles. These text styles distinguish different kinds of information.

Code words, variable sand Python values, used within the main body of the text, are shown using a `Courier` font. For example:

This program creates a top-level window (the `wx.Frame`) and gives it a title. It also creates a label (a `wx.StaticText` object) to be displayed within the frame.

In the above paragraph, wx.Frame and wx.StaticText are classes available in a Python graphical user interface library.

A block of Python code is set out as shown here:

```
num = int(input('Enter another number: '))
if num > 0:
    print(num, 'is positive')
    print(num, 'squared is ', num * num)
print('Bye')
```

Note that keywords and strings are shown in bold font.

Any command line or user input is shown in italics:

```
> python hello.py
```

Or

```
Hello, world
Enter your name: John
Hello John
```

Example Code and Sample Solutions

The examples used in this book (along with sample solutions for the exercises at the end of most chapters) are available in a GitHub repository. GitHub provides both a server environment hosting Git and a web based interface to that environment.

Git is a version control system typically used to manage source code files (such as those used to create systems in programming languages such as Python but also Java, C#, C++, Scala, etc). Systems such as Git are very useful for collaborative development as they allow multiple people to work on an implementation and to merge their work together. They also provide a useful historical view of the code (which also allows developers to roll back changes if modifications prove to be unsuitable).

If you already have Git installed on your computer, then you can clone (obtain a copy of) the repository locally using:

```
git clone https://github.com/johnehunt/beginnerspython3.git
```

If you do not have Git, then you can obtain a zip file of the examples using

```
https://github.com/johnehunt/beginnerspython3/archive/master.zip
```

You can of course install Git yourself if you wish. To do this, see https://git-scm.com/downloads. Versions of the Git client for Mac OS, Windows, and Linux/Unix are available here.

However, many IDEs such as PyCharm come with Git support and so offer another approach to obtaining a Git repository.

For more information on Git, see http://git-scm.com/doc. This Git guide provides a very good primer and is highly recommended.

Bath, UK   John Hunt

Contents

Chapter 1
Introduction

1.1 What Is Python?

Python is a general-purpose programming language in a similar vein to other programming languages that you might have heard of such as C++, JavaScript or Microsoft's C# and Oracle's Java.

It has been around for some considerable time having been originally conceived back in the 1980s by Guido van Rossum at Centrum Wiskunde & Informatica (CWI) in the Netherlands. The language is named after one of Guido's favourite programs "Monty Pythons Flying Circus", a classic and somewhat anarchic British comedy sketch show originally running from 1969 to 1974 (but which has been rerun on various stations ever since) and with several film spin offs. You will even find various references to this show in the documentation available with Python.

As a language it has gained in interest over recent years, particularly within the commercial world, with many people wanting to learn the language. This increased interest in Python is driven by several different factors:

1. Its flexibility and simplicity which makes it easy to learn.
2. Its use by the Data Science community where it provides a more standard programming language than some rivals such as R.
3. Its suitability as a scripting language for those working in the DevOps field where it provides a higher level of abstraction than alternative languages traditionally used.
4. Its ability to run on (almost) any operating system, but particularly the big three operating systems Windows, MacOS and Linux.
5. The availability of a wide range of libraries (modules) that can be used to extend the basic features of the language.
6. It is free!

© Springer Nature Switzerland AG 2019
J. Hunt, *A Beginners Guide to Python 3 Programming*,
Undergraduate Topics in Computer Science,
https://doi.org/10.1007/978-3-030-20290-3_1

Python itself is now managed by the not-for-profit Python Software Foundation (see https://en.wikipedia.org/wiki/Python_Software_Foundation) which was launched in March 2001. The mission of the foundation is to foster development of the Python community; it is also responsible for various processes within the Python community, including developing the core Python distribution, managing intellectual rights and supporting developer conferences including PyCon.

1.2   Python Versions

Currently there are two main versions of Python called Python 2 and Python 3.

- Python 2 was launched in October 2000 and has been, and still is, very widely used.
- Python 3 was launched in December 2008 and is a major revision to the language that is not backward compatible.

The issue between the two versions can be highlighted by the simple print facility:

- In Python 2 this is written as `print 'Hello World'`
- In Python 3 this is written as `print ('Hello World')`

It may not look like much of a difference but the inclusion of the `'()'` marks a major change and means that any code written for one version of Python will probably not run on the other version. There are tools available, such as the 2–3 utility, that will (partially) automate translation from Python 2 to Python 3 but in general you are still left with significant work to do.

This then raises the question which version to use?

Although interest in Python 3 is steadily increasing there are many organisations that are still using Python 2. Choosing which version to use is a constant concern for many companies.

However, the Python 2 end of life plan was initially announced back in 2015 and although it has been postponed to 2020 out of concern that a large body of existing code could not easily be forward-ported to Python 3, it is still living on borrowed time. Python 3 is the future of the Python language and it is this version that has introduced many of the new and improved language and library features (that have admittedly been back ported to Python 2 in many cases). This book is solely focussed on Python 3.

In the remainder of this book when we refer to Python we will always be referring to Python 3.

1.3 Python Programming

There are several different programming paradigms that a programming language may allow developers to code in, these are:

- **Procedural Programming** in which a program is represented as a sequence of instructions that tell the computer what it should do explicitly. Procedures and/ or functions are used to provide structure to the program; with control structures such as *if statements* and *loop constructs* to manage which steps are executed and how many times. Languages typifying this approach include C and Pascal.
- **Declarative Programming** languages, such as Prolog, that allow developers to describe how a problem should be solved, with the language/environment determining how the solution should be implemented. SQL (a database query language) is one of the most common declarative languages that you are likely to encounter.
- **Object Oriented Programming** approaches that represent a system in terms of the objects that form that system. Each object can hold its own data (also known as state) as well as define behaviour that defines what the object can do. A computer program is formed from a set of these objects co-operating together. Languages such as Java and C# typify the object oriented approach.
- **Functional Programming** languages decompose a problem into a set of functions. Each function is independent of any external state, operating only on the inputs they received to generate their outputs. The programming language Haskell is an example of a functional programming language.

Some programming languages are considered to be *hybrid* languages; that is they allow developers to utilise a combination of difference approaches within the same program. Python is an example of a hybrid programming language as it allows you to write very procedural code, to use objects in an object oriented manner and to write functional programs. Each of these approaches is covered in this book.

1.4 Python Libraries

As well as the core language, there are very many libraries available for Python. These libraries extend the functionality of the language and make it much easier to develop applications. These libraries cover

- web frameworks such as Django/Flask,
- email clients such as smtplib (a SMTP email client) and imaplib (an IMAP4 email client),
- content management operations such as the Zope library,
- lightweight concurrency (running multiple operations at the same time) using the Stackless library,
- the Generation of Microsoft Excel files using the Python Excel library,
- graphics libraries such as Matplotlib and PyOpenGL,
- machine learning using libraries such as SKLearn and TensorFlow.

A very useful resource to look at, which introduces many of these libraries (also known as modules), is the 'Python 3 module of the Week' web site which can be found at https://pymotw.com/3. This lists many of the libraries/modules available and provides a short introduction to what they do and how to use them.

1.5   Python Execution Model

Python is not a precompiled language in the way that some other languages you may have come across are (such as C++). Instead it is what is known as an interpreted language (although even this is not quite accurate). An interpreted language is one that does not require a separate compilation phase to convert the human readable format into something that can be executed by a computer. Instead the plain text version is fed into another program (generally referred to as the interpreter) which then executes the program for you.

Python actually uses an intermediate model in that it actually converts the plain text English style Python program into an intermediate 'pseudo' machine code format and it is this intermediate format that is executed. This is illustrated below:

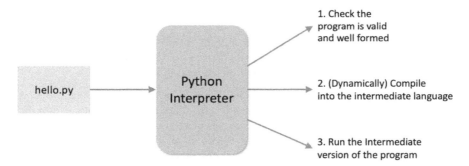

The way in which the Python interpreter processes a Python program is broken down into several steps. The steps shown here are illustrative (and simplified) but the general idea is correct.

1. First the program is checked to make sure that it is valid Python. That is a check is made that the program follows all the rules of the language and that each of the commands and operations etc. is understood by the Python environment.
2. It then translates the plain text, English like commands, into a more concise intermediate format that is easier to execute on a computer. Python can store this intermediate version in a file which is named after the original file but with a '.pyc' extension instead of a '.py' extension (the 'c' in the extension indicates it contains the compiled version of the code).
3. The compiled intermediate version is then executed by the interpreter.

When this program is rerun, the Python interpreter checks to see if a '.pyc' file is present. If no changes have been made to the source file since the '.pyc' was created, then the interpreter can skip steps 1 and 2 and immediately run the '.pyc' version of the program.

One interesting aspect of Python's usage is that it can be (and often is) used in an interactive fashion (via the REPL), with individual commands being entered and executed one at a time, with context information being built up. This can be useful in debugging situations.

1.6 Running Python Programs

There are several ways in which you can run a Python program, including

- Interactively using the Python interpreter
- Stored in a file and run using the Python command
- Run as a script file specifying the Python interpreter to use within the script file
- From within a Python IDE (Integrated Development Environment) such as PyCharm.

1.6.1 Interactively Using the Python Interpreter

It is quite common to find that people will use Python in interactive mode. This uses the Python REPL (named after **R**ead **E**valuate **P**rint **L**oop style of operation).

Using the REPL, Python statements and expressions can be typed into the Python prompt and will then be executed directly. The values of variables will be remembered and may be used later in the session.

To run the Python REPL, Python must have been installed onto the computer system you are using. Once installed you can open a Command Prompt window (Windows) or a Terminal window (Mac) and type python into the prompt. This is shown for a Windows machine below:

```
Command Prompt - python                                         —    □    ×
Microsoft Windows [Version 10.0.15063]
(c) 2017 Microsoft Corporation. All rights reserved.

C:\Users\john>python
Python 3.7.1 (v3.7.1:260ec2c36a, Oct 20 2018, 14:05:16) [MSC v.1915 32 bit (Intel)] on win32
Type "help", "copyright", "credits" or "license" for more information.
>>> print('Hello World')
Hello World
>>> 5 + 4
9
>>> name = 'John'
>>> print(name)
John
>>>
```

In the above example, we interactively typed in several Python commands and the Python interpreter 'Read' what we have typed in, 'Evaluated' it (worked out what it should do), 'Printed' the result and then 'Looped' back ready for further input. In this case we

- Printed out the string 'Hello World'.
- Added 5 and 4 together and got the result 9.
- Stored the string 'John' in a variable called name.
- Printed out the contents of the variable name.

To leave the interactive shell (the REPL) and go back to the console (the system shell), press Ctrl-Z and then Enter on Windows, or Ctrl-D on OS X or Linux. Alternatively, you could also run the Python command exit() or quit().

1.6.2   Running a Python File

We can of course store the Python commands into a file. This creates a program file that can then be run as an argument to the python command.

For example, given a file containing the following file (called hello.py) with the 4 commands in it:

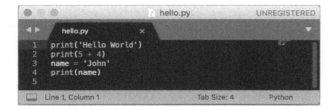

To run the hello.py program on a PC using Windows we can use the python command followed by the name of the file:

We can also run the same program on an Apple Mac using MacOS via the python interpreter. For example on a Mac we can do the following:

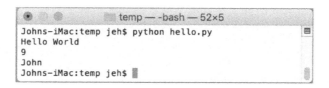

This makes it very easy to create Python programs that can be stored in files and run when needed on whatever platform is required (Windows, Linux or Mac). This illustrates the cross platform nature of Python and is just one of the reasons why Python is so popular.

1.6.3   Executing a Python Script

It is also possible to transform a file containing a stored Python program into a Script. A script is a stand-alone file that can be run directly without the need to (explicitly) use the `python` command.

This is done by adding a special line to the start of the Python file that indicates the Python command (or interpreter) to use with the rest of the file. This line must start with '#!' and must come at the start of the file.

To convert the previous section's file into a Script we would need to add the `path` to the `python` interpreter. Here *path* refers to the route that the computer must take to find the specified Python interpreter (or executable).

The exact location of the Python interpreter on your computer depends on what options were selected when you (or whoever installed Python) set it up. Typically on a Windows PC Python will be found in the 'Program Files' directory or it might be installed in its own 'Python' directory.

Whatever the location of the Python interpreter, to create a script we will need to add a first line to our hello.py file. This line must start with a #!. This combination of characters is known as a shebang and indicates to Linux and other Unix like operating systems (such as MacOS) how the remainder of the file should be executed.

For example, on a Apple Mac we might add:

`/Library/Frameworks/Python.framework/Versions/3.7/bin/python3`

When added to the `hello.py` file we now have:

However, we cannot just run the file as it stands. If we tried to run the file without any changes then we will get an error indicating that the permission to execute the file has been denied:

```
$ ./hello.py
-bash: ./hello.py: Permission denied
$
```

This is because by default you can't just run a file. We need to mark it as executable. There are several ways to do this, however one of the easiest on a Mac or Linux box is to use the chmod command (which can be used to modify the permissions associated with the file). To make the file executable we can change the file permissions to allow the file to be run by using the following command from a terminal window when we are in the same directory as the hello.py file:

```
$ chmod +x hello.py
```

Where +x indicates that we want to add the executable permission to the file.

Now if we try to run the file directly it executes and the results of the commands within the file are printed out:

```
● ● ●                    temp — -bash — 58×6
Johns-iMac:temp jeh$ chmod +x hello.py
Johns-iMac:temp jeh$ ./hello.py
Hello World
9
John
Johns-iMac:temp jeh$ █
```

Note the use of the './' preceding the file name in the above; this is used on Linux and Macs to tell the operating system to look in the current directory for the file to execute.

Different systems will store Python in different locations and thus might need different first lines, for example on a Linux we might write:

```
#!/usr/local/bin/python3
print('Hello, world')
print(5 + 4)
name = 'John'
print(name)
```

By default Windows does not have the same concept. However, to promote cross platform portability, the Python Launcher for Windows can also support this style of operation. It allows scripts to indicate a preference for a specific Python version using the same #! (Shebang) format as Unix style operating systems. We can now indicate that the rest of the file should be interpreted as a Python script; if multiple versions of Python are installed this may require Python 3 to be explicitly specified. The launcher also understands how to translate the Unix version into Windows versions so that /user/local/bin/python3 will be interpreted as indicating that python3 is required.

An example of the hello.py script for a Windows or Linux machine is given below using Notepad++ on a Windows box.

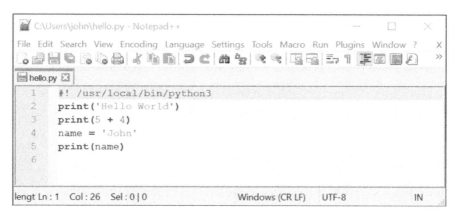

When the launcher was installed it should have been associated with Python files (i.e. files that have a '.py' extension). This means that if you double-click on one of these files from the Windows Explorer, then the Python launcher will be used to run the file.

1.6.4 Using Python in an IDE

We can also use an IDE such as PyCharm to writing and execute our Python program. The same program is shown using PyCharm below:

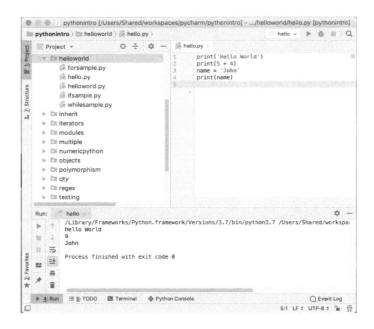

In the above figure, the simple set of commands are again listed in a file called `hello.py`. However, the program has been run from within the IDE and the output is shown in an output console at the bottom of the display.

1.7   Useful Resources

There are a wide range of resources on the web for Python; we will highlight a few here that you should bookmark. We will not keep referring to these to avoid repetition but you can refer back to this section whenever you need to:

- https://en.wikipedia.org/wiki/Python_Software_Foundation   Python   Software Foundation.
- https://docs.python.org/3/ The main Python 3 documentation site. It contains tutorials, library references, set up and installation guides as well as Python how-tos.
- https://docs.python.org/3/library/index.html A list of all the builtin features for the Python language—this is where you can find online documentation for the various class and functions that we will be using throughout this book.
- https://pymotw.com/3/ the Python 3 Module of the week site. This site contains many, many Python modules with short examples and explanations of what the modules do. A python module is a library of features that build on and expand

the core Python language. For example, if you are interested in building games using Python then pyjama is a module specifically designed to make this easier.
- https://www.fullstackpython.com/email.html is a monthly newsletter that focusses on a single Python topic each month, such as a new library or module.
- http://www.pythonweekly.com/ is a free weekly summary of the latest Python articles, projects, videos and upcoming events.

Chapter 2
Setting Up the Python Environment

2.1 Introduction

In this chapter we will check to see if you have Python installed on your computer. If you do not have Python installed we will step through the process of installing Python. This is necessary because when you run a Python program it looks for the `python` interpreter that is used to execute your program or script. Without the `python` interpreter installed on your machine Python programs are just text files!

2.2 Check to See If Python Is Installed

The first thing you should do is to see if Python 3 is already installed on your computer. First check to see that you don't have Python installed. If it is you don't need to do anything unless it is a very old version of Python 3 such as 3.1 or 3.2.

On a Windows machine you can check the version installed by opening a Command Prompt window (this can be done by searching for Cmd in the 'Type here to search' box in Windows 10).

Once the Command window is open try typing in `python`. This is illustrated below:

© Springer Nature Switzerland AG 2019
J. Hunt, *A Beginners Guide to Python 3 Programming*,
Undergraduate Topics in Computer Science,
https://doi.org/10.1007/978-3-030-20290-3_2

```
Command Prompt
Microsoft Windows [Version 10.0.15063]
(c) 2017 Microsoft Corporation. All rights reserved.

C:\Users\john>python
'python' is not recognized as an internal or external command,
operable program or batch file.

C:\Users\john>python3
'python3' is not recognized as an internal or external command,
operable program or batch file.

C:\Users\john>_
```

Note the above has tried both python and python3 in case the latest version has been installed using that name.

On a system such as a Mac you can use the Terminal and do the same thing. You will probably find that at least python (2) is pre-installed for you. For example, if you type in python on a Mac you will get something like this:

```
                                 jeh — Python — 80×9
Johns-iMac:~ jeh$ python
Python 2.7.15 (v2.7.15:ca079a3ea3, Apr 29 2018, 20:59:26)
[GCC 4.2.1 Compatible Apple LLVM 6.0 (clang-600.0.57)] on darwin
Type "help", "copyright", "credits" or "license" for more information.
>>>
```

This indicates that the above user has version 2.7.15 installed (note you may have another 2.x version installed).

However, be careful if you find that you have Python 2 installed on your machine; this book is focussed solely on Python 3.

If you have started a Python interpreter then

- Use quit() or exit() to exit the Python interpreter; exit() is an alias for quit() and is provided to make Python easier to use.

If Python 3 was not available, then the following steps will help you to install it.

If the correct version of Python is already available on your computer then you can skip to the next chapter.

2.3   Installing Python on a Windows PC

Step 1: Downloading Python

Python is available for a wide range of platforms from Windows, to Mac OS and Linux; you will need to ensure that you download the version for your operating system.

Python can be downloaded from the main Python web site which can be found at http://www.python.org

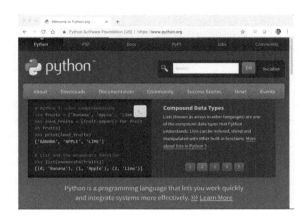

As you will see the 'Downloads' link is the second from the left on the large menu bar below the search field. Click on this and you will be taken to the download page; the current Python 3 version at the time of writing is Python 3.7 which is the version we will download. Click on the Download Python link. For example, for a Windows machine you will see:

This will download an installer for your operating system. Even if a newer version of Python is available (which is likely as the version is updated quiet frequently) the steps should be fundamentally the same.

Step 2: Running the Installer

You will now be prompted for the location to install Python, for example:

Note that it is easiest if you click on the 'Add Python 3.7 to PATH' option as this will make it available from the command line. If you don't do this then don't worry, we can add Python to the PATH later on (the PATH environment variable is used by Windows to find the location of programs such as the Python interpreter).

Next select the 'Install Now' option and follow the installation steps.

If everything went as expected you should now see an confirmatory dialog such as:

If you are on Windows now close any command windows that you have open (the PATH variable is not updated for existing Command Windows). This can be done by typing in 'exit' or closing the window.

Step 3: Set Up the PATH (optional)
If you did not select 'Add Python 3.7 to PATH' at the start of the installation you
will now need to set up the PATH environment variable. If you did then skip onto
the next step.

You can set the PATH environment variable using the system environment
variables editor.

The easiest way to find this is to type 'envir' into the Windows search box, it
will then list all applications which match this pattern including the 'Edit the system
environment variables' editor. If you are logged into your machine as a user with
'admin' rights use the first one listed, if you are logged in as a user without admin
rights select the 'Edit environment variables for your account;' option.

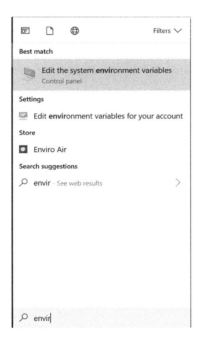

One the resulting dialog select the 'Environment Variables …' button at the
bottom of the page:

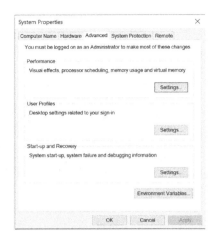

One the next dialog select the `PATH` environment variable and select Edit:

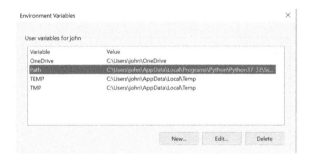

Now add the locations in which you installed Python, by default this will be something like

```
C:\Users\<username>\AppData\Local\Programs\Python\Python37-32
C:\Users\<username>\AppData\Local\Programs\Python\Python37-32\Scripts
```

Note Python37-32 should be replaced by the version of Python you are installing if it is different.

The end result should look something like:

Now click on OK until all the windows are closed.

Step 4: Verify the Installation

Next open a new Command Prompt window and type in `python` as shown below:

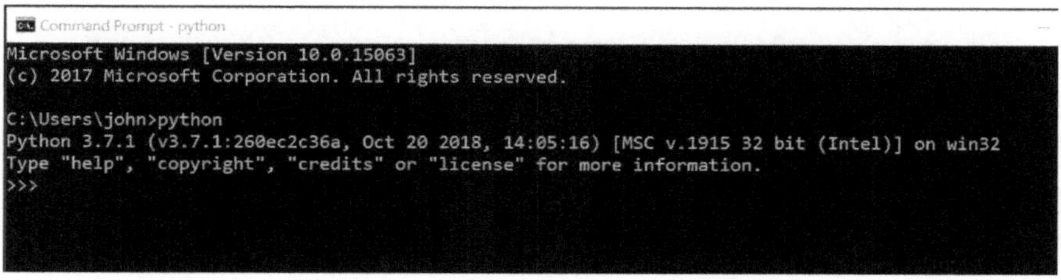

Congratulations you have installed Python and run the `python` interpreter!

Step 5: Run Some Python

Now at the '>>>' prompt type in

```
print('Hello World')
```

Be careful to make sure you use all lowercase letters for the 'print' function; Python is very case sensitive which means that as far as Python is concerned `print('Hello World')` and `Print('Hello World')` are completely different things.

Also make sure that you have single quotes around the *Hello World* text this makes it a string. If you get this right then on Windows you should see:

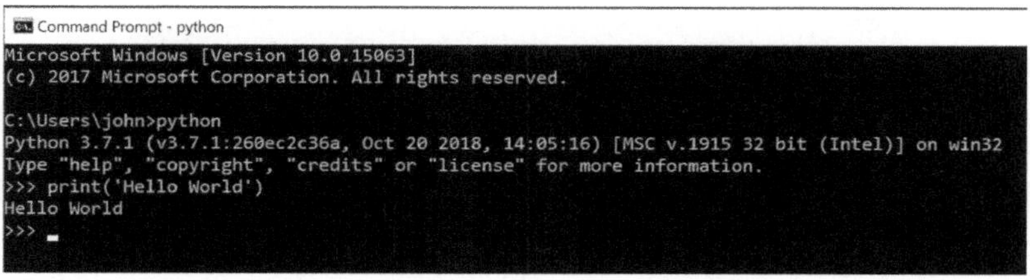

You have now run your first Python program. In this case your program printed out the message `'Hello World'` (a traditional first program in most programming languages).

Step 6: Exit the Python Interpreter

To exit the Python interpreter use `exit()` or Ctrl-Z plus Return.

```
Command Prompt

C:\Users\john>python
Python 3.7.1 (v3.7.1:260ec2c36a, Oct 20 2018, 14:05:16) [MSC v.1915 32 bit (Intel)] on win32
Type "help", "copyright", "credits" or "license" for more information.
>>> print('Hello World')
Hello World
>>> exit()

C:\Users\john>_
```

2.4   Setting Up on a Mac

Installing Python on a Mac is similar to installing it on a Windows machine in that you can download the Python installer for the Apple Mac from the Python Software Foundation web site (https://www.python.org). Of course this time you need to make sure you select the Mac OS version of the download as shown below:

From here you can select the macOS 64-bit installer (make sure you select the appropriate one for your version of the operating system). This will download an Apple package that can be installed (it will have a name similar to python-3.7.2-macos10.9.pkg although the version number of Python and the Mac OS operating system may be different). You will need to run this installer.

When you run this installer the Python Installer wizard dialog will open as shown below:

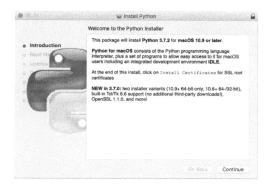

Step through the dialogs presented to you by the installer wizard accepting each option until the installation starts. Once the installation has completed you will be presented with a summary screen confirming the installation was successful. You can now close the installer.

This will have created a new folder in your Applications folder for Python 3.7.

Note that on a Mac which already has Python 2 installed (which is installed by default), Python 3 can be installed along side it and can be accessible via the `python3` command (as shown below). You should confirm that Python has been installed successfully by opening a Terminal window and entering the Python 3 REPL:

```
Last login: Tue Mar  5 17:56:21 on ttys000
Johns-iMac:~ jeh$ python3
Python 3.7.2 (v3.7.2:9a3ffc0492, Dec 24 2018, 02:44:43)
[Clang 6.0 (clang-600.0.57)] on darwin
Type "help", "copyright", "credits" or "license" for more information.
>>>
```

Now at the '>>>' prompt type in

```
print('Hello World')
```

Be careful to make sure you use all lowercase letters for the 'print' function; as Python is very case sensitive which means that as far as Python is concerned `print('Hello World')` and `Print('Hello World')` are completely different things.

The result should be as shown below:

```
●  ○  ○                    ⌂ jeh — Python — 75×10
Johns-iMac:~ jeh$ python3
Python 3.7.2 (v3.7.2:9a3ffc0492, Dec 24 2018, 02:44:43)
[Clang 6.0 (clang-600.0.57)] on darwin
Type "help", "copyright", "credits" or "license" for more information.
>>> print('Hello World')
Hello World
>>>
```

You can now exit the REPL using the `exit()` or `quit()`.

2.5   Online Resources

See the Python Standard Library documentation for:

- https://docs.python.org/3/using/index.html with documentation for Python setup and usage.
- https://docs.python.org/3/faq/windows.html Python on Windows FAQ.
- https://www.jetbrains.com/pycharm/ The PyCharm IDE home page.

Chapter 3
A First Python Program

3.1 Introduction

In this chapter we will return to the Hello World program and look at what it is doing. We will also modify it to become more interactive and will explore the concept of Python variables.

3.2 Hello World

As mentioned in the previous chapter, it is traditional to get started in a new programming language with writing a *Hello World* style program. This is very useful as it ensures that your environment, that is the interpreter, any environmental settings, your editor (or IDE) etc. are all set up appropriately and can process (or compile) and execute (or run) your program. As the 'Hello World' program is about the simplest program in any language, you are doing this without the complexities of the actual language being used.

Our 'Hello World' program has already been presented in the first chapter of this book, however we will return to it here and take a closer look at what is going on.

In Python the simplest version of the *Hello World* program merely prints out a string with the welcome message:

```
print('Hello World')
```

You can use any text editor or IDE (Integrated Development Editor) to create a Python file. Examples of editors commonly used with Python include Emacs, Vim, Notepad++, Sublime Text or Visual Studio Code; examples of IDEs for Python include PyCharm and Eclipse. Using any of these tools we can create file with a

© Springer Nature Switzerland AG 2019
J. Hunt, *A Beginners Guide to Python 3 Programming*,
Undergraduate Topics in Computer Science,
https://doi.org/10.1007/978-3-030-20290-3_3

.py extension. Such a file can contain one or more Python statements that represent a Python program or Script.

For example, we can create a file called `hello.py` containing the above `print()` function in it.

One question this raises is where does the `print()` function come from?

In fact, `print()` is a predefined function that can be used to *print things out*, for example to the user. The output is actually printed to what is known as the output stream. This handles a stream (sequence) of data such as letters and numbers. This output stream of data can be sent to an output window such as the terminal on a Mac or Command Window on a Windows PC. In this case we are printing the string `'Hello World'`.

By *predefined* here we mean that it is built into the Python environment and is understood by the Python interpreter. This means that the interpreter knows where to find the definition of the `print()` function which tells it what to do when it encounters the `print()` function.

You can of course write your own functions and we will be looking at how to do that later in this book.

The `print()` function actually tries to print whatever you give it,

- when it is given a string it will print a string,
- if it is given an integer such as `42` it will print `42` and
- if it is a given a floating point number such as `23.56` then it will print 23.56.

Thus, when we run this program, the string 'Hello World' is printed out to the console window.

Also note that the text forming the Hello World string is wrapped within two single quote characters; these characters delimit the start and end of the string; if you miss one of them out then there will be an error.

To run the program, if you are using an IDE such as PyCharm, then you can select the file in the left hand tree and from the right mouse button select Run. If you want to run this program again you can merely click on the green arrow in the tool bar at the top of the IDE.

If you are running it from the command line type in `python` followed by the name of the file, for example:

```
> python hello.py
```

This should be done in the directory where you created the file.

3.3 Interactive Hello World

Let us make our program a little more interesting; lets get it to ask us our name and say hello to us personally.

The updated program is:

```
print('Hello, world')
user_name = input('Enter your name: ')
print('Hello ', user_name)
```

Now after printing the original 'Hello World' string, the program then has two additional statements.

The result of running this program is:

```
Hello, world
Enter your name: John
Hello John
```

We will look at each of the new statements separately.
The first statement is:

```
user_name = input('Enter your name: ')
```

This statement does several things. It first executes another function called `input()`. This function is passed a string—which is known as an argument—to use when it prompts the user for input.

This function `input()`, is again a *built-in* function that is part of the Python language. In this case it will display the string you provide as a prompt to the user and wait until the user types something in followed by the return key.

Whatever the user types in is then returned as the result of executing the `input()` function. In this case that result is then stored in the *variable* `user_name`.

A *variable* is a named area of the computers' memory that can be used to hold things (often referred to as data) such as strings, numbers, boolean such as True/False etc. In this case the variable *user_name* is acting as a label for an area of memory which will hold the string entered by the user. The basic idea is illustrated in the following diagram:

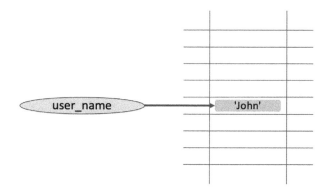

This simplified picture illustrates how a variable, such as `user_name`, can reference an area of memory containing actual data. In this diagram the memory is shown as a two dimensional grid of memory *locations*. Each location has an address associated with it. This address is unique within the memory and can be used to return to the data held at that location. This address is often referred to as the memory address of the data. It is this memory address that is actually held in the variable `user_name`; this is why the `user_name` variable is shown as pointing to the area in memory containing the string 'John'.

Thus the variable `user_name` allows us to access this area of memory easily and conveniently.

For example, if we want to get hold of the name entered by the user in another statement, we can do so merely by referencing the variable `user_name`. Indeed, this is exactly what we do in the second statement we added to our program. This is shown below:

```
print('Hello', user_name)
```

The last statement again uses the built-in `print()` function, but this time it takes two arguments. This is because the `print()` function can actually take a variable number of arguments (data items that we pass into it). Each argument is separated by a comma. In this case we have passed in the string 'Hello' and whatever value is referenced by (present at the memory address indicated by) the variable `user_name`.

3.4   Variables

You may wonder why the element holding the user's name above is referred to as a *variable*. It is a called a variable because the value it references in memory can vary during the lifetime of the program.

For example we can modify our *Hello World* program to ask the user for the name of their best friend and print out a welcome message to that best friend. If we want to, we can *reuse* the variable to hold the name of that best friend. For example:

```
print('Hello, world')
name = input('Enter your name: ')
print('Hello', name)
name = input('What is the name of your best friend: ')
print('Hello Best Friend', name)
```

When we run this version of the program and the user enters 'John' for their name and 'Denise' for their best friends' name we will see:

```
Hello, world
Enter your name: John
Hello John
What is the name of your best friend: Denise
Hello Best Friend Denise
```

As you can see from this when the string 'Hello Best Friend' is printed, it is the name 'Denise' that is printed alongside it.

This is because the area of memory that previously held the string 'John' now holds the string 'Denise'.

In fact, in Python the variable name is not restricted to holding a string such as 'John' and 'Denise'; it can also hold other types of data such as numbers or the values True and False. For example:

```
my_variable = 'John'
print(my_variable)
my_variable = 42
print(my_variable)
my_variable = True
print(my_variable)
```

The result of running the above example is

```
John
42
True
```

As you can see my_variable first holds (or references the area of memory containing) the string 'John', it then holds the number 42 and finally it holds the Boolean value True (Boolean values can only be True or False).

This is referred to in Python as *Dynamic Typing*. That is the *type* of the data held by a variable can *Dynamically* change as the program executes. Although this may seem like the obvious way to do things; it is not the approach used by many programming languages such as Java and C# where variables are instead *Statically Typed*. The word static is used here to indicate that the type of data that a variable can hold will be determined when the program is first processed (or compiled). Later on it will not be possible to change the type of data it can hold; thus if a variable is to hold a number it cannot later on hold a String. This is the approach adopted by languages such as Java and C#.

Both approaches have their pros and cons; but for many people the flexibility of Pythons variables are one of its major advantages.

3.5   Naming Conventions

You may have noticed something above some of the variable names we have
introduced above such as `user_name` and `my_variable`. Both these variable
names are formed of a set of characters with an underbar between the 'words' in the
variable name.

Both these variable names highlight a very widely used naming convention in
Python, which is that variable names should:

- be all lowercase,
- be in general more descriptive than variable names such as *a* or *b* (although
  there are some exceptions such as the use of variables *i* and *j* in looping
  constructs).
- with individual words separated by underscores as necessary to improve
  readability.

This last point is very important as in Python (and most computer programming
languages) spaces are treated as separators which can be used to indicate where one
thing ends and another starts. Thus it is not possible to define a variable name such
as:

- user name

As the space is treated by Python as a separator and thus Python thinks you are
defining two things 'user' and 'name'.

When you create your own variables, you should try to name then following the
Python accepted style thus name such as:

- `my_name, your_name, user_name, account_name`
- `count, total_number_of_users, percentage_passed, pass_`
  `rate`
- `where_we_live, house_number,`
- `is_okay, is_correct, status_flag`

  are all acceptable but

- `A, Aaaaa, aaAAAaa`
- `Myname, myName, MyName or MYName`
- `WHEREWELIVE`

  Do not meet the accepted conventions.

However, it is worth mentioning that these are merely commonly adhered to
conventions and even Python itself does not always comply with these conventions.
Thus if you define a variable name that does not conform to the convention Python
will not complain.

3.6 Assignment Operator

One final aspect of the statement shown below has yet to be considered

```
user_name = input('Enter your name: ')
```

What exactly is this '=' between the user_name variable and the input() function?

It is called the *assignment* operator. It is used to assign the value returned by the function input() to the variable user_name. It is probably the most widely used operator in Python. Of course, it is not just used to assign values from functions as the earlier examples illustrated. For example, we also used it when we stored a string into a variable directly:

```
my_variable = 'Jason'
```

3.7 Python Statements

Throughout this chapter we have used the phrase statement to describe a portion of a Python program, for example the following line of code is a statement that prints out a string 'Hello' and the value held in user_name.

```
print('Hello', user_name)
```

So what do we mean by a statement? In Python a statement is an instruction that the Python interpreter can execute. This statement may be formed of a number of elements such as the one above which includes a call to a function and an assignment of a value to a variable. In many cases a statement is a single line in your program but it is also possible for a statement to extend over several lines particularly if this helps the readability or layout of the code. For example, the following is a single statement but it is laid out over 6 lines of code to make it easier to read:

```
print('The total population for',
      city,
      'was',
      number_of_people_in_city,
      'in',
      year)
```

As well as statements there are also expressions. An expression is essentially a computation that generates a value, for example:

```
4 + 5
```

This is an expression that adds 4 and 5 together and generates the value 9.

3.8   Comments in Code

It is common practice (although not universally so) to add comments to code to help anyone reading the code to understand what the code does, what its intent was, any design decisions the programmer made etc.

Comments are sections of a program that are ignored by the Python interpreter—they are not executable code.

A comment is indicated by the '#' character in Python. Anything following that character to the end of the line will be ignored by the interpreter as it will be assumed to be a comment, for example:

```
# This is a comment
name = input('Enter your name: ')
# This is another comment
print(name)  # this is a comment to the end of the line
```

In the above, the two lines starting with a # are comments—they are for our human eyes only. Interestingly the line containing the `print()` function also has a comment—that is fine as the commend starts with the # and runs to the end of the line, anything *before* the # character is not part of the comment.

3.9   Scripts Versus Programs

Python can be run in several ways:

- Via the Python interpreter by entering the REPL; the interactive Python session.
- By having the Python interpreter run a file containing stored Python commands.
- By setting up an association at the operating system level so that any files ending with `.py` are always run by the Python interpreter.
- By indicating the Python interpreter to use at the start of the Python file. This is done by including a first line in a file with something similar to '`#!/usr/bin/env python`'. This indicates that the rest of the file should be passed to the Python interpreter.

All of these can be defined as a way to run a Python program or indeed a Python script.

However, for the purposes of this book we will treat a file containing a first line specifying the Python interpreter to use as a script. All other Python code that represents some code to execute for a specific purpose will be called a Python program. However, this is really only a distinction being made here to simplify terminology.

3.10 Online Resources

See the Python Standard Library documentation for:

- https://docs.python.org/3/reference/simple_stmts.html   For   information   on statements in Python.

3.11 Exercises

At this point you should try to write your own Python program. It is probably easiest to start by modifying the *Hello World* program we have already been studying. The following steps take you through this:

1. If you have not yet run the *Hello World* program, then do so now. To run your program you have several options. The easiest if you have set up an IDE such as PyCharm is to use the 'run' menu option. Otherwise if you have set up the Python interpreter on your computer, you can run it from a command prompt (on Windows) or a Terminal window (on a Mac/Linux box).
2. Now ensure that you are comfortable with what the program actually does. Try commenting out some lines—what happens; is that the behaviour you expected? check that you are happy with what it does.
3. Once you have done that, modify the program with your own prompts to the user (the string argument given to the input function). Make sure that each string is surrounded by the single quote characters ("); remember these denote the start and end of a string.
4. Try creating your own variables and storing values into those instead of the variable user_name.
5. Add a print() function to the program with your own prompt.
6. Include an assignment that will add two numbers together (for example 4 + 5) and then assign the result to a variable.
7. Now print out that variables value once it has been assigned a value.
8. Make sure you can run the program after each of the above changes. If there is an error reported attempt to fix that issue before moving on.

You must also be careful with the indentation of your program—Python is very sensitive to how code is laid out and at this point all statements should start at the beginning of the line.

Chapter 4
Python Strings

4.1 Introduction

In the previous chapter we used strings several times, both as prompts to the user and as output from the `print()` function. We even had the user type in their name and store it in a variable that could be used to access this name at a later point in time. In this chapter we will explore what a string is and how you can work with and manipulate them.

4.2 What Are Strings?

During the description of the *Hello World* program we referred to Python strings several times, but what is a string?

In Python a string is a series, or sequence, of characters in order. In this definition a *character* is anything you can type on the keyboard in one keystroke, such as a letter 'a', 'b', 'c' or a number '1', '2', '3' or a special characters such as '\', '[', '$' etc. a space is also a character ' ', although it does not have a visible representation.

It should also be noted that strings are *immutable*. Immutable means that once a string has been created it cannot be changed. If you try to change a string you will in fact create a new string, containing whatever modifications you made, you will not affect the original string in anyway. For the most part you can ignore this fact but it means that if you try to get a sub string or split a string you must remember to store the result—we will see this later on in this chapter.

To define the start and end of a string we have used the single quote character ', thus all of the following are valid strings:

- `'Hello'`
- `'Hello World'`
- `'Hello Andrea2000'`
- `'To be or not to be that is the question!'`

We can also define an empty string which has no characters in it (it is defined as a single quote followed immediately by a second single quote with no gap between them). This is often used to initialise or reset a variable holding a reference to a string, for example

- `some_string = ''`

4.3   Representing Strings

As stated above; we have used single quotes to define the start and end of a string, however in Python single or double quotes can be used to define a string, thus both of the following are valid:

- `'Hello World'`
- `"Hello World"`

In Python these forms are exactly the same, although by convention we default to using single quotes. This approach is often referred to as being more Pythonic (which implies it is more the convention used by experienced Python programmers) but the language does not enforce it.

You should note however, that you cannot mix the two styles of start and end strings, that is you cannot start a string with a single quote and end a string with a double quote, thus the following are both illegal in Python:

- `'Hello World" # This is illegal`
- `"Hello World' # So is this`

The ability to use both " and ' however, comes in useful if your string needs to contain one of the other type of string delimiters. This is because a single quote can be embedded in a string defined using double quotes and vice versa, thus we can write the following:

```
print("It's the day")
print('She said "hello" to everyone')
```

The output of these two lines is:

```
It's the day
She said "hello" to everyone
```

A third alternative is the use of triple quotes, which might at first hand seem a bit unwieldy, but they allow a string to support multi-line strings, for example:

```
z = """
Hello
 World
"""
```
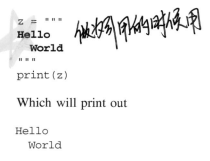

```
print(z)
```

Which will print out

```
Hello
 World
```

4.4   What Type Is String

It is often said that Python is untyped; but this is not strictly true—as was stated in an earlier chapter it is a dynamically typed language with all data having an associated type.

The type of an item of data (such as a string) determines what it is legal to do with the data and what the effect of various actions will be. For example, what the effect of using a '+' operator is will depend on the *types* involved; if they are numbers then the plus operator will add them together; if however strings are involved then the strings will be concatenated (combined) together etc.

It is possible to find out what type a variable currently holds using the built-in type() function. This function takes a variable name and will return the type of the data held by that variable, for example:

```
my_variable = 'Bob'
print(type(my_variable))
```

The result of executing these two lines of code is the output:

```
<class 'str'>
```

This is a shorthand for saying that what is held in my_variable is currently a class (type) of string (actually string is a class and Python supports ideas from Object Oriented Programming such as classes and we will encounter them later in the book).

4.5   What Can You Do with Strings?

In Python terms this means what operations or functions are their available or built-in that you can use to work with strings. The answer is that there are very many. Some of these are described in this section.

4.5.1 String Concatenation

You can concatenate two strings together using the '+' operator (an operator is an operation or behaviour that can be applied to the types involved). That is you can take one string and add it to another string to create a new third string:

```
string_1 = 'Good'
string_2 = " day"
string_3 = string_1 + string_2
print(string_3)
print('Hello ' + 'World')
```

The output from this is

```
Good day
Hello World
```

Notice that the way in which the string is defined does not matter here, string_1 used single quotes but string_2 used double quotes; however they are both just strings.

4.5.2 Length of a String

It can sometimes be useful to know how long a string is, for example if you are putting a string into a user interface you might need to know how much of the string will be displayed within a field. To find out the length of a string in Python you use the len() function, for example:

```
print(len(string_3))
```

This will print out the length of the string currently being held by the variable string_3 (in terms of the number of characters contained in the string).

4.5.3 Accessing a Character

As a string is a fixed sequence of letters, it is possible to use square brackets and an index (or position) to retrieve a specific character from within a string. For example:

```
my_string = 'Hello World'
print(my_string[4])
```

However, you should note that strings are indexed from *Zero!* This means that the first character is in position 0, the second in position 1 etc. Thus stating [4] indicates that we want to obtain the fifth character in the string, which in this case is the letter 'o'. This form of indexing elements is actually quite common in programming languages and is referred to a *zero based indexing*.

4.5.4   Accessing a Subset of Characters

It is also possible to obtain a subset of the original string, often referred to as a substring (of the original string). This can again be done using the square brackets notation but using a ':' to indicate the start and end points of the sub string. If one of the positions is omitted then the start or end of the string is assumed (depending upon the omission), for example:

```
my_string = 'Hello World'
print(my_string[4])    # characters at position 4
print(my_string[1:5])  # from position 1 to 5
print(my_string[:5])   # from start to position 5
print(my_string[2:])   # from position 2 to the end
```

Will generate

```
o
ello
Hello
llo World
```

As such `my_string[1:5]` returns the substring containing the 2nd to 6th letters (that is `'ello'`). In turn `my_string[:5]` returned the substring containing the 1st to 6th letters and `my_string[2:]` the sub string containing the 3rd to the last letters.

4.5.5   Repeating Strings

We can also use the '*' operator with strings. In the case of strings this means repeat the given string a certain number of times. This generates a new string containing the original string repeated *n* number of times. For example:

```
print('*' * 10)
print('Hi' * 10)
```

Will generate

```
**********
HiHiHiHiHiHiHiHiHiHi
```

4.5.6 Splitting Strings

A very common requirement is the need to split a string up into multiple separate strings based on a specific character such as a space or a comma.

This can be done with the split() function, that takes a string to used in identifying how to split up the receiving string. For example:

```
title = 'The Good, The Bad, and the Ugly'
print('Source string:', title)
print('Split using a space')
print(title.split(' '))
print('Split using a comma')
print(title.split(','))
```

This produces as output

```
Source string: The Good, The Bad, and the Ugly
Split using a space
['The', 'Good,', 'The', 'Bad,', 'and', 'the', 'Ugly']
Split using a comma
['The Good', ' The Bad', ' and the Ugly']
```

As can be seen from this the result generated is either a list of each word in the string or three strings as defined by the comma.

You may have noticed something odd about the way in which we wrote the call to the split operation. We did not pass the string into split() rather we used the format of the variable containing the string followed by '.' and then split().

This is because split() is actually what is referred to as a *method*. We will return to this concept more when we explore classes and objects. For the moment merely remember that methods are *applied* to things like string using the *dot* notation.

For example, given the following code

```
title = 'The Good, The Bad, and the Ugly'
print(title.split(' '))
```

This means take the string held by the variable title and split it based on the character space.

4.5.7 Counting Strings

It is possible to find out how many times a string is repeated in another string. This is done using the count() operation for example

```
my_string = 'Count, the number     of spaces'
print("my_string.count(' '):", my_string.count(' '))
```

Which has the output

```
my_string.count(' '): 8
```

indicating that there are 8 spaces in the original string.

4.5.8   Replacing Strings

One string can replace a substring in another string. This is done using the replace() method on a string. For example:

```
welcome_message = 'Hello World!'
print(welcome_message.replace("Hello", "Goodbye"))
```

The output produced by this is thus

```
Goodbye World!
```

4.5.9   Finding Sub Strings

You can find out if one string is a substring of another string using the find() method. This method takes a second string as a parameter and checks to see if that string is in the string receiving the find() method, for example:

```
string.find(string_to_find)
```

The method returns −1 if the string is not present. Otherwise it returns an index indicating the start of the substring. For example

```
print('Edward Alun Rawlings'.find('Alun'))
```

This prints out the value 5 (the index of the first letter of the substring 'Alun' note strings are indexed from Zero; thus the first letter is at position Zero, the second at position one etc.

In contrast the following call to the find() method prints out −1 as 'Alun' is no longer part of the target string:

```
print('Edward John Rawlings'.find('Alun'))
```

4.5.10   Converting Other Types into Strings

If you try to use the '+' concatenation operator with a string and some other type such as a number then you will get an error. For example if you try the following:

```
msg = 'Hello Lloyd you are ' + 21
print(msg)
```

You will get an *error* message indicating that you can only concatenate strings with strings not integers with strings. To concatenate a number such as 21 with a string you must convert it to a string. This can be done using the str() function. This contest any type into a string representation of that type. For example:

```
msg = 'Hello Lloyd you are ' + str(21)
print(msg)
```

This code snippet will print out the message:

```
Hello Lloyd you are 21
```

4.5.11   Comparing Strings

To compare one string with another you can use the '==' equality and '!=' not equals operators. These will compare two strings and return either True or False indicating whether the strings are equal or not. For example:

```
print('James' == 'James')  # prints True
print('James' == 'John')   # prints False
print('James' != 'John')   # prints True
```

You should note that strings in Python are case sensitive thus the string 'James' does not equal the string 'james'. Thus:

```
print('James' == 'james') # prints False
```

4.5.12   Other String Operations

There are in fact very many different operations available for strings, including checking that a string starts or ends with another string, that is it upper or lower case etc. It is also possible to replace part of a string with another string, convert strings to upper, lower or title case etc.

Examples of these are given below (note all of these operations use the dot notation):

```
some_string = 'Hello World'
print('Testing a String')
print('-' * 20)
print('some_string', some_string)
print("some_string.startswith('H')",
some_string.startswith('H'))
print("some_string.startswith('h')",
some_string.startswith('h'))
print("some_string.endswith('d')", some_string.endswith('d'))
print('some_string.istitle()', some_string.istitle())
print('some_string.isupper()', some_string.isupper())
print('some_string.islower()', some_string.islower())
print('some_string.isalpha()', some_string.isalpha())

print('String conversions')
print('-' * 20)
print('some_string.upper()', some_string.upper())
print('some_string.lower()', some_string.lower())
print('some_string.title()', some_string.title())
print('some_string.swapcase()', some_string.swapcase())
print('String leading, trailing spaces', "   xyz   ".strip())
```

The output from this is

```
Testing a String
--------------------
some_string Hello World
some_string.startswith('H') True
some_string.startswith('h') False
some_string.endswith('d') True
some_string.istitle() True
some_string.isupper() False
some_string.islower() False
some_string.isalpha() False
String conversions
--------------------
some_string.upper() HELLO WORLD
some_string.lower() hello world
some_string.title() Hello World
some_string.swapcase() hELLO wORLD
String leading, trailing spaces xyz
```

4.6   Hints on Strings

4.6.1   Python Strings Are Case Sensitive

In Python the string 'l' is not the same as the string 'L'; one contains the lower-case letter 'l' and one the upper-case letter 'L'. If case sensitively does not matter to you then you should convert any strings you want to compare into a common case before doing any testing; for example using `lower()` as in

```
some_string.lower().startswith('h')
```

4.6.2   Function/Method Names

Be very careful with capitalisation of function/method names; in Python `isupper()` is a completely different operation to `isUpper()`. If you use the wrong case Python will not be able to find the required function or method and will generate an error message. Do not worry about the terminology regarding functions and methods at this point—for now they can be treated as the same thing and only differ in the way that they recalled or invoked.

4.6.3   Function/Method Invocations

Also be careful of always including the round brackets when you call a function or method; even if it takes no parameters/arguments. There is a significant difference between `isupper` and `isupper()`. The first one is the *name* of an operation on a string while the second is a call to that operation so that the operation executes. Both formats are legal Python but the result is very different, for example:

```
print(some_string.isupper)
print(some_string.isupper())
```

produces the output:

```
<built-in method isupper of str object at 0x105eb19b0>
False
```

Notice that the first print out tells you that you are referring to the built-in method called `isupper` defined on the type String; while the second actually runs `isupper()` for you and returns either `True` or `False`.

4.7 String Formatting

Python provides a sophisticated formatting system for strings that can be useful for printing information out or logging information from a program.

The string formatting system uses a special string known as the *format* string that acts as a pattern defining how the final string will be laid out. This format string can contain placeholders that will be replaced with actual values when the final string is created. A set of values can be applied to the format string to fill the placeholders using the `format()` method.

The simplest example of a *format* string is one that provides a single placeholder indicated by two curly braces (e.g. `{}`). For example, the following is a *format* string with the pattern 'Hello' followed by a placeholder:

```
format_string = 'Hello {}!'
```

This can be used with the `format()` string method to provide a value (or populate) the placeholder, for example:

```
print(format_string.format('Phoebe'))
```

The output from this is:

```
Hello Phoebe!
```

A *format* string can have any number of placeholders that must be populated, for example the next example has two placeholders that are populated by providing two values to the `format()` method:

```
# Allows multiple values to populate the string
name = "Adam"
age = 20
print("{} is {} years old".format(name, age))
```

In this case the output is:

```
Adam is 20 years old
```

It also illustrates that variables can be used to provide the values for the `format` method as well as literal values. A literal value is a fixed value such as 42 or the string 'John'.

By default the values are bound to the placeholders based on the order that they are provided to the `format()` method; however this can be overridden by providing an *index* to the placeholder to tell it which value should be bound, for example:

```
# Can specify an index for the substitution
format_string = "Hello {1} {0}, you got {2}%"
print(format_string.format('Smith', 'Carol', 75))
```

In this case the second string 'Carol' will be bound the first placeholder; note that the parameters are numbered from *Zero* not one.

The output from the above example is:

```
Hello Carol Smith, you got 75%
```

Of course when ordering the values it is quiet easy to get something wrong either because a developer might think the strings are indexed from 1 or just because they get the order wrong.

An alternative approach is to use *named* values for the placeholders. In this approach the curly brackets surround the name of the value to be substituted, for example {artist}. Then in the format() method a *key=value* pair is provided where the key is the name in the *format* string; this is shown below:

```
# Can use named substitutions, order is not significant
format_string = "{artist} sang {song} in {year}"
print(format_string.format(artist='Paloma Faith',
song='Guilty', year=2017))
```

In this example the order no longer matters as the name associated with the parameter passed into the format() method is used to obtain the value to be substituted. In this case the output is:

```
Paloma Faith sang Guilty in 2017
```

It is also possible to indicate alignment and width within the format string. For example, if you wish to indicate a width to be left for a placeholder whatever the actual value supplied, you can do this using a colon (':') followed by the width to use. For example to specify a gap of 25 characters which can be filled with a substitute value you can use {:25} as shown below:

```
print('|{:25}|'.format('25 characters width'))
```

In the above the vertical bars are merely being used to indicate where the string starts and ends for reference, they have no meaning within the format method. This produces the output:

```
|25 characters width      |
```

Within this gap you can also indicate an alignment where:

- < Indicates left alignment (the default),
- > Indicates right alignment,
- ^ Indicates centered.

These follow the colon (':') and come before the size of the gap to use, for example:

```
print('|{:<25}|'.format('left aligned')) # The default
print('|{:>25}|'.format('right aligned'))
print('|{:^25}|'.format('centered'))
```

Which produces:

```
|left aligned             |
|            right aligned|
|         centered        |
```

Another formatting option is to indicate that a number should be formatted with separators (such as a comma) to indicate thousands:

```
# Can format numbers with comma as thousands separator
print('{:,}'.format(1234567890))
print('{:,}'.format(1234567890.0))
```

Which generates the output:

```
1,234,567,890
1,234,567,890.0
```

There are in fact numerous options available to control the layout of a value within the format string and the Python documentation should be referenced for further information.

4.8 String Templates

An alternative to using string formatting is to use string *Templates*. These were introduced into Python 2.4 as a simpler, less error prone, solution to most string formatting requirements.

A string template is a class (type of thing) that is created via the `string`. `Template()` function. The template contains one or more *named* variables preceded with a $ symbol. The Template can then be used with a set of values that replace the template variables with actual values.

For example:

```
import string

# Initialise the template with ¢variables that
# will be substitute with actual values
template = string.Template('$artist sang $song in $year')
```

Note that it is necessary to include an *import* statement at the start of the program as Templates are not provided by default in Python; they must be loaded from a library of additional string features. This library is part of Python but you need to tell Python that you want to access these extra string facilities.

We will return to the import statement later in the book; for now just except that it is needed to access the Template functionality.

The Template itself is created via the string.Template() function. The string passed into the string.Template() function can contain any characters plus the template variables (which are indicated by the $ character followed by the name of the variable such as $artist above).

The above is thus a template for the pattern '*some-artist* sang *some-song* in *some-year*'.

The actual values can be substituted into the template using the substitute() function. The substitute function takes a set of *key=value* pairs, in which the *key* is the name of the template variable (minus the leading $ character) and the *value* is the value to use in the string.

```
print(template.substitute(artist='Freddie Mercury', song='The
Great Pretender', year=1987))
```

In this example $artist will be replaced by 'Freddie Mercury', $song by 'The Great Pretender' and $year by 1987. The substitute function will then return a new string containing

```
'Freddie Mercury sang The Great Pretender in 1987'
```

This is illustrated in the following code:

```
import string

# Initialise the template with $variables that
# will be substitute with actual values
template = string.Template('$artist sang $song in $year')

# Replace / substitute template variables with actual values
# Can use a key = value pairs where the key is the name of
# the template Variable and the value is the value to use
# in the string
print(template.substitute(artist='Freddie Mercury', song='The
Great Pretender', year=1987))
```

This produces:

```
Freddie Mercury sang The Great Pretender in 1987
```

We can of course reuse the template by substituting other values for the template variables, each time we call the `substitute()` method it will generate a new string with the template variables replaced with the appropriate values:

```
print(template.substitute(artist='Ed Sheeran', song='Galway
Girl', year=2017))
print(template.substitute(artist='Camila Cabello',
song='Havana', year=2018))
```

With the above producing:

```
Ed Sheeran sang Galway Girl in 2017
Camila Cabello sang Havana in 2018
```

Alternatively you can create what is known as a dictionary. A dictionary is a structure comprised of *key:value* pairs in which the key is unique. This allows a *data structure* to be created containing the values to use and then applied to the substitute function:

```
d = dict(artist = 'Billy Idol', song='Eyes Without a Face',
year = 1984)
print(template.substitute(d))
```

This produces a new string:

```
Billy Idol sang Eyes Without a Face in 1984
```

We will discuss dictionaries in greater detail later in the book.

Template strings can contain template variables using the format `$name-of-variable`; however there are a few variations that are worth noting:

- `$$` allows you to include a '$' character in the string without Python interpreting it as the start of a template variable this the double '$$' is replaced with a single $. This is known as *escaping a control* character.
- `${template_variable}` is equivalent to `$template_variable`. It is required when valid identifier characters follow the placeholder but are not part of the placeholder, such as "`${noun}ification`".

Another point to note about the `template.substitute()` function is that if you fail to provide all the template variables with a value then an *error* will be generated. For example:

```
print(template.substitute(artist='David Bowie', song='Rebel
Rebel'))
```

Will result in the program failing to execute and an error message being generated:

```
Traceback (most recent call last):
  File "/emplate_examples.py", line 16, in <module>
    print(template.substitute(artist='David Bowie', song='Rebel
Rebel'))
  File "/Library/Frameworks/Python.framework/Versions/3.7/lib/
python3.7/string.py", line 132, in substitute
    return self.pattern.sub(convert, self.template)
  File "/Library/Frameworks/Python.framework/Versions/3.7/lib/
python3.7/string.py", line 125, in convert
    return str(mapping[named])
KeyError: 'year'
```

This is because the template variable $year has not been provided with a value.

If you do not want to have to worry about providing all the variables in a template with a value then you should use the safe_substitute() function:

```
print(template.safe_substitute(artist='David Bowie',
song='Rebel Rebel'))
```

This will populate the template variables provided and leave any other template variables to be incorporated into the string as they are, for example:

```
David Bowie sang Rebel Rebel in $year
```

4.9   Online Resources

There is a great deal of online documentation available on strings in Python including:

- https://docs.python.org/3/library/string.html which presents common string operations.
- https://docs.python.org/3/library/stdtypes.html#text-sequence-type-str this provides information on strings and the str class in Python.
- https://pyformat.info has a simple introduction to Python string formatting.
- https://docs.python.org/3/library/string.html#format-string-syntax which presents detailed documentation on Python string formatting.
- https://docs.python.org/3/library/string.html#template-strings for documentation on string templates.

4.10 Exercises

We are going to try out some of the string related operations.

1. Explore replacing a string
   Create a string with words separated by ',' and replace the commas with spaces; for example replace all the commas in 'Denyse,Marie,Smith,21,London,UK' with spaces. Now print out the resulting string.
2. Handle user input
   The aim of this exercise is to write a program to ask the user for two strings and concatenate them together, with a space between them and store them into a new variable called `new_string`.

   Next:

- Print out the value of `new_string`.
- Print out how long the contents of `new_string` is.
- Now convert the contents of `new_string` to all upper case.
- Now check to see if `new_string` contains the string 'Albus' as a substring.

Chapter 5
Numbers, Booleans and None

5.1 Introduction

In this chapter we will explore the different ways that numbers can be represented by the *built-in* types in Python. We will also introduce the Boolean type used to represent True and False. As part of this discussion we will also look at both numeric and assignment operators in Python. We will conclude by introducing the special value known as None.

5.2 Types of Numbers

There are three types used to represent numbers in Python; these are integers (or integral) types, floating point numbers and complex numbers.

This begs the question why? Why have different ways of representing numbers; after all humans can easily work with the number 4 and the number 4.0 and don't need completely different approaches to writing them (apart from the '.' of course).

This actually comes down to efficiency in terms of both the amount of memory needed to represent a number and the amount of processing power needed to work with that number. In essence integers are simpler to work with and can take up less memory than real numbers. Integers are whole numbers that do not need to have a fractional element. When two integers are added, multiplied or subtracted they will always generate another integer number.

In Python real numbers are represented as floating point numbers (or floats). These can contain a fractional part (the bit after the decimal point). Computers can best work with integers (actually of course only really 1s and 0s). They therefore need a way to represent a floating point or real number. Typically this involves representing the digits before and after the decimal point.

© Springer Nature Switzerland AG 2019
J. Hunt, *A Beginners Guide to Python 3 Programming*,
Undergraduate Topics in Computer Science,
https://doi.org/10.1007/978-3-030-20290-3_5

The term floating point is derived from the fact that there is no fixed number of digits before or after the decimal point; that is, the decimal point can float.

Operations on floating point numbers such as addition, subtract, multiplication etc. will generate new real numbers which must also be represented. It is also much harder to ensure that the results are correct as potentially very small and very large fractional parts may be involved. Indeed, most floating-point numbers are actually represented as approximations. This means that one of the challenges in handling floating-point numbers is in ensuring that the approximations lead to reasonable results. If this is not done appropriately, small discrepancies in the approximations can snowball to the point where the final results become meaningless.

As a result, most computer programming languages treat integers such as 4 as being different from real numbers such as 4.000000004.

Complex numbers are an extension of real numbers in which all numbers are expressed as a sum of a real part and an imaginary part. Imaginary numbers are real multiples of the imaginary unit (the square root of -1), where the imaginary part is often written in mathematics using an 'i' while in engineering it is often written using a 'j'.

Python has built-in support for complex numbers, which are written using the engineering notation; that is the imaginary part is written with a j suffix, e.g. 3 + 1j.

5.3   Integers

All integer values, no matter how big or small are represented by the integral (or int) type in Python 3. For example:

```
x = 1
print(x)
print(type(x))
x =
10000000000000000000000000000000000000000000000000000000000000001
print(x)
print(type(x))
```

If this code is run then the output will show that both numbers are of type int:

```
1
<class 'int'>
10000000000000000000000000000000000000000000000000000000000000001
<class 'int'>
```

This makes it very easy to work with integer numbers in Python. Unlike some programming languages such as C# and Java have different integer types depending on the size of the number, small numbers having to be converted into larger types in some situations.

5.3.1 Converting to Ints

It is possible to convert another type into an integer using the int() function. For example, if we want to convert a string into an int (assuming the string contains a integer number) then we can do this using the int() function. For example

```
total = int('100')
```

This can be useful when used with the input() function.

The input() function always returns a string. If we want to ask the user to input an integer number, then we will need to convert the string returned from the input() function into an int. We can do this by wrapping the call to the input() function in a call to the int() function, for example:

```
age = int(input('Please enter your age:'))
print(type(age))
print(age)
```

Running this gives:

```
Please enter your age: 21
<class 'int'>
21
```

The int() function can also be used to convert a floating point number into an int, for example:

```
i = int(1.0)
```

5.4 Floating Point Numbers

Real numbers, or floating point numbers, are represented in Python using the IEEE 754 double-precision binary floating-point number format; for the most part you do not need to know this but it is something you can look up and read about if you wish.

The type used to represent a floating point number is called float.

Python represents floating point numbers using a decimal point to separate the whole part from the fractional part of the number, for example:

```
exchange_rate = 1.83
print(exchange_rate)
print(type(exchange_rate))
```

This produces output indicating that we are storing the number 1.83 as a floating point number:

```
1.83
<class 'float'>
```

5.4.1   Converting to Floats

As with integers it is possible to convert other types such as an int or a string into a float. This is done using the float() function:

```
int_value = 1
string_value = '1.5'
float_value = float(int_value)
print('int value as a float:', float_value)
print(type(float_value))
float_value = float(string_value)
print('string value as a float:', float_value)
print(type(float_value))
```

The output from this code snippet is:

```
int value as a float: 1.0
<class 'float'>
string value as a float: 1.5
<class 'float'>
```

5.4.2   Converting an Input String into a Floating Point Number

As we have seen the input() function returns a string; what happens if we want the user to input a floating point (or real) number? As we have seen above, a string can be converted into a floating point number using the float() function and therefore we can use this approach to convert an input from the user into a float:

```
exchange_rate = float(input("Please enter the exchange rate to use: "))
print(exchange_rate)
print(type(exchange_rate))
```

Using this we can input the string 1.83 and convert it to a floating-point number:

```
Please enter the exchange rate to use: 1.83
1.83
<class 'float'>
```

5.5 Complex Numbers

Complex numbers are Pythons third type of built-in numeric type. A complex number is defined by a real part and an imaginary part and has the form $a + bi$ (where i is the imaginary part and a and b are real numbers):

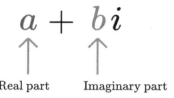

Real part   Imaginary part

The real part of the number (a) is the real number that is being added to the pure imaginary number.

The imaginary part of the number, or b, is the real number coefficient of the pure imaginary number.

The letter 'j' is used in Python to represent the imaginary part of the number, for example:

```
c1 = 1j
c2 = 2j
print('c1:', c1, ', c2:', c2)
print(type(c1))
print(c1.real)
print(c1.imag)
```

We can run this code and the output will be:

```
c1: 1j , c2: 2j
<class 'complex'>
0.0
1.0
```

As you can see the type of the number is 'complex' and when the number is printed directly it is done so by printing both the real and imaginary parts together.

Don't worry if this is confusing; it is unlikely that you will need to use complex numbers unless you are doing some very specific coding, for example within a scientific field.

5.6 Boolean Values

Python supports another type called Boolean; a Boolean type can only be one of `True` or `False` (and nothing else). Note that these values are `True` (with a capital T) and `False` (with a capital F); true and false in Python are not the same thing and have no meaning on their own.

The equivalent of the int or float class for Booleans is bool.

The following example illustrates storing the two Boolean values into a variable all_ok:

```
all_ok = True
print(all_ok)
all_ok = False
print(all_ok)
print(type(all_ok))
```

The output of this is

```
True
False
<class 'bool'>
```

The Boolean type is actually a sub type of integer (but with only the values True and False) so it is easy to translate between the two, using the functions int() and bool() to convert from Booleans to Integers and vice versa. For example:

```
print(int(True))
print(int(False))
print(bool(1))
print(bool(0))
```

Which produces

```
1
0
True
False
```

You can also convert strings into Booleans as long as the strings contain either True or False (and nothing else). For example:

```
status = bool(input('OK to proceed: '))
print(status)
print(type(status))
```

When we run this

```
OK to proceed: True
True
<class 'bool'>
```

5.7 Arithmetic Operators

Arithmetic operators are used to perform some form of mathematical operation such as addition, subtraction, multiplication and division etc. In Python they are represented by one or two characters. The following table summarises the Python arithmetic operators:

Operator	Description	Example
+	Add the left and right values together	1 + 2
−	Subtract the right value from the left value	3 − 2
*	Multiple the left and right values	3 * 4
/	Divide the left value by the right value	12/3
//	Integer division (ignore any remainder)	12//3
%	Modulus (aka the remainder operator)—only return any remainder	13%3
**	Exponent (or power of) operator—with the left value raised to the power of the right	3 ** 4

5.7.1 Integer Operations

Two integers can be added together using +, for example `10 + 5`. In turn two integers can be subtracted (`10 − 5`) and multiplied (`10 * 4`). Operations such as +, − and * between integers always produce integer results.

This is illustrated below:

```
home = 10
away = 15
print(home + away)
print(type(home + away))

print(10 * 4)
print(type(10*4))

goals_for = 10
goals_against = 7
print(goals_for - goals_against)
print(type(goals_for - goals_against))
```

The output from this is

```
25
<class 'int'>
40
<class 'int'>
3
<class 'int'>
```

However, you may notice that we have missed out division with respect to integers, why is this? It is because it depends on which division operator you use as to what the returned type actually is.

For example, if we divide the integer 100 by 20 then the result you might reasonably expect to produce might be 5; but it is not, it is actually 5.0:

```
print(100 / 20)
print(type(100 / 20))
```

The output is

```
5.0
<class 'float'>
```

And as you can see from this the type of the result is float (that is a floating point number). So why is this the case?

The answer is that division does not know whether the two integers involved divide into one another exactly or not (i.e. is there a remainder). It therefore defaults to producing a floating point (or real) number which can have a fractional part. This is of course necessary in some situations, for example if we divide 3 by 2:

```
res1 = 3/2
print(res1)
print(type(res1))
```

In this case 3 cannot be exactly divided by 2, we might say that 2 goes into 3 once with a remainder. This is what is shown by Python:

```
1.5
<class 'float'>
```

The result is that 2 goes into 3, 1.5 times with the type of the result being a float.

If you are only interested in the number of times 2 does go into 3 and are happy to ignore the fractional part then there is an alternative version of the divide operator //. This operator is referred to as the integer division operator:

```
res1 = 3//2
print(res1)
print(type(res1))
```

which produces

```
1
<class 'int'>
```

But what if you are only interested in the remainder part of a division, the integer division operator has lost that? Well in that case you can use the modulus operation ('%'). This operator returns the remainder of a division operation: for example:

```
print('Modulus division 4 % 2:', 4 % 2)
print('Modulus division 3 % 2:', 3 % 2)
```

Which produces:

```
Modulus division 4 % 2: 0
Modulus division 3 % 2: 1
```

A final integer operator we will look at is the power operator that can be used to raise an integer by a given power, for example 5 to the power of 3. The power operator is '**', this is illustrated below:

```
a = 5
b = 3
print(a ** b)
```

Which generates the number 125.

5.7.2 Negative Number Integer Division

It is also worth just exploring what happens in integer and true division when negative numbers are involved. For example,

```
print('True division 3/2:', 3 / 2)
print('True division 3//2:', -3 / 2)
print('Integer division 3//2:', 3 // 2)
print('Integer division 3//2:', -3 // 2)
```

The output from this is:

```
True division 3/2: 1.5
True division 3//2: -1.5
Integer division 3//2: 1
Integer division 3//2: -2
```

The first three of these might be exactly what you expect given our earlier discussion; however, the output of the last example may seem a bit surprising, why does $3//2$ generate 1 but $-3//2$ generates -2?

The answer is that Python always rounds the result of *integer* division towards minus infinity (which is the smallest negative number possible). This means it pulls the result of the integer division to the smallest possible number, 1 is smaller than 1.5 but -2 is smaller than -1.5.

5.7.3 Floating Point Number Operators

We also have the multiple, subtract, add and divide operations available for floating point numbers. All of these operators produce new floating point numbers:

```
print(2.3 + 1.5)
print(1.5 / 2.3)
print(1.5 * 2.3)
print(2.3 - 1.5)
print(1.5 - 2.3)
```

These statements produce the output given below:

```
3.8
0.6521739130434783
3.4499999999999997
0.7999999999999998
-0.7999999999999998
```

5.7.4 Integers and Floating Point Operations

Any operation that involves both integers and floating point numbers will always produce a floating point number. That is, if one of the sides of an operation such as add, subtract, divide or multiple is a floating point number then the result will be a floating point number. For example, given the integer 3 and the floating point number 0.1, if we multiple them together then we get a floating point number:

```
i = 3 * 0.1
print(i)
```

Executing this we get

```
0.30000000000000004
```

Which may or may not have been what you expected (you might have expected 0.3); however this highlights the comment at the start of this chapter relating to floating point (or real) numbers being represented as an approximation within a computer system. If this was part of a larger calculation (such as the calculation of the amount of interest to be paid on a very large loan over a 10 year period) then the end result might well be out by a significant amount.

It is possible to overcome this issue using one of Pythons modules (or libraries). For example, the decimal module provides the Decimal class that will appropriately handle multiplying 3 and 0.1.

5.7.5 Complex Number Operators

Of course you can use operators such as multiply, add, subtract and divide with complex numbers. For example:

```
c1 = 1j
c2 = 2j
c3 = c1 * c2
print(c3)
```

We can run this code and the output will be:

```
(-2+0j)
```

You can also convert another number or a string into a complex number using the complex() function. For example:

```
complex(1) # generates (1+0j)
```

In addition the math module provides mathematical functions for complex numbers.

5.8 Assignment Operators

In Chap. 3 we briefly introduced the assignment operator ('=') which was used to assign a value to a variable. There are in fact several different assignment operators that could be used with numeric values.

These assignment operators are actually referred to as *compound operators* as they combine together a numeric operation (such as add) with the assignment operator. For example, the += compound operator is a combination of the add operator and the = operator such that

```
x = 0
x += 1    # has the same behaviour as x = x + 1
```

Some developers like to use these compound operators as they are more concise to write and can be interpreted more efficiently by the Python interpreter.

The following table provides a list of the available compound operators

Operator	Description	Example	Equivalent
+=	Add the value to the left-hand variable	x += 2	x = x + 2
−=	Subtract the value from the left-hand variable	x −= 2	x = x − 2
*=	Multiple the left-hand variable by the value	x *= 2	x = x * 2
/=	Divide the variable value by the right-hand value	x /= 2	x = x/2
//=	Use integer division to divide the variable's value by the right-hand value	x //= 2	x = x//2
%=	Use the modulus (remainder) operator to apply the right-hand value to the variable	x %= 2	x = x % 2
**=	Apply the power of operator to raise the variable's value by the value supplied	x **= 3	x = x ** 3

5.9 None Value

Python has a special type, the `NoneType`, with a single value, `None`.

This is used to represent null values or *nothingness*.

It is not the same as `False`, or an empty string or 0; it is a *non-value*. It can be used when you need to create a variable but don't have an initial value for it. For example:

```
winner = None
```

You can then test for the presence of `None` using `'is'` and `'is not'`, for example:

```
print(winner is None)
```

This will print out `True` if and only if the variable `winner` is currently set to `None`.

Alternatively you can also write:

```
print(winner is not None)
```

Which will print out `True` only if the value of `winner` is *not* `None`.

Several example using the value `None` and the 'is' and is not' operators are given below:

```
winner = None
print('winner:', winner)
print('winner is None:', winner is None)
print('winner is not None:', winner is not None)
print(type(winner))
print('Set winner to True')
winner = True
print('winner:', winner)
print('winner is None:', winner is None)
print('winner is not None:', winner is not None)
print(type(winner))
```

The output of this code snippet is:

```
winner: None
winner is None: True
winner is not None: False
<class 'NoneType'>
Set winner to True
winner: True
winner is None: False
winner is not None: True
<class 'bool'>
```

5.10   Online Resources

See the Python Standard Library documentation for:

- https://docs.python.org/3/library/stdtypes.html#numeric-types-int-float-complex Numeric Types.
- https://docs.python.org/3/library/stdtypes.html#truth-value-testing Boolean values and boolean testing.
- https://docs.python.org/3/library/decimal.html which provides information on the Python decimal module.
- https://docs.python.org/3/library/cmath.html which discusses mathematical functions for complex numbers.

If you are interested in how floating point numbers are represented then a good starting points are:

- https://en.wikipedia.org/wiki/Double-precision_floating-point_format   which provides an overview of floating point representation.
- https://en.wikipedia.org/wiki/IEEE_754 which is the Wikipedia page on the IEEE 754 Double-precision floating-point number format.

5.11   Exercises

The aim of the exercises in this chapter is to explore the numeric types we have been looking at.

5.11.1 General Exercise

Try to explore the different number types available in Python.

You should try out the different numeric operators available and mix up the numbers being used, for example, 1 and well as 1.0 etc.

Check to see the results you get are what you expect.

5.11.2 Convert Kilometres to Miles

The aim of this exercise is to write a program to convert a distance in Kilometres into a distance in miles.

1. Take input from the user for a given distance in Kilometres. This can be done using the input() function.
2. Convert the value returned by the input() function from a string into an integer using the int() function.
3. Now convert this value into miles—this can be done by dividing the kilometres by 0.6214
4. Print out a message telling the user what the kilometres are in miles.

Chapter 6
Flow of Control Using If Statements

6.1 Introduction

In this chapter we are going to look at the `if` statement in Python. This statement is used to control the flow of execution within a program based on some condition. These conditions represent some choice point that will be evaluated to `True` or `False`. To perform this evaluation it is common to use a comparison operator (for example to check to see if the temperature is greater than some threshold). In many cases these comparisons need to take into account several values and in these situations logical operators can be used to combine two or more comparison expressions together.

This chapter first introduces comparison and logical operators before discussing the `if` statement itself.

6.2 Comparison Operators

Before exploring `if` statements we need to discuss *comparison operators*. These are operators that return Boolean values. They are key to the conditional elements of flow of control statements such as `if`.

A comparison operator is an operator that performs some form of test and returns `True` of `False`.

These are operators that we use in everyday life all the time. For example, do I have enough money to buy lunch, or is this shoe in my size etc.

© Springer Nature Switzerland AG 2019
J. Hunt, *A Beginners Guide to Python 3 Programming*,
Undergraduate Topics in Computer Science,
https://doi.org/10.1007/978-3-030-20290-3_6

In Python there are a range of comparison operators represented by typically one or two characters. These are:

Operator	Description	Example
==	Tests if two values are equal	3 == 3
!=	Tests that two values are *not* equal to each other	2 != 3
<	Tests to see if the left-hand value is less than the right-hand value	2 < 3
>	Tests if the left-hand value is greater than the right-hand value	3 > 2
<=	Tests if the left-hand value is less than *or* equal to the right-hand value	3 <= 4
>=	Tests if the left-hand value is greater than or equal to the right-hand value	5 >= 4

6.3 Logical Operators

In addition to comparison operators, Python also has logical operators.

Logical operators can be used to combined Boolean expressions together. Typically, they are used with comparison operators to create more complex conditions. Again, we use these every day for example we might consider whether we can afford an ice cream *and* whether we will be having our dinner soon etc.

There are three logical operators in Python these are listed below:

Operator	Description	Example
and	Returns True if both left and right are true	(3 < 4) and (5 > 4)
or	Returns two if either the left or the right is truce	(3 < 4) or (3 > 5)
not	Returns true if the value being tested is False	not 3 < 2

6.4 The If Statement

An `if` statement is used as a form of conditional programming; something you probably do every day in the real world. That is, you need to decide whether you are going to have tea or coffee or to decide if you will have toast or a muffin for breakfast etc. In each of these cases you are making a choice, usually based on some information such as I had coffee yesterday, so I will have tea today.

In Python such choices are represented programmatically by the `if` condition statement.

In this construct if some condition is true some action is performed, optionally if it is not true some other action may be performed instead.

6.4.1 Working with an If Statement

In its most basic from, the `if` statement is

```
if <condition-evaluating-to-boolean>:
    statement
```

Note that the condition must evaluate to `True` or `False` (or an equivalent value—see later in this chapter). If the condition is `True` then we will execute the indented statement.

Note that indentation, this is *very* important in Python; indeed, layout of the code is *very*, *very* important in Python. Indentation is used to determine how one piece of code should be associated with another piece of the code.

Let us look at a simple example,

```
num = int(input('Enter a number: '))
if num < 0:
    print(num, 'is negative')
```

In this example, the user has input a number; if it is less than zero a message noting this will be printed to the user. If the number is positive; then nothing will be output.

For example,

```
Enter a number: -1
-1  is negative
```

If we wish to execute multiple statements when our condition is `True` we can indent several lines; in fact all lines indented to the same level after the `if` statement will automatically be part of the `if` statement. For example;

```
num = int(input('Enter another number: '))
if num > 0:
    print(num, 'is positive')
    print(num, 'squared is ', num * num)

print('Bye')
```

If we now run this program and input 2 then we will see

```
Enter another number: 2
2  is positive
2  squared is  4
Bye
```

However, if we enter the value −1 then we get

```
Enter another number: -1
Bye
```

Note that neither of the indented lines was executed.

This is because the two indented lines are associated with the if statement and will only be executed if the Boolean condition evaluates (returns) True. However, the statement print('Bye') is not part of the if statement; it is merely the next statement to executed after the if statement (and its associated print() statements) have finished.

6.4.2   Else in an If Statement

We can also define an *else* part of an if statement; this is an optional element that can be run if the conditional part of the if statement returns False. For example:

```
num = int(input('Enter yet another number: '))
if num < 0:
    print('Its negative')
else:
    print('Its not negative')
```

Now when this code is executed, if the number entered is less than zero then the first print() statement will be run otherwise (else) the second print() statement will be run. However, we are *guaranteed* that at least one (and at most one) of the print() statements will execute.

For example, in run 1 if we enter the value 1:

```
Enter yet another number: 1
Its not negative
```

And in run 2 if we enter the value −1:

```
Enter yet another number: -1
Its negative
```

6.4.3   The Use of elif

In some cases there may be several conditions you want to test, with each condition being tested if the previous one failed. This *else-if* scenario is supported in Python by the elif element of an if statement.

The `elif` element of an `if` statement follows the `if` part and comes before any (optional) `else` part. It has the format:

```
elif <condition-evaluating-to-boolean>:
    statement
```

For example *为什么这是 float 然后？*

```
savings = float(input("Enter how much you have in savings: "))
if savings == 0:
    print("Sorry no savings")
elif savings < 500:
    print('Well done')
elif savings < 1000:
    print('Thats a tidy sum')
elif savings < 10000:
    print('Welcome Sir!')
else:
    print('Thank you')
```

If we run this:

```
Enter how much you have in savings: 500
Thats a tidy sum
```

Here we can see that the first `if` condition failed (as savings is not equal to 0). However, the next `elif` also must have returned `False` as savings were greater than 500. In fact it was the second `elif` statement that returned `True` and thus the associated `print('Thats a tidy sum')` statement was executed. Having executed this statement the `if` statement then terminated (the remaining `elif` and `else` parts were ignored).

6.5   Nesting If Statements

It is possible to *nest* one `if` statement inside another. This term *nesting* indicates that one `if` statement is located within part of the another `if` statement and can be used to refine the conditional behaviour of the program.

An example is given below. Note that it allows some behaviour to be performed before and after the nested `if` statement is executed/run. Also note that indentation is key here as it is how Python works out whether the `if` statements are nested or not.

```
snowing = True
temp = -1
if temp < 0:
    print('It is freezing')
    if snowing:
        print('Put on boots')
    print('Time for Hot Chocolate')
print('Bye')
```

In this example, if the temperature if less than Zero then we will enter the `if` block of code. If it is not less than zero we will skip the whole `if` statement and jump to the `print('Bye')` statement which is after both If statements.

In this case the temperature is set to −1 and so we will enter the If statement. We will then print out the 'It is freezing' string. At this point another `if` statement is *nested* within the first `if` statement. A check will now be made to see if it is snowing. Notice that `snowing` is already a Boolean value and so will be either True or False and illustrates that a Boolean value on its own can be used here.

As it is snowing, we will print out 'Put on boots'.

However, the statement printing out 'Time for Hot Chocolate' is not part of the nested `if`. It is part of the outer `if` (this is where indentation is important). If you wanted it to only be printed out if it was snowing then it must be indented to the same level as the first statement in the nested `if` block, for example:

```
snowing = True
temp = -1
if temp < 0:
    print('It is freezing')
    if snowing:
        print('Put on boots')
        print('Time for Hot Chocolate')
print('Bye')
```

This now changes the inner (or nested) if to have two `print` statements associated with it.

This may seem subtle, but it is *key* to how Python uses layout to link together individual statements.

6.6   If Expressions

An if expression is a short hand form of an `if` statement that returns a value. In fact, the difference between an expression and a statement in a programming language is just that; expressions return a value; statements do not.

It is quite common to want to assign a specific value to a variable dependent on some condition. For example, if we wish to decide if someone is a teenager or not then we might check to see if they are over 12 and under 20. We could write this as:

```
age = 15
status = None
if (age > 12) and age < 20:
    status = 'teenager'
else:
    status = 'not teenager'
print(status)
```

If we run this, we get the string 'teenager' printed out.

However, this is quite long and it may not be obvious that the real intent of this code was to assign an appropriate value to status.

An alternative is an *if expression*. The format of an if expression is

```
<result1> if <condition-is-met> else <result2>
```

That is the result returned from the if expression is the first value unless the condition fails in which case the result returned will be the value after the else. It may seem confusing at first, but it becomes easier when you see an example.

For example, using the if expression we can perform a test to determine the value to assign to status and return it as the result of the if expression. For example:

```
status = ('teenager' if age > 12 and age < 20 else 'not
teenager')
print(status)
```

Again, the result printed out is 'teenager' however now the code is much more concise, and it is clear that the purpose of the test is to determine the result to assign to status.

6.7 A Note on True and False

Python is actually quite flexible when it comes to what actually is used to represent True and False, in fact the following rules apply

- 0, '' (empty strings), None equate to False
- Non zero, non empty strings, any object equate to True.

However, we would recommend sticking to just True and False as it is often a cleaner and safer approach.

6.8   Hints

One thing to be very careful of in Python is layout.

Unlike language such as Java and C# the layout of your program is *part of your program*. It determines how statements are associated together and how flow of control elements such as if statements effect which statements are executed.

Also, be careful with the `if` statement and its use of the ':' character. This character is key in separating out the conditional part of the `if` statement from the statements that will be executed depending upon whether the condition is `True` or `False`.

6.9   Online Resources

See the Python Standard Library documentation for:

- https://docs.python.org/3/library/stdtypes.html#boolean-operations-and-or-not
  Boolean Operations.
- https://docs.python.org/3/library/stdtypes.html#comparisons   Comparison
  operators.
- https://docs.python.org/3/tutorial/controlflow.html the online Python flow of
  control tutorial.

6.10   Exercises

There are three different exercises in this section, you can select which you are interested in or do all three.

6.10.1   Check Input Is Positive or Negative

The aim of this exercise is to write a small program to test if an integer is positive or negative.

Your program should:

1. Prompt the user to input a number (use the input() function). You can assume that the input will be some sort of number.
2. Convert the string into an integer using the int() function.
3. Now check whether the integer is a positive number or a negative number.
4. You could also add a test to see if the number is Zero.

6.10.2   Test if a Number Is Odd or Even

The exercises requires you to write a program to take input from the user and determine if the number is odd or even. Again you can assume that the user will enter a valid integer number.

Print out a message to the user to let them know the result.

To test if a number is even you can use

```
(num % 2) == 0
```

Which will return True if the number is even (note the brackets are optional but make it easier to read).

6.10.3   Kilometres to Miles Converter

In this exercise you should return to the kilometres to miles converter you wrote in the last chapter.

We will add several new tests to your program:

1. Modify your program such that it verify that the user has entered a positive distance (i.e. they cannot enter a negative number).
2. Now modify your program to verify that the input is a number; if it is not a number then do nothing; otherwise convert the distance to miles.

To check to see if a string contains only digits use the method isnumeric() for example '42'.isnumeric(); which returns True if the string only contains numbers. Note this method only works for positive integers; but this is sufficient for this example.

Chapter 7
Iteration/Looping

7.1 Introduction

In this section we will look at the `while` loop and the `for` loop available in Python. These loops are used to control the repeated execution of selected statements.

7.2 While Loop

The `while` loop exists in almost all programming languages and is used to iterative (or repeat) one or more code statements as long as the test condition (expression) is `True`. This iteration construct is usually used when the number of times we need to repeat the block of code to execute is not known. For example, it may need to repeat until some solution is found or the user enters a particular value.

The behaviour of the while loop is illustrated in below.

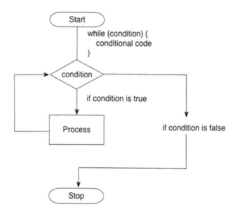

© Springer Nature Switzerland AG 2019
J. Hunt, *A Beginners Guide to Python 3 Programming*,
Undergraduate Topics in Computer Science,
https://doi.org/10.1007/978-3-030-20290-3_7

The Python while loop has the basic form:

```
while <test-condition-is-true>:
    statement or statements
```

As shown both in the diagram and can be inferred from the code; *while* the test condition/expression is `True` then the statement or block of statements in the `while` loop will be executed.

Note that the test is performed *before* each iteration, including the first iteration; therefore, if the condition fails the first time around the loop the statement or block of statements may never be executed at all.

As with the `if` statement, indentation is key here as the statements included in the while statement are determined by indentation. Each statement that is indented to the same level after the while condition is part of the `while` loop.

However, as soon as a statement is no longer following the `while` block; then it is no longer part of the `while` loop and its execution is no longer under the control of the test-condition.

The following illustrates an example `while` loop in Python:

```
count = 0
print('Starting')
while count < 10:
    print(count, ' ', end='')  # part of the while loop
    count += 1                 # also part of the while loop
print()  # not part of the while loop
print('Done')
```

In this example while some variable `count` is less than the value 10 the `while` loop will continue to iterate (will be repeated). The `while` loop itself contains two statements; one prints out the value of count variable while the other increments `count` (remember `count +=1` is equivalent to `count = count + 1`).

We have used the version of `print()` that does not print a carriage return when it prints out a value (this is indicated by the `end=' '` option passed to the `print()` function).

The result of running this example is:

```
Starting
0 1 2 3 4 5 6 7 8 9
Done
```

As you can see the statements printing the starting and done messages are only run once. However, the statement printing out the `count` variable is run 10 times (printing out the values 0–9).

Once the value of `count` is equal to 10 then the loop finishes (or terminates).

Note that we needed to initialise the `count` variable before the loop. This is because it needs to have a value for the first iteration of the `while` loop. That is before the `while` loop does anything the program needs to already know the first value of count so that it can perform that very first test. This is a feature of the while loops behaviour.

7.3   For Loop

In many cases we know how many times we want to iterative over one or more statements (as indeed we did in the previous section). Although the `while` loop can be used for such situations, the `for` loop is a far more concise way to do this. It typically also clearer to another programmer that the loop must iterate for a specific number of iterations.

The `for` loop is used to step a *variable* through a series of values until a given test is met. The behaviour of the `for` loop is illustrated in below.

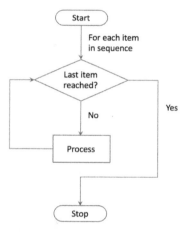

This flow chart shows that some sequence of values (for example all integer values between 0 and 9) will be used to iterate over a block of code to process. When the last item in the sequence has been reached, the loop will terminate.

Many languages have a `for` loop of the form:

```
for i = from 0 to 10
    statement or statements
```

In this case a variable `'i'` would take the values 0, 1, 2, 3 etc. up to 10.

In Python the approach is slightly different as the values from 0 up to 10 are represented by a *range*. This is actually a function that will generate the *range* of values to be used as the sequence in the `for` loop. This is because the Python for loop is very flexible and can loop over not only a range of integer values but also a set of values held in data structures such as a list of integers or strings. We will return to this feature of the `for` loop when we look at collections/containers of data in a later chapter.

The format of the Python `for` loop when using a range of values is

```
for <variable-name> in range(...):
    statement
    statement
```

An example is shown below which equates to the `while` loop we looked at earlier:

```
# Loop over a set of values in a range
print('Print out values in a range')
for i in range(0, 10):
    print(i, ' ', end='')
print()
print('Done')
```

When we run this code, the output is:

```
Print out values in a range
0  1  2  3  4  5  6  7  8  9
Done
```

As can be seen from the above; the end result is that we have generated a `for` loop that produces the same set of values as the earlier `while` loop. However,

- the code is more concise,
- it is clear we are processing a range of values from 0 to 9 (note that it is up to but not including the final value) and
- we did not need to define the loop variable first.

For these reasons *for* loops are more common in programs in general than *while* loops.

One thing you might notice though is that in the `while` loop we are not constrained to incrementing the `count` variable by one (we just happened to do this). For example, we could have decided to increment `count` by 2 each time round the loop (a very common idea). In fact, `range` allows us to do exactly this; a third argument that can be provided to the `range` function is the value to increment the loop variable by each time round the loop, for example:

```
# Now use values in a range but increment by 2
print('Print out values in a range with an increment of 2')
for i in range(0, 10, 2):
    print(i, ' ', end='')
print()
print('Done')
```

When we run this code, the output is

```
Print out values in a range with an increment of 2
0   2   4   6   8
Done
```

Thus the value of the loop variable has jumped by 2 starting at 0. Once its value was 10 or more then the loop terminates. Of course, it is not only the value 2 we could use; we could increment by any meaningful integer, 3, 4 or 5 etc.

One interesting variation on the for loop is the use of a wild card (a '_') instead of a looping variable; this can be useful if you are only interested in looping a certain number of times and not in the value of the loop counter itself, for example:

```
# Now use an 'anonymous' loop variable
for _ in range(0,10):
    print('.', end='')
print()
```

In this case we are not interested in the values generated by the range per se only in looping 10 times thus there is no benefit in recording the loop variable. The loop variable is represented by the underbar character ('_').

Note that in actual fact this is a valid variable and can be referenced within the loop; however by convention it is treated as being anonymous.

7.4 Break Loop Statement

Python allows programmers to decide whether they want to *break* out of a loop early or not (whether we are using a for loop or a while loop). This is done using the break statement.

The break statement allows a developer to alter the normal cycle of the loop based on some criteria which may not be predictable in advance (for example it may be based on some user input).

The break statement, when executed, will terminate the current loop and jump the program to the first line after the loop. The following diagram shows how this works for a for loop:

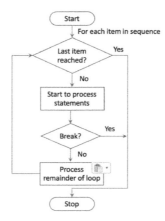

Typically, a guard statement (if statement) is placed on the break so that the break statement is conditionally applied when appropriate.

This is shown below for a simple application where the user is asked to enter a number which may or may not be in the range defined by the for loop. If the number is in the range, then we will loop until this value is reached and then break the loop (that is terminate early without processing the rest of the values in the loop):

```
print('Only print code if all iterations completed')
num = int(input('Enter a number to check for: '))
for i in range(0, 6):
    if i == num:
        break
    print(i, ' ', end='')
print('Done')
```

If we run this and enter the value 7 (which is outside of the range) then all the values in the loop should be printed out:

```
Enter a number to check for: 7
0 1  2  3  4  5 Done
```

However, if we enter the value 3 then only the values 0, 1 and 2 will be printed out before the loop breaks (terminates) early:

```
Enter a number to check for: 3
0 1  2  Done
```

Note that the string 'Done' is printed out in both cases as it is the first line after the for loop that is not indented and is thus not part of the for loop.

Note that the `break` statement can come anywhere within the block of code associated with the loop construct (whether that is a `for` loop or a `while` loop). This means that there can be statements before it and after it.

7.5   Continue Loop Statement

The `continue` statement also affects the flow of control within the looping constructs `for` and `while`. However, it does not terminate the whole loop; rather it only terminates the current iteration round the loop. This allows you to skip over part of a loop's iteration for a particular value, but then to continue with the remaining values in the sequence.

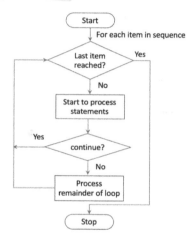

A guard (`if` statement) can be used to determine when the `continue` statement should be executed.

As with the `break` statement, the `continue` statement can come anywhere within the body of the looping construct. This means that you can have some statements that will be executed for every value in the sequence and some that are only executed when the continue statement is not run.

This is shown below. In this program the `continue` statement is executed only for odd numbers and thus the two `print()` statements are only run if the value of `i` is even:

```
for i in range(0, 10):
    print(i, ' ', end='')
    if i % 2 == 1:
        continue
    print('hey its an even number')
    print('we love even numbers')
print('Done')
```

When we run this code we get

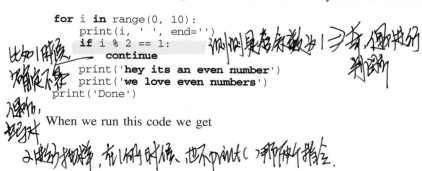

```
0   hey its an even number
we love even numbers
1   2   hey its an even number
we love even numbers
3   4   hey its an even number
we love even numbers
5   6   hey its an even number
we love even numbers
7   8   hey its an even number
we love even numbers
9   Done
```

As you can see, we only print out the messages about a number being even when the values are 0, 2, 4, 6 and 8.

7.6   For Loop with Else

A for loop can have an *optional* else block at the end of the loop. The else part is executed if and only if all items in the sequence are processed. The for loop may fail to process all elements in the loop if for some reason an error occurs in your program (for example if you have a syntax error) or if you break the loop.

Here is an example of a for loop with an else part:

```
# Only print code if all iterations completed over a list
print('Only print code if all iterations completed')
num = int(input('Enter a number to check for: '))
for i in range(0, 6):
    if i == num:
        break
    print(i, ' ', end='')
else:
    print()
    print('All iterations successful')
```

If we run this code and enter the integer value 7 as the number to check for; then the else block executes as the if test within the for statement is never True and thus the loop is never broken, and all values are processed:

```
Only print code if all iterations completed
Enter a number to check for: 7
0   1   2   3   4   5
All iterations successful
```

However, if we enter the value 3 as the number to check for; then the if statement will be True when the loop variable 'i' has the value 3; thus only the values 0, 1 and 2 will be processed by the loop. In this situation the else part will *not* be executed because not all the values in the sequence were processed:

```
Only print code if all iterations completed
Enter a number to check for: 3
0  1  2
```

7.7   A Note on Loop Variable Naming

Earlier in the book we said that variable names should be meaningful and that names such as 'a' and 'b' were not in general a good idea. The one exception to this rule relates to loop variable names used with for loops over ranges. It is very common to find that these loop variables are called 'i', 'j' etc.

It is such a common convention that if a variable is called 'i' or 'j' people expect it to be a loop variable. As such

- you should consider using these variable names in looping constructs,
- and avoid using them elsewhere.

But this does raise the question why 'i' and 'j'; the answer is that it all goes back to a programming language called Fortran which was first developed in the 1950s. In this programming language loop variables had to be called 'i' and 'j' etc. Fortran was so ubiquitous for mathematical and scientific programming, where loops are almost *di rigour*, that this has become the convention in other languages which do not have this restriction.

7.8   Dice Roll Game

The following short program illustrates how a while loop can be used to control the execution of the main body of code. In this game we will continue to roll a pair of dice until the user indicates that they do not want to roll again (we use the random module for this which is discussed in the next chapter). When this occurs the while loop will terminate:

```
import random

MIN = 1
MAX = 6

roll_again = 'y'

while roll_again == 'y':
    print('Rolling the dices...')
    print('The values are....')
    dice1 = random.randint(MIN, MAX)
    print(dice1)
    dice2 = random.randint(MIN, MAX)
    print(dice2)
    roll_again = input('Roll the dices again? (y / n): ')
```

When we run this program the results of rolling two dice are shown. The program will keep looping and printing out the two dice values until the user indicates that they no longer want to roll the dice:

```
Rolling the dices...
The values are....
2
6
Roll the dices again? (y / n): y
Rolling the dices...
The values are....
4
1
Roll the dices again? (y / n): y
Rolling the dices...
The values are....
3
6
Roll the dices again? (y / n): n
```

7.9 Online Resources

See the Python Standard Library documentation for:

• https://docs.python.org/3/tutorial/controlflow.html the online Python flow of control tutorial.

7.10 Exercises

There are two exercises for this chapter. The first exercise will require a simple `for` loop while the second is more complicated requiring nested `for` loops and a `break` statement.

7.10.1 Calculate the Factorial of a Number

Write a program that can find the factorial of any given number. For example, find the factorial of the number 5 (often written as 5!) which is 1 * 2 * 3 * 4 * 5 and equals 120.

The factorial is not defined for negative numbers and the factorial of Zero is 1; that is 0! = 1.

Your program should take as input an integer from the user (you can reuse your logic from the last chapter to verify that they have entered a positive integer value using `isnumeric()`).

You should

1. If the number is less than Zero return with an error message.
2. Check to see if the number is Zero—if it is then the answer is 1—print this out.
3. Otherwise use a loop to generate the result and print it out.

7.10.2 *Print All the Prime Numbers in a Range*

A Prime Number is a positive whole number, greater than 1, that has no other divisors except the number 1 and the number itself.

That is, it can only be divided by itself and the number 1, for example the numbers 2, 3, 5 and 7 are prime numbers as they cannot be divided by any other whole number. However, the numbers 4 and 6 are not because they can both be divided by the number 2 in addition the number 6 can also be divided by the number 3.

You should write a program to calculate prime number starting from 1 up to the value input by the user.

If the user inputs a number below 2, print an error message.

For any number greater than 2 loop for each integer from 2 to that number and determine if it can be divided by another number (you will probably need two for loops for this; one nested inside the other).

For each number that cannot be divided by any other number (that is its a prime number) print it out.

Chapter 8
Number Guessing Game

8.1 Introduction

In this chapter we are going to bring everything we have learned so far together to create a simple number guessing game.

This will involve creating a new Python program, handling user input, using the if statement as well as using looping constructs.

We will also, use an additional library or module, that is not by default available by default to your program; this will be the random number generator module.

8.2 Setting Up the Program

We want to make sure that we don't overwrite whatever you have done so far, and we would like this Python program to be separate from your other work. As such we will create a new Python file to hold this program. The first step will be to create a new Python file. If you are using the PyCharm IDE you can do it using the New>PythonFile menu option.

8.2.1 Add a Welcome Message

To make sure everything is working correctly we will add a simple print() statement to the file so that we can test out running it.

You can add anything you like, including printing out 'Hello World', however the example shown below shows a welcome message that can be used at the start of the game in the PyCharm IDE:

© Springer Nature Switzerland AG 2019
J. Hunt, *A Beginners Guide to Python 3 Programming*,
Undergraduate Topics in Computer Science,
https://doi.org/10.1007/978-3-030-20290-3_8

8.2.2 Running the Program

We can now run our embryonic program. If you are using PyCharm then to do this we can select the file in the left-hand view and use the right mouse menu to select the 'Run' option:

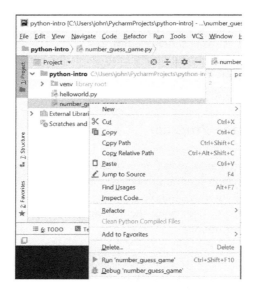

When we do this the Python console will be opened at the bottom of the IDE and the output displayed:

From now on you can rerun the `number_guess_game` program merely by clicking on the little green arrow at the top right-hand side of PyCharm (it allows you to rerun the last program that PyCharm executed).

8.3   What Will the Program Do?

The aim of our number guess game is to guess the number that the program has come up with.

The main flow of the program is shown in the following diagram:

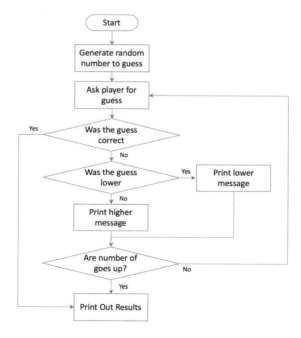

Essentially the program logic is

- The program randomly selects a number between 1 and 10.
- It will then ask the player to enter their guess.
- It will then check to see if that number is the same as the one the computer randomly generated; if it is then the player has won.
- If the player's guess is not the same, then it will check to see if the number is higher or lower than the guess and tell the player.
- The player will have 4 goes to guess the number correctly; if they don't guess the number within this number of attempts, then they will be informed that they have lost the game and will be told what the actual number was.

8.4   Creating the Game

8.4.1   Generate the Random Number

We will start off by looking at how we can generate a random number. Up to this point we have only used the built-in functions that are provided by Python automatically. In actual fact Python comes with very many modules provided by the Python organisation itself, by third party vendors and by the open source (typically free) software community.

The Python `random` module or library is one that is provided with Python as part of the default environment; but the functions within it are not automatically loaded or made available to the programmer. This is partly because there are so many facilities available with Python that it could become overwhelming; so for the most part Python only makes available by default the most commonly used facilities. Programmers can then explicitly specify when they want to use some facilities from one of the other libraries or modules.

The `random` module provides implementations of pseudo-random number generators for use in application programs. These random number generators are referred to as *pseudo* because it is very hard for a computer to truly generate a series of random numbers; instead it does its best to mimic this using an algorithm; which by its very nature will be based on some logic which will mean that it is not impossible to predict the next number—hence it is not truly random. For our purposes this is fine but there are applications, such as security and encryption, where this can be a real problem.

To access the `random` module in Python you need to *import* it; this makes the module visible in the rest of the Python file (in our case to our program). This is done using

```
import random
number_to_guess = random.randint(1,10)
```

Once we have imported it, we can use the functions within this module, such as
randint. This function returns a random integer between the first and second
arguments. In the above example it means that the random number generated will
be between 1 and 10 inclusive.

The variable number_to_guess will now hold an integer which the player of
the game must guess.

8.4.2 Obtain an Input from the User

We now need to obtain input from the user representing their guess. We have
already seen how to do this in previous chapters; we can use the input() function
which returns a string and then the integer function that will convert that string into
an integer (we will ignore error checking to make sure they have typed in a number
at this point). We can therefore write:

```
guess = int(input('Please guess a number between 1 and 10: '))
```

This will store the number they guessed into the variable guess.

8.4.3 Check to See If the Player Has Guessed the Number

We now need to check to see whether the player has guessed the correct number.

We could use an if statement for this, however we are going to want to repeat
this test until either they have guessed correctly or until they have run out of goes.

We will therefore use a while loop and check to see if their guess equals the
number to be guessed:

```
guess = int(input('Please guess a number between 1 and 10: '))
while number_to_guess != guess:
```

The loop above will be repeated if the number they entered did not match the
number to be guessed.

We can therefore print a message telling the player that their guess was wrong:

```
guess = int(input('Please guess a number between 1 and 10: '))
while number_to_guess != guess:
    print('Sorry wrong number')
```

Now we need the player to make another guess otherwise the program will never terminate, so we can again prompt them to enter a number:

```
guess = int(input('Please guess a number between 1 and 10: '))
while number_to_guess != guess:
    print('Sorry wrong number')
    # TBD ...
    guess = int(input('Please guess again: '))
```

8.4.4 Check They Haven't Exceeded Their Maximum Number of Guess

We also said above that the player can't play forever; they have to guess the correct number within 4 goes. We therefore need to add some logic which will stop the game once they exceed this number.

We will therefore need a variable to keep track of the number of attempts they have made.

We should call this variable something meaningful so that we know what it represents, for example we could call it count_number_of_tries and initialise it with the value 1:

```
count_number_of_tries = 1
```

This needs to happen before we enter the while loop.

Inside the while loop we need to do two things

- check to see if the number of tries has been exceeded,
- increment the number of tries if they are still allowed to play the game.

We will use an if statement to check to see if the number of tries has been met; if it has we want to terminate the loop; the easiest way to this is via a break statement.

```
if count_number_of_tries == 4:
    break
```

If we don't break out of the loop we can increment the count using the '+=' operator. We thus now have:

```
count_number_of_tries = 1
guess = int(input('Please guess a number between 1 and 10: '))
while number_to_guess != guess:
    print('Sorry wrong number')
    if count_number_of_tries == 4:
        break
    # TBD ...
    guess = int(input('Please guess again: '))
    count_number_of_tries += 1
```

8.4.5 Notify the Player Whether Higher or Lower

We also said at the beginning that to make it easier for the player to guess the number; we should indicate whether their guess was higher or lower than the actual number. To do this we can again use the if statement; if the guess is lower we print one message but if it was higher we print another.

At this point we have a choice regarding whether to have a separate if statement to that used to decide if the maximum goes has been reached or to extend that one with an elif. Each approach can work but the latter indicates that these conditions are all related so that is the one we will use.

The while loop now looks like:

```
count_number_of_tries = 1
guess = int(input('Please guess a number between 1 and 10: '))
while number_to_guess != guess:
    print('Sorry wrong number')
    if count_number_of_tries == 4:
        break
    elif guess < number_to_guess:
        print('Your guess was lower than the number')
    else:
        print('Your guess was higher than the number')
    guess = int(input('Please guess again: '))
    count_number_of_tries += 1
```

Notice that the if statement has a final else which indicates that the guess was higher; this is fine as by this point it is the only option left.

8.4.6   End of Game Status

We have now covered all the situations that can occur while the game is being played; all that is left for us to do is to handle the end of game messages.

If the player has guessed the number correctly, we want to congratulate them; if they did not guess the number, we want to let them know what the actual number was. We will do this using another if statement which checks to see if the player guessed the number of not. After this we will print an end of game message:

```
if number_to_guess == guess:
    print('Well done you won!')
    print('You took', count_number_of_tries ,
        'goes to complete the game')
else:
    print('Sorry - you loose')
    print('The number you needed to guess was',
        number_to_guess)
print('Game Over')
```

8.5   The Complete Listing

For ease of reference the complete listing is provided below:

```
import random

print('Welcome to the number guess game')

# Initialise the number to be guessed
number_to_guess = random.randint(1,10)

# Initialise the number of tries the player has made
count_number_of_tries = 1

# Obtain their initial guess
guess = int(input('Please guess a number between 1 and 10: '))
while number_to_guess != guess:
    print('Sorry wrong number')

    # Check to see they have not exceeded the maximum
    # number of attempts if so break out of loop otherwise
```

许的缩进在 while 的下面

```python
    # give the user come feedback
    if count_number_of_tries == 4:
        break
    elif guess < number_to_guess:
        print('Your guess was lower than the number')
    else:
        print('Your guess was higher than the number')

    # Obtain their next guess and increment number of attempts
    guess = int(input('Please guess again: '))
    count_number_of_tries += 1

# Check to see if they did guess the correct number
if number_to_guess == guess:
    print('Well done you won!')
    print('You took', count_number_of_tries , 'goes to complete
the game')
else:
    print("Sorry - you loose")
    print('The number you needed to guess was',
        number_to_guess)

print('Game Over')
```

And a sample run of the program is shown here:

```
Welcome to the number guess game
Please guess a number between 1 and 10: 5
Sorry wrong number
Your guess was higher than the number
Please guess again: 3
Sorry wrong number
Your guess was lower than the number
Please guess again: 4
Well done you won!
You took 3 goes to complete the game
Game Over
```

8.6   Hints

8.6.1   *Initialising Variables*

In Python it is not necessary to declare a variable before you assign to it; however, it is necessary to give it an initial value before you reference it. Here *reference it* refers to obtaining the value held by a variable. For example

```
count = count + 1
```

what this says is obtain the value held by count, add 1 to it and then store the new value back into count.

If count does not have a value before you try to do this then you are trying to get hold of nothing and add 1 to it; which you can't do and thus an error will be generated in your program, such as:

```
NameError: name 'count_number_of_tries' is not defined
```

This is also true for

```
count += 1
```

Remember this is just a shorthand form of count = count + 1 and thus still relies on count having a value before this statement.

This is why we needed to initialise the count_number_of_tries variable before we used it.

8.6.2   *Blank Lines Within a Block of Code*

You may have noticed that we have used blank lines to group together certain lines of code in this example. This is intended to make it easier to read the code and are perfectly allowable in Python. Indeed, the Python layout guidelines encourage it.

It is also possible to have a blank line within an indented block of code; the block of statements is not terminated until another line with valid Python on it is encountered which is not indented to the same level.

8.7   Exercises

For this chapter the exercises all relate to adding additional features to the game:

1. Provide a cheat mode, for example if the user enters −1 print out the number they need to guess and then loop again. This does not count as one of their goes.
2. If their guess is within 1 of the actual number tell the player this.
3. At the end of the game, before printing 'Game Over', modify your program so that it asks the user if they want to play again; if they say yes then restart the whole thing.

Chapter 9
Recursion

9.1 Introduction

Recursion is a very powerful way to implement solutions to a certain class of problems. This class of problems is one where the overall solution to a problem can be generated by breaking that overall problem down into smaller instances of the same problem. The overall result is then generated by combining together the results obtained for the smaller problems.

9.2 Recursive Behaviour

A recursive solution in a programming language such as Python is one in which a function calls itself one or more times in order to solve a particular problem. In many cases the result of calling itself is combined with the functions current state to return a result.

In most cases the recursive call involves calling the function but with a smaller problem to solve. For example, a function to traverse a tree data structure might call itself passing in a sub-tree to process. Alternatively a function to generate a factorial number might call itself passing in a smaller number to process etc.

The key here is that an overall problem can be solved by breaking it down into smaller examples of the same problem.

Functions that solve problems by calling themselves are referred to as *recursive* functions.

However, if such a function does not have a termination point then the function will go on calling itself to infinity (at least in theory). In most languages such a situation will (eventually) result in an error being generated.

© Springer Nature Switzerland AG 2019
J. Hunt, *A Beginners Guide to Python 3 Programming*,
Undergraduate Topics in Computer Science,
https://doi.org/10.1007/978-3-030-20290-3_9

For a recursive function to the useful it must therefore have a *termination condition*. That is a condition under which they do not call themselves and instead just return (often with some result). The termination condition may be because:

- A solution has been found (some data of interest in a tree structure).
- The problem has become so small that it can be solved without further recursion. This is often referred to as a base case. That is, a base case is a problem that can be solved without further recursion.
- Some maximum level of recursion has been reached, possibly without a result being found/generated.

We can therefore say that a recursive function is a function defined in terms of itself via self-referential expressions. The function will continue to call itself with smaller variations of the overall problem until some termination condition is met to stop the recursion. All recursive functions thus share a common format; they have a recursive part and a termination point which represents the base case part.

9.3   Benefits of Recursion

The key benefit of recursion is that some algorithms (solutions to computer problems) are expressed far more elegantly and with a great deal less code when implemented recursively than when using an iterative approach.

This means that the resulting code can be easier to write and easier to read.

These twin ideas are important both for the developers who initially create the software but also for those developers who must maintain that software (potentially a significant amount of time later).

Code that is easier to write tends to be less error prone. Similarly code that is easier to read tends to be easier to maintain, debug, modify and extend.

Recursion is also well suited to producing functional solutions to a problem as by its very nature a recursive function relies on its inputs and outputs and does not hold any hidden state. We will return to this in a later chapter on Functional Programming.

9.4   Recursively Searching a Tree

As an example of a problem that is well suited to a recursive solution, we will example how we might implement a program to traverse a binary tree data structure.

A binary tree is a tree data structure made up of nodes in which each node has a value, a left pointer and a right pointer.

The root node is the top most node in the tree. This root node then references a left and right subtree. This structure is repeated until a leaf node. A leaf node is a node in which both the right and left pointers are empty (that is they have the value None).

This is shown below for a simple binary tree:

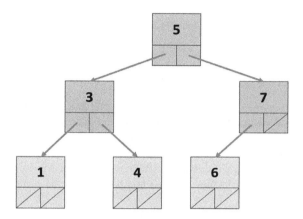

Thus a binary tree is either empty (represented by a null pointer), or is made of a single node, where the left and right pointers each point to a binary tree.

If we now want to find out if a particular value is in the tree then we can start at the root node.

If the root node holds the value we print it; otherwise we can call the search function on the child nodes of the current node. If the current node has no children we just return without a result.

The pseudo code for this might look like:

```
search(value_to_find, current_node):
    If current_node.value == value_to_find:
        print('value found:', current_node.value)
    Else If current.node.has_children:
        search(value, current_node.left)
        search(current_node.right)
```

This illustrates how easy it is to write a recursive function that can solve what might at first appear to be a complex problem.

9.5   Recursion in Python

Most computer programs support the idea of recursion and Python is no exception. In Python it is perfectly legal to have a function that calls itself (that is within the body of the function a call is made to the same function). When the function is executed it will therefore call itself.

In Python we can write a recursive function such as:

```python
def recursive_function():
    print('calling recursive_function')
    recursive_function()
```

Here the function `recursive_function()` is defined such that it prints out a message and then calls itself. Note that no special syntax is required for this as a function does not need to have been completely defined before it is used.

Of course in the case of `recursive_function()` this will result in infinite recursion as there is no *termination* condition. However, this will only become apparent at runtime when Python will eventually generate an error:

```
Traceback (most recent call last):
  File "recursion_example.py", line 5, in <module>
RecursionError: maximum recursion depth exceeded while calling
a Python object
```

However, as already mentioned a recursive function should have a *recursive* part and a *termination* or base case part. The termination condition is used to identify when the base case applies. We should therefore add a condition to identify the termination scenario and what the base case behaviour is. We will do this in the following section as we look at how a factorial for a number can be generated recursively.

9.6   Calculating Factorial Recursively

We have already seen how to create a program that can calculate the factorial of a number using iteration as one of the exercises in the last chapter; now we will create an alternative implementation that uses recursion instead.

Recall that the factorial of a number is the result of multiplying that number by each of the integer values up to that number, for example, to find the factorial of the number 5 (written as 5!) we can multiple 1 * 2 * 3 * 4 * 5 which will generate the number 120.

We can create a recursive solution to the Factorial problem by defining a function that takes an integer to generate the factorial number for. This function will return the value 1 if the number passed in is 1—this is the base case. Otherwise it will multiple the value passed into it with the result of calling itself (the `factorial()` function) with n − 1 which is the recursive part.

The function is given below:

```
def factorial(n):
    if n == 1: # The termination condition
        return 1 # The base case
    else:
        res = n * factorial(n-1) # The recursive call
        return res

print(factorial(5))
```

The key to understanding this function is that it has:

1. A termination condition that is guaranteed to execute when the value of n is 1. This is the base case; we cannot reduce the problem down any further as the factorial of 1 is 1!
2. The function recursively calls itself but with n − 1 as the argument; this means each time it calls itself the value of n is *smaller*. Thus the value returned from this call is the result of a smaller computation.

To clarify how this works we can add some print statements (and a depth indicator) to the function to indicate its behaviour:

```
def factorial(n, depth = 1):
    if n == 1:
        print('\t' * depth, 'Returning 1')
        return 1
    else:
        print('\t'*depth,'Recursively calling factorial(',n-
1,')')
        result = n * factorial(n-1, depth + 1)
        print('\t' * depth, 'Returning:', result)
        return result


print('Calling factorial( 5 )')
print(factorial(5))
```

When we run this version of the program then the output is:

```
Calling factorial( 5 )
    Recursively calling factorial( 4 )
        Recursively calling factorial( 3 )
            Recursively calling factorial( 2 )
                Recursively calling factorial( 1 )
                Returning 1
                Returning: 2
            Returning: 6
        Returning: 24
    Returning: 120
120
```

Note that the depth parameter is used merely to provide some indentation to the `print` statements.

From the output we can see that each call to the `factorial` program results in a simpler calculation until the point where we are asking for the value of 1! which is 1. This is returned as the result of calling `factorial(1)`. This result is multiplied with the value of n prior to that; which was 2. The causes `factorial(2)` to return the value 2 and so on.

9.7   Disadvantages of Recursion

Although Recursion can be a very expressive way to define how a problem can be solved, it is not as efficient as iteration. This is because a function call is more expensive for Python to process that a `for` loop. In part this is because of the infrastructure that goes along with a function call; that is the need to set up the stack for each separate function invocation so that all local variables are independent of any other call to that function. It is also related to associated unwinding the stack when a function returns. However, it is also affected by the increasing amount of memory each recursive call must use to store all the data on the stack.

In some languages optimisations are possible to improve the performance of a recursive solution. One typical example relates to a type of recursion known as *tail recursion*. A tail recursive solution is one in which the calculation is performed before the recursive call. The result is then passed to the recursive step, which results in the last statement in the function just calling the recursive function. In such situations the recursive solution can be expressed (internally to the computer system) as an iterative problem. That is the programmer write the solution as a recursive algorithm but the interpreter or compiler converts it into an iterative solution. This allows programmers to benefit from the expressive nature of recursion while also benefiting from the performance of an iterative solution.

You might think that the `factorial` function presented earlier is tail recursive; however it is not because the last statement in the function performs a calculation that multiples n by the result of recursive call.

However, we can refactor the `factorial` function to be tail recursive. This version of the `factorial` function passes the evolving result along via the `accumulator` parameter. It is given for reference here:

```python
def tail_factorial(n, accumulator=1):
    if n == 0:
        return accumulator
    else:
        return tail_factorial(n - 1, accumulator * n)

print(tail_factorial(5))
```

However, it should be noted that Python currently does not perform tail recursion optimisation; so this is a purely a theoretical exercise.

9.8   Online Resources

The following provides some references on recursion available on line:

- https://en.wikipedia.org/wiki/Recursion_(computer_science) Provides wikipedias introduction to recursion.
- https://www.sparknotes.com/cs/recursion/whatisrecursion/section1/ provides an introduction to the concept of recursion.

9.9   Exercises

In this set of exercises you will get the chance to explore how to solve problems using recursion in Python.

1. Write a program to determine if a given number is a *Prime Number* or not. Use recursion to implement the solution. The following code snippet illustrates how this might work:

```
print('is_prime(3):', is_prime(3)) # True
print('is_prime(7):', is_prime(7)) # True
print('is_prime(9):', is_prime(9)) # False
print('is_prime(31):', is_prime(31)) # True
```

2. Write a function which implements Pascal's triangle for a specified number of rows. Pascals triangle is a triangle of the binomial coefficients. The values held in the triangle are generated as follows: In row 0 (the topmost row), there is a unique nonzero entry 1. Each entry of each subsequent row is constructed by adding the number above and to the left with the number above and to the right, treating blank entries as 0. For example, the initial number in the first (or any other) row is 1 (the sum of 0 and 1), whereas the numbers 1 and 3 in the third row are added together to generate the number 4 in the fourth row. An example of Pascals triangle for 4 rows is given below:

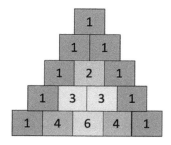

For example, your function might be called `pascals_traingle()` in which case the following application illustrates how you might use it:

```
triangle = pascals_triangle(5)
for row in triangle:
    print(row)
```

The output from this might be:

```
[1]
[1, 1]
[1, 2, 1]
[1, 3, 3, 1]
[1, 4, 6, 4, 1]
```

Chapter 10
Introduction to Structured Analysis

10.1 Introduction

In the preceding chapters what we have seen is typical of the procedural approach to programming. In the next chapter we will begin to explore the definition of functions which allow a more modular style of programming.

In this chapter we will introduce an approach to the analysis and design of software systems called Structured Analysis/Design. Within this area there are many specific and well documented methods including SSADM (Structured Systems Analysis and Design Method) and the Yourden structured method. However, we will not focus on any one specific approach; instead we will outline the key ideas and the two basic elements of most Structured Analysis methods; Functional Decomposition and Data Flow Analysis. We will then present Flowcharts for designing algorithms.

10.2 Structured Analysis and Function Identification

The Structured Analysis methods typically employ a process driven approach (with a set of prescribed steps or stages) which in one way or another consider what the inputs and outputs of the system are and how those inputs are transformed into the outputs. This transformation involves the application of one or more functions. The steps involved in Structured Analysis identify these functions and will typically iteratively break them down into smaller and smaller functions until an appropriate level of detail has been reached. This process is known as Functional Decomposition.

Although simple Python programs may only contain a sequence of statements and expressions; any program of a significant size will need to be structured such that it can be:

© Springer Nature Switzerland AG 2019
J. Hunt, *A Beginners Guide to Python 3 Programming*,
Undergraduate Topics in Computer Science,
https://doi.org/10.1007/978-3-030-20290-3_10

- understood easily by other developers,
- tested to ensure that it does what is intended,
- maintained as new and existing requirements evolve,
- debugged to resolve unexpected or undesirable behaviour.

Given these requirements it is common to want to organise your Python program in terms of functions and sub functions.

Functional Decomposition supports the analysis and identification of these functions.

10.3 Functional Decomposition

Functional Decomposition is one way in which a system can be broken down into its constituent parts. For example, for a computer payroll system to calculate how much an hourly paid employee should receive it might be necessary to:

1. Load the employee's details from some form of permanent storage (such as a file or a database).
2. Load how many hours the employee has worked for that week (possibly from another system that records the number of hours worked).
3. Multiple the hours worked by the employee's hourly rate.
4. Record how much the employee is to be paid in a payroll database or file.
5. Print out the employee's pay slip.
6. Transfer the appropriate funds from the company's bank account to the employees bank account.
7. Record in the payroll database the everything has been completed.

Each of the above steps could represent a function performed by the system.

These top level functions could themselves be broken down into lower level functions. For example, printing out the employees payroll slip may involve printing their name and address in a particular format, printing the employee number, social security number etc. As well as printing historical information such as how much they have been paid in the current financial year, how much tax they have paid etc. All in addition to printing the actual amount they are being paid.

This process of breaking down higher level functions into lower level functions helps with:

- testing the system (functions can be tested in isolation),
- understanding the system as the organisation of the functions can give meaning to the code, as well as allowing each function to be understood in isolation from the rest of the system,
- maintaining the system as only those functions that need to be changed may be affected by new or modified requirements,

- debugging the system as issues can be isolated to specific functions which can be examined independently of the rest of the application.

It is also known as a top-down refinement approach. The term top-down refinement (also known as stepwise design) highlights the idea that we are breaking down a system into the sub-systems that make it up.

It is common to represent the functions identified in the form of a tree illustrating the relationships between the higher level functions and lower level functions. This is illustrated below:

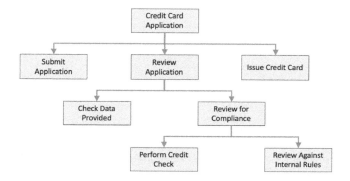

This diagram illustrates how a credit card approval process can be broken down into sub functions.

10.3.1 Functional Decomposition Terminology

The key terms used within Functional Decomposition are:

- **Function**. This is a task that is performed by a device, system or process.
- **Decomposition**. This is the process by which higher level functions are broken down into lower level functions where each function represents part of the functionality of the higher level function.
- **Higher Level Function**. This is a function that has one or more sub functions. This higher level function depends on the functionality of the lower level functions for its behaviour.
- **Sub Function**. This is a function that provides some element of the behaviour of a higher level function. A sub function can also be broken down into its own sub functions in a hierarchical manner. In the above diagram the *Review for Compliance* function is both a sub function and has its own sub functions.

- **Basic Function**. A basic function is a function that has no smaller sub functions. The *Perform Credit Check* and *Review Against internal Rules* functions are both Basic Functions.

10.3.2   *Functional Decomposition Process*

At a very high level, Functional Decomposition consists of a series of steps such as those outlined below:

1. Find/Identify the inputs and outputs of the system.
2. Define how the inputs are converted to the outputs. This will help identify the top most, high level function(s).
3. Look at the current function(s) and try to break them down into a list of sub functions. Identify what each sub function should do and what its inputs and outputs are.
4. Repeat step 2 for each function identified until the functions identified can't or should not be decomposed further.
5. Draw a diagram of the function hierarchy you have created. Viewing the functions and their relationships is a very useful thing to do as it allows developers to visualise the system functionally. There are many CASE (Computer Aided Software Engineering) tools that help with this but any drawing tool (such as Visio) can be used.
6. Examine the diagram for any repeating functions. That is, functions that do the same thing but appear in different places in the design. These are probably more generic functions that can be reused. Also examine the diagram to see if you can identify any missing functions.
7. Refine/Design the interfaces between one function and another. That is, what data/information is passed to and from a function to a sub function as well as between functions.

10.3.3   *Calculator Functional Decomposition Example*

As an example of Functional Decomposition let us consider a simple calculator program.

We want this program to be able to perform a set of mathematical operations on two numbers, such as add, subtract, multiple and divide. We might therefore draw a Functional Decomposition Diagram (or FDD) such as:

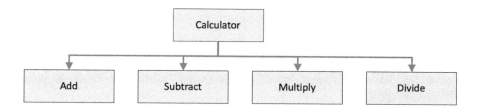

This illustrates that the Calculator function can be decomposed into the add, subtract multiply and Divide functions.

We might then identify the need to enter the two numbers to be operated on. This would result in one or more new functions being added:

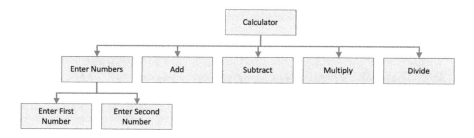

We might also identify the need to determine which numerical operation should be performed based on user input. This function might sit above the numerical functions or along side them. This is in fact an example of a design decision that the designer/developer must make based on their understanding of the problem and how the software will be developed/tested/used etc.

In the following version of the Functional Decomposition Diagram the *operation selection* function is placed at the same level as the numerical operations as it provides information back to the top level function.

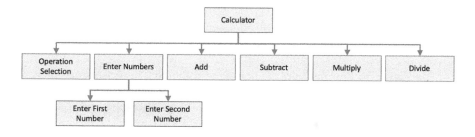

10.4   Functional Flow

Although the decomposition hierarchy presented in the Functional Decomposition Diagram illustrates the functions and their hierarchical relationships; it does not capture how the data flows between the functions or the order in which the functions are invoked.

There are several approaches to describing the interactions between the functions identified by Functional Decomposition including the use of pseudo code, Data Flow Diagrams and Sequence diagrams:

- **Pseudo Code**. This is a form of structured english that is not tied to any particular programming language but which can be used to express simple ideas including conditional choices (similar to if statements) and iteration (as typified by looping constructs). However, as it is a pseudo language, developers are not tied to a specific syntax and can include functions without the need to define those functions in detail.
- **Data Flow Diagrams**. These diagrams are used to chart the inputs, processes, and outputs of the functions in a structured graphical form. A data-flow diagram typically has no control flow, there are no decision rules and no loops. For each data flow, there must be at least one input and one end point. Each process (function) can be refined by another lower-level data-flow diagram, which subdivides this process into sub-processes.
- **Sequence Diagrams**. These are used to represent interactions between different entities (or objects) in sequence. The functions invoked are represented as being called from one entity to another. Sequence diagrams are more typically used with Object Oriented systems.

10.5   Data Flow Diagrams

A Data Flow Diagram consists of a set of inputs and outputs, processes (functions), flows, data stores (also known as warehouses) and terminators.

- **Process**. This is the process (or function or transformation) that converts inputs into outputs. The name of the process should be descriptive indicating what it does.
- **Data Flow**. The flow indicates the transfer of data/information from one element to another (that is a flow has a direction). The flow should have a name that suggests what information/data is being exchanged. Flows link processes, data stores and terminators.
- **Data Store/Warehouse**. A data store (which may be something such as a file, folder, database, or other repository of data) is used to store data for later use. The name of the data store is a plural noun (e.g. employees). The flow from the data store usually represents the reading of the data stored in the data store, and

the flow to the waredata storehouse usually expresses data entry or updating (sometimes also deleting data).
- **Terminator**. The Terminator represents an external entity (to the system) that communicates with the system. Examples of entities might be human users or other systems etc.

An example of a Data Flow Diagram is given below using the functions identified for the calculator:

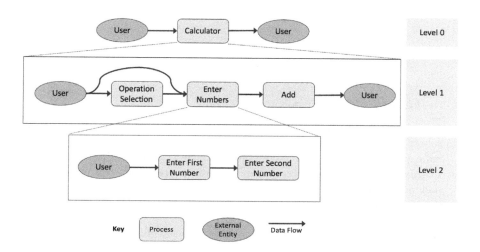

In this diagram the hierarchy of DFDs is indicated by the levels which expand on how the function in the previous level is implemented by the functions at the next level. This DFD also only presents the data flow for the situation where the user selects the add function as the numerical operation to apply.

10.6 Flowcharts

A flowchart is a graphical representation of an algorithm, workflow or process for a given problem.

Flowcharts are used in the analysis, design and documentation of software systems. As with other forms of notation (such as DFDs) Flowcharts help designers and developers to visualise the steps involved in a solution and thus aid in understanding the processes and algorithms involved.

The steps in the algorithm are represented as various types of boxes. The ordering of the steps is indicated by arrows between the boxes. The flow of control is represented by decision boxes.

There are a number of common notations used with Flowcharts and most of those notations use the following symbols:

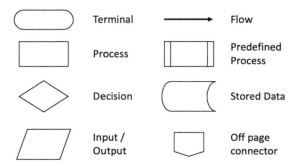

The meaning of these symbols is given below:

- **Terminal**. This symbol is used to indicate the start or end of a program or subprocess. They usually contain the words 'Start', 'End' or 'Stop' or a phrase indicating the start or end of some process such as 'Starting Print Run'.
- **Process**. This symbol represents one or more operations (or programming statements/expressions) that in some way apply behaviour or change the state of the system. For example they may add two numbers together, run some form of calculation or change a boolean flag etc.
- **Decision**. This represents a decision point in the algorithm; that is it represents a decision point which will alter the flow of the program (typically between two different paths). The decision point is often represented as a question with a 'yes'/'no' response and this is indicated on the flow chart by the use of 'yes' (or 'y') and 'no' (or 'n') labels on the flow chart. In Python this decision point may be implemented using an if statement.
- **Input/Output**. This box indicates the input or output of data from the algorithm. This might represent obtaining input data from the user or printing out results to the user.
- **Flow**. These arrows are used to represent the algorithms order of execution of the boxes.
- **Predefined Process**. This represents a process that has been defined elsewhere.
- **Stored Data**. Indicates that data is stored in some form of persistent storage system.
- **Off Page Connector**. A labelled connector for use when the target is on another page (another flowchart).

Using the above symbols we can create a Flowchart for our simple integer calculator program:

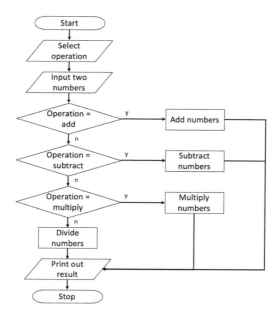

The above flowchart shows the basic operation of the calculator; the user selects which operation to perform, enters the two numbers and then depending upon the operation the selected operation is performed. The result is then printed out.

10.7   Data Dictionary

Another element commonly associated with Structured Analysis/Design is the Data Dictionary. The Data Dictionary is a structured repository of data elements in the system. It stores the descriptions of all Data Flow Diagram data elements. That is it records details and definitions of data flows, data stores, data stored in data stores, and the processes. The format used for a data dictionary varies from method to method and project to project. It can be as simple as an Excel spreadsheet to an enterprise wide software system such as Semanta (https://www.semantacorp.com/data-dictionary).

10.8   Online Resources

There are many online resources available that discuss functional decomposition, both from a theoretical a practical Python oriented, point of view including:

- https://en.wikipedia.org/wiki/Structured_analysis   Wikipedia   Structured Analysis Page.
- https://en.wikipedia.org/wiki/Top-down_and_bottom-up_design   Wikipedia page on Top Down and Bottom Up design.
- https://en.wikipedia.org/wiki/Edward_Yourdon#Yourdon_Structured_Method Wikipedia page on the Yourden method.
- https://en.wikipedia.org/wiki/Structured_systems_analysis_and_design_method Wikipedia page on SSADM.
- https://en.wikipedia.org/wiki/Functional_decomposition The wikipedia page on Functional Decomposition.
- https://docs.python.org/3/howto/functional.html The Python standard documentation on functional decomposition.
- https://en.wikipedia.org/wiki/Data-flow_diagram Wikipedia page on Data Flow Diagrams (DFDs).
- https://en.wikipedia.org/wiki/Sequence_diagram Wikipedia page on Sequence Diagrams.
- https://en.wikipedia.org/wiki/Data_dictionary   Wikipedia   page   on   Data Dictionaries.
- https://en.wikipedia.org/wiki/Flowchart Wikipedia Flowchart page.

Chapter 11
Functions in Python

11.1 Introduction

As discussed in the last chapter; when you build an application of any size you will want to break it down into more manageable units; these units can then be worked on separately, tested and maintained separately. One way in which these units can be defined is as Python functions.

This chapter will introduce Python functions, how they are defined, how they can be referenced and executed. It considers how parameters work in Python functions and how values can be returned from functions. It also introduces *lambda* or anonymous functions.

11.2 What Are Functions?

In Python functions are groups of related statements that can be called together, that typically perform a specific task, and which may or may not take a set of parameters or return a value.

Functions can be defined in one place and called or invoked in another. This helps to make code more modular and easier to understand.

It also means that the same function can be called multiple times or in multiple locations. This help to ensure that although a piece of functionality is used in multiple places; it is only defined once and only needs to be maintained and tested in one location.

The original version of this chapter was revised: text has been replaced. The correction to this chapter is available at https://doi.org/10.1007/978-3-030-20290-3_38

© Springer Nature Switzerland AG 2019, corrected publication 2020
J. Hunt, *A Beginners Guide to Python 3 Programming*,
Undergraduate Topics in Computer Science,
https://doi.org/10.1007/978-3-030-20290-3_11

11.3   How Functions Work

We have said what they are and a little bit about why they might be good but not really how they work.

When a function is called (or invoked) the flow of control a program jumps from where the function was called to the point where the function was defined. The body of the function is then executed before control returns back to where it was called from.

As part of this process, all the values that were in place when the function was called, are stored away (on something called the stack) so that if the function defines its own versions, they do not overwrite each other.

The invocation of a function illustrated below:

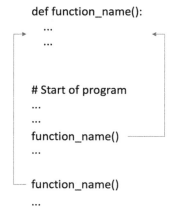

```
def function_name():
    ...
    ...

# Start of program
...
...
function_name()
...

function_name()
...
```

Each time the call is made to function_name() the program flow jumps to the body of the function and executes the statements there. Once the function finishes it returns to the point at which the function was called.

In the above this happens twice as the function is called at two separate points in the program.

11.4   Types of Functions

Technically speaking there are two types of functions in Python; *built-in* functions and *user-defined* functions.

Built-in functions are those provided by the language and we have seen several of these already. For example, both print() and input() are built-in functions. We did not need to define them ourselves as they are provided by Python.

In contrast *user-defined* functions are those written by developers. We will be defining user-defined functions in the rest of this chapter and it is likely that in many cases, most of the programs that you will write will include user-defined functions of one sort or another.

11.5   Defining Functions

The basic syntax of a function is illustrated below:

```
def function_name(parameter list):
    """docstring"""
    statement
    statement(s)
```

This illustrates several things:

1. All (named) functions are defined using the *keyword* `def`; this indicates the start of a function definition. A keyword is a part of the syntax of the Python language and cannot be redefined and is not a function.
2. A function can have a name which uniquely identifies it; you can also have anonymous functions, but we will leave those until later in this chapter.
3. The naming conventions that we have been adopting for variables also applies to functions, they are all lower case with the different elements of the function name separated by an '_'.
4. A function can (optionally) have a list of parameters which allow data to be passed into the function. These are optional as not all functions need to be supplied with parameters.
5. A colon is used to mark the end of the *function header* and the start of the *function body*. The function header defines the signature of the function (what its called and the parameters it takes). The function body defines what the function does.
6. An optional documentation string (the `docstring`) can be provided that describes what the function does. We typically use the triple double quote string format as this allows the documentation string to go over multiple lines if required.
7. One or more Python statements make up the function body. These are indented relative to the function definition. All lines that are indented are part of the function until a line which is intended at the same level as the `def` line.
8. It is common to use 4 spaces (not a tab) to determine how much to indent the body of a function by.

11.5.1   An Example Function

The following is one of the simplest functions you can write; it takes no parameters and has only a single statement that prints out the message 'Hello World':

```
def print_msg():
    print('Hello World!')
```

This function is called `print_msg` and when called (also known as invoked) it will run the body of the function which will print out the string, for example

```
print_msg()
```

Will generate the output

```
Hello World!
```

Be careful to include the round brackets `()` when you call the function. This is because if you just use the function's name then you are merely referring to the location in memory where the function is stored, and you are not invoking it.

We could modify the function to make it a little more general and reusable by providing a parameter. This parameter could be used to supply the message to be printed out, for example:

```
def print_my_msg(msg):
    print(msg)
```

Now the `print_my_msg` function takes a single parameter and this parameter becomes a variable which is available within the body of the function. However, this parameter only exists within the body of the function; it is not available outside of the function.

This now means that we can call the `print_my_msg` function with a variety of different messages:

```
print_my_msg('Hello World')
print_my_msg('Good day')
print_my_msg('Welcome')
print_my_msg('Ola')
```

The output from calling this function with each of these strings being supplied as the parameter is:

```
Hello World
Good day
Welcome
Ola
```

11.6   Returning Values from Functions

It is very common to want to return a value from a function. In Python this can be done using the `return` statement. Whenever a `return` statement is encountered within a function then that function will terminate and return any values following the `return` keyword.

This means that if a value is provided, then it will be made available to any calling code.

For example, the following defines a simple function that squares whatever value has been passed to it:

```
def square(n):
    return n * n
```

When we call this function, it will multiple whatever it is given by itself and then return that value. The returned value can then be used at the point that the function was invoked, for example:

```
# Store result from square in a variable
result = square( 4)
print(result)
# Send the result from square immediately to another function
print(square( 5))
# Use the result returned from square in a conditional
expression
if square(3) < 15:
    print(' Still less than 15  ')
```

When this code is run, we get:

```
16
25
Still less than 15
```

It is also possible to return multiple values from a function, for example in this swap function the order in which the parameters are supplied is swapped when they are returned:

```
def swap(a, b):
    return b, a
```

We can then assign the values returned to variables at the point when the function is called:

```
a = 2
b = 3
x, y = swap(a, b)
print(x, ',', y)
```

Which produces

```
3 , 2
```

In actual fact the result returned from the swap function is what is called a *tuple* which is a simple way to grouping data together. This means that we could also have written:

```
z = swap(a, b)
print(z)
```

Which would have printed the tuple out:

```
(3, 2)
```

We will look at tuples more when we consider collections of data.

11.7 Docstring

So far our example functions have not included any documentation strings (the docstring). This is because the docstring is *optional* and the functions we have written have been very simple.

However, as functions become more complex and may have multiple parameters the documentation provided can become more important.

The docstring allows the function to provide some guidance on what is expected in terms of the data passed into the parameters, potentially what will happen if the data is incorrect,as well as what the purpose of the function is in the first place.

In the following example, the docstring is being used to explain the behaviour of the function and how the parameter is used.

```python
def get_integer_input(message):
    """
    This function will display the message to the user
    and request that they input an integer.

    If the user enters something that is not a number
    then the input will be rejected
    and an error message will be displayed.

    The user will then be asked to try again."""

    value_as_string = input(message)
    while not value_as_string.isnumeric():
        print('The input must be an integer')
        value_as_string = input(message)
    return int(value_as_string)
```

When used this method will guarantee that a valid integer will be returned to the calling code:

```python
age = get_integer_input('Please input your age: ')
print('age is', age)
```

An example of what happens when this is run is given below:

```
Please input your age: John
The input must be an integer
Please input your age: 21
age is 21
```

The docstring can be read directly from the code but is also available to IDEs such as PyCharm so that they can provide information about the function. It is even available to the programmer via a very special property of the function called __doc__ that is accessible via the name of the function using the dot notation:

```
print(get_integer_input.__doc__)
```

Which generates

```
This function will display the message to the user
and request that they input an integer.

If the user enters something that is not a number
then the input will be rejected
and an error message will be displayed.

The user will then be asked to try again.
```

11.8   Function Parameters

Before we go any further it is worth clarifying some terminology associated with passing data into functions. This terminology relates to the parameters defined as part of the function header and the data passed into the function via these parameters:

- A *parameter* is a variable defined as part of the function header and is used to make data available within the function itself.
- An *argument* is the actual value or data passed into the function when it is called. The data will be held within the parameters.

Unfortunately many developers use these terms interchangeably but it is worth being clear on the distinction.

11.8.1   Multiple Parameter Functions

So far the functions we have defined have only had zero or one parameters; however that was just a choice. We could easily have defined a function which defined two or more parameters. In these situations, the parameter list contains a list of parameter names separated by a comma.

For example

```
def greeter(name, message):
    print('Welcome', name, '-', message)

greeter('Eloise', 'Hope you like Rugby')
```

Here the greeter function takes defines two parameters; name and message. These parameters (which are local to the function and cannot be seen outside of the function) are then used within the body of the function.

The output is

```
Welcome Eloise - Hope you like Rugby
```

You can have any number of parameters defined in a function (prior to Python 3.7 there was a limit of 256 parameters—although if you have this many then probably you have a major problem with the design of your function—however this limit has now gone).

11.8.2   Default Parameter Values

Once you have one or more parameters you may want to provide *default* values for some or all of those parameters; particular for ones which might not be used in most cases.

This can be done very easily in Python; all that is required is that the default value must be declared in the function header along with the parameter name.

If a value is supplied for the parameter, then it will override the default. If no value is supplied when the function is called, then the default will be used.

For example, we can modify the greeter() function from the previous section to provide a default message such as 'Live Long and Prosper'.

```
def greeter(name, message = 'Live Long and Prosper'):
    print('Welcome', name, '-', message)

greeter('Eloise')
greeter('Eloise', 'Hope you like Python')
```

Now we can call the greeter() function with one or two arguments. When we run this example, we will get:

```
Welcome Eloise - Live Long and Prosper
Welcome Eloise - Hope you like Python
```

As you can see from this in the first example (where only one argument was provided) the default message was used. However, in the second example where a message was provided, along with the name, then that message was used instead of the default.

Note we can use the terms *mandatory* and *optional* for the parameters in `greeter()`. In this case

- name is a mandatory field/parameter
- message is an optional field/parameter (as it has a default value).

One subtle point to note is that any number of parameters in a function's parameter list can have a default value; however once one parameter has a default value all remaining parameters to the right of that parameter must also have default values. For example, we could *not* define the greeter function as

```
def greeter(message = 'Live Long and Prosper', name):
    print('Welcome', name, '-', message)
```

As this would generate an *error* indicating that name must have a default value as it comes after (to the right) of a parameter with a default value.

11.8.3 Named Arguments

So far we have relied on the position of a value to be used to determine which parameter that value is assigned to. In many cases this is the simplest and cleanest option.

However, if a function has several parameters, some of which have default values, it may become impossible to rely on using the position of a value to ensure it is given to the correct parameter (because we may want to use some of the default values instead).

For example, let us assume we have a function with four parameters

```
def greeter(name,
            title = 'Dr',
            prompt = 'Welcome',
            message = 'Live Long and Prosper'):
    print(prompt, title, name, '-', message)
```

This now raises the question how do we provide the `name` and the `message` arguments when we would like to have the default `title` and `prompt`?

The answer is to use *named* arguments (or *keyword* arguments). In this approach we provide the name of the parameter we want an argument/value to be assigned to; position is no longer relevant. For example:

```
greeter(message = 'We like Python', name = 'Lloyd')
```

In this example we are using the default values for `title` and `prompt` and have changed the order of `message` and `name`. This is completely legal and results in the following output:

```
Welcome Dr Lloyd - We like Python
```

We can actually mix *positional* and *named* arguments in Python, for example:
Here 'Lloyd' is bound to the `name` parameter as it is the first parameter, but 'We like Python' is bound to `message` parameter as it is a named argument.

```
greeter('Lloyd', message = 'We like Python')
```

However, you cannot place positional arguments after a named argument, so we cannot write:

```
greeter(name='John', 'We like Python')
```

As this will result in Python generating an error.

11.8.4   Arbitrary Arguments

In some cases, you do not know how many arguments will be supplied when a function is called. Python allows you to pass an arbitrary number of arguments into a function and then process those arguments inside the function.

To define a parameter list as being of arbitrary length, a parameter is marked with an asterisk (*). For example:

```
def greeter(*args):
    for name in args:
        print('Welcome', name)

greeter('John', 'Denise', 'Phoebe', 'Adam', 'Gryff', 'Jasmine')
```

This generates

```
Welcome John
Welcome Denise
Welcome Phoebe
Welcome Adam
Welcome Gryff
Welcome Jasmine
```

Note that this is another use of the for loop; but this time it is a sequence of strings rather than a sequence of integers that is being used.

11.8.5   Positional and Keyword Arguments

Some functions in Python are defined such that the arguments to the methods can either be provided using a variable number of positional or keyword arguments. Such functions have two arguments *args and **kwargs (for positional arguments and keyword arguments).

They are useful if you do not know exactly how many of either position or keyword arguments are going to be provided.

For example, the function my_function takes both a variable number of positional and keyword arguments:

```
def my_function(*args, **kwargs):
    for arg in args:
        print('arg:', arg)
    for key in kwargs.keys():
        print('key:', key, 'has value: ', kwargs[key])
```

This can be called with any number of arguments of either type:

```
my_function('John', 'Denise', daughter='Phoebe', son='Adam')
print('-' * 50)
my_function('Paul', 'Fiona', son_number_one='Andrew',
son_number_two='James', daughter='Joselyn')
```

Which produces the output:

```
arg: John
arg: Denise
key: son has value:  Adam
key: daughter has value:  Phoebe
---------------------------------------------------
arg: Paul
arg: Fiona
key: son_number_one has value:  Andrew
key: son_number_two has value:  James
key: daughter has value:  Joselyn
```

Also note that the keywords used for the arguments are not fixed.

You can also define methods that only use one of the *args and **kwargs depending on your requirements (as we saw with the greeter() function above), for example:

```python
def named(**kwargs):
    for key in kwargs.keys():
        print('arg:', key, 'has value:', kwargs[key])

named(a=1, b=2, c=3)
```

In this case, the named function only supports the provision of keyword arguments. Its output in the above case is:

```
arg:  a has value:  1
arg:  c has value:  3
arg:  b has value:  2
```

In general, these facilities are most likely to be used by those creating libraries as they allow for great flexibility in how the library can be used.

11.9   Anonymous Functions

All the functions we have defined in this chapter have had a *name* that they can be referenced by, such as greeter or get_integer_input etc. This means that we can reference and reuse these functions as many times as we like.

However, in some cases we want to create a function and use it only once; giving it a name for this one time can *pollute* the namespace of the program (i.e. there are lots of names around) and also means that someone might call it when we don't expect them to.

Python therefore another option when defining a function; it is possible to define an *anonymous* function. In Python an anonymous function is one that does not have a name and can only be used at the point that it is defined.

Anonymous functions are defined using the keyword `lambda` and for this reason they are also known as *lambda* functions.

The syntax used to define an anonymous function is:

```
lambda arguments: expression
```

Anonymous functions can have any number of arguments but only one expression (that is a statement that returns a value) as their body. The expression is executed, and the value generated from it is returned as the result of the function.

As an example, let us define an anonymous function that will square a number:

```
double = lambda i : i * i
```

In this example the lambda definition indicates that there is one parameter to the anonymous function ('i') and that the body of the function is defined after the colon ':' which multiples i * i; the value of which is returned as the result of the function. The whole anonymous function is then stored into a variable called `double`.

We can store the anonymous function into the variable as all functions are instances of the class `function` and can be referenced in this way (we just haven't done this so far).

To invoke the function, we can access the reference to the function held in the variable `double` and then use the round brackets to cause the function to be executed, passing in any values to be used for the parameters:

```
print(double(10))
```

When this is executed the value `100` is printed out.

Other examples of lambda/anonymous functions are given below (illustrating that an anonymous function can take any number of arguments):

```
func0 = lambda: print('no args')
func1 = lambda x: x * x
func2 = lambda x, y: x * y
func3 = lambda x, y, z: x + y + z
```

These can be used as shown below:

```
func0()
print(func1(4))
print(func2(3, 4))
print(func3(2, 3, 4))
```

The output from this code snippet is:

```
no args
16
12
9
```

11.10   Online Resources

See the Python Standard Library documentation for:

- https://docs.python.org/3/library/functions.html for a list of built-in functions in Python.
- https://www.w3schools.com/python/python_functions.asp the W3 Schools brief introduction to Python functions.
- https://www.w3schools.com/python/python_lambda.asp a short summary of lambda functions.

11.11   Exercises

For this chapter the exercises involve the number_guess_game you created in the last chapter:

Take the number guess game and break it up into a number of functions. There is not necessarily a right or wrong way to do this; look for functions that are meaningful to you within the code, for example:

1. You could create a function to obtain input from the user.
2. You could create another function that will implement the main game playing loop.
3. You could also provide a function that will print out a message indicating if the player won or not.
4. You could create a function to print a welcome message when the game starts up.

Chapter 12
Scope and Lifetime of Variables

12.1 Introduction

We have already defined several variables in the examples we have being working with in this book. In practice, most of these variables have been what are known as *global* variables. That is there are (potentially) accessible anywhere (or globally) in our programs.

In this chapter we will look at *local* variables as defined within a function, at global variables and how they can be referenced within a function and finally we will consider *nonlocal* variables.

12.2 Local Variables

In practice developers usually try to limit the number of global variables in their programs as global variables can be accessed anywhere and can be modified anywhere and this can result in unexpected behaviours (and has been the cause of many, many bugs in all sorts of programs over the years).

However, not all variables are global. When we define a function, we can create variables which are scoped only to that function and are not accessible or visible outside of the function. These variables are referred to as local variables (as they are local to the function).

This is a great help in developing more modular code which has been proven to be easier to maintain and in fact develop and test.

In the following function local variable called `a_variable` has been created and initialised to hold the value 100.

© Springer Nature Switzerland AG 2019
J. Hunt, *A Beginners Guide to Python 3 Programming*,
Undergraduate Topics in Computer Science,
https://doi.org/10.1007/978-3-030-20290-3_12

```
def my_function():
    a_variable = 100
    print(a_variable)

my_function()
```

When this function is called a_variable will be initialised to 100 and will then be printed out to the console:

```
100
```

Thus when we ran the my_function() it successfully printed out the value 100 which was held in the local (to the function) variable a_variable.

However if we attempt to access a_variable outside the function, then it will not be defined and we will generate an error, for example:

```
my_function()
print(a_variable)
```

When we run this code, we get the number 100 printed out from the call the my_function(). However, an error is then reported by Python:

```
100
Traceback (most recent call last):
  File "localvars.py", line 7, in <module>
    print(a_variable)
NameError: name 'a_variable' is not defined
```

This indicates that a_variable is *undefined* at the top level (which is the global scope). Thus, we can say that a_variable is not globally defined.

This is because a_variable only exists and only has meaning inside my_function; outside of that function it cannot be seen.

In fact, each time the function is called, a_variable comes back into existence as a *new* variable, so the value in a_variable is not even seen from one invocation of the function to another.

This raises the question what happens if a *global* variable called a_variable is defined? For example, if we have the following:

```
a_variable = 25
my_function()
print(a_variable)
```

Actually, this is fine and is supported by Python. There are now two versions of a_variable in the program; one of which is defined *globally* and one of which is defined within the *context* of the function.

Python does not get confused between these and treats then as completely separately. This is just like having two people called *John* in the same class in school. If they were only called John this might cause some confusion, but if they have different surnames then it is easy to distinguish between them via their full names such as *John Jones* and *John Smith*.

In this case we have *global* a_variable and my_function a_variable.
Thus if we run the above code we get

```
100
25
```

The value 100 does not overwrite the value 25 as they are completely different
variables.

12.3   The Global Keyword

But what happens if what you want is to reference the global variable within a
function.

As long as Python does not think you have defined a local variable then all will
be fine. For example

```
max = 100
def print_max():
    print(max)
print_max()
```

This prints out the value 100.

However, things go a bit astray if you try to modify the global variable inside the
function. At this point Python thinks you are creating a local variable. If as part of
the assignment you try to reference the current value of that (now) local variable
you will get an error indicating that it currently does not have a value. For example,
if we write:

```
def print_max():
    max = max + 1
    print(max)
print_max()
```

And then run this example, we will get

```
Traceback (most recent call last):
  File "localvars.py", line 17, in <module>
    print_max()
  File "localvars.py", line 14, in print_max
    max = max + 1
UnboundLocalError: local variable 'max' referenced before
assignment
```

Indicating that we have referenced max before it was assigned a value—even
though it was assigned a value *globally* before the function was called!

Why does it do this? To protect us from ourselves—Python is really saying 'Do you really want to modify a global variable here?'. Instead it is treating max as a *local* variable and as such it is being referenced before a value has been assigned to it.

To tell Python that we know what we are doing and that we want to reference the global variable at this point we need to use the keyword global with the name of the variable. For example:

```
max = 100

def print_max():
    global max
    max = max + 1
    print(max)

print_max()
print(max)
```

Now when we try to update the variable max inside the function print_max(), Python knows we mean the *global* version of the variable and uses that one. The result is that we now print out the value 101 and max is updated to 101 for everyone everywhere!

12.4   Nonlocal Variables

It is possible to define functions inside other functions, and this can be very useful when we are working with collections of data and operations such as map() (which maps a function to all the elements of a collection of data).

However, local variables are local to a specific function; even functions defined within another function cannot modify the outer functions local variables (as the inner function is a separate function). They can reference it, just as we could reference the global variable earlier; the issue is again modification.

The global keyword is no help here as the outer function's variables are not global, they are local to a function.

For example, if we define a nested function (inner) inside the parent outer function (outer) and want the inner function to modify the local field we have a problem:

```
def outer():
    title = 'original title'

    def inner():
        title = 'another title'
        print('inner:', title)

    inner()
    print('outer:', title)

outer()
```

In this example both `outer()` and `inner()` functions modify the `title` variable. However, they are not the same `title` variable and as long as this is what we need then that is fine; both functions have their own version of a `title` local variable.

This can be seen in the output where the outer function maintains its own value for `title`:

```
inner: another title
outer: original title
```

However, if what we want is for the `inner()` function to modify the `outer()` function's `title` variable then we have a problem.

This problem can be solved using the `nonlocal` keyword. This indicates that a variable is not global but is also not local to the current function and Python should look within the scope in which the function is defined to fund a local variable with the same name:

If we now declare `title` as `nonlocal` in the `inner()` function, then it will use the `outer()` functions version of `title` (it will be shared between them) and thus when the `inner()` function changes the `title` it will change the it for both functions:

```python
def outer():
    title = 'original title'
    def inner():
        nonlocal title
        title = 'another title'
        print('inner:', title)
    inner()
    print('outer:', title)

outer()
```

The result of running this is

```
inner: another title
outer: another title
```

12.5 Hints

Points to note about the scope and lifetime of variables

1. The scope of a variable is the part of a program where the variable is known. Parameters and variables defined inside a function are not visible from outside. Hence, they have a local scope.
2. The lifetime of a variable is the period throughout which the variable exits in the memory of your Python program. The lifetime of variables inside a function is as long as the function executes. These local variables are destroyed as soon as the function returns or terminates. This means that the function does not store the values in a variable from one invocation to another.

12.6   Online Resources

See the Python Standard Library documentation for:

- https://docs.python.org/3/faq/programming.html#what-are-the-rules-for-local-and-global-variables-in-python which provides further information on the Python rules for local and global variables.

12.7   Exercise

Return to the number guess game—did you have to make any compromises with the variables to overcome the global variable issue? If so can you resolve them now with the use of the `global`?

Chapter 13
Implementing a Calculator Using Functions

13.1 Introduction

In this chapter we will step through the development of another Python program; this time the program will be to provide a simple calculator which can be used to add, subtract, multiple and divide numbers. The implementation of the calculator is base on the Function Decomposition performed earlier in the book in the Introduction to Structured Analysis chapter.

The calculator will be implemented using Python functions to help modularise the code.

13.2 What the Calculator Will Do

This will be a purely command driven application that will allow the user to specify

- the operation to perform and
- the two numbers to use with that operation.

When the program starts up it can use a loop to keep processing operations until the user indicates that they wish to terminate the application.

We can also use an if statement to select the operation to perform etc.

As such it will also build on several other features in Python that we have already been working with.

© Springer Nature Switzerland AG 2019
J. Hunt, *A Beginners Guide to Python 3 Programming*,
Undergraduate Topics in Computer Science,
https://doi.org/10.1007/978-3-030-20290-3_13

13.3   Getting Started

The first step will be to create a new Python file. If you are using the PyCharm IDE you can do it using the New>PythonFile menu option (look back at the number guess game chapter if you can't remember how to do this). The file can be called anything you like, but *calculator* seems like a reasonable name.

In the newly created (and empty) `calculator.py` file type in a welcome print message such as:

```python
print('Simple Calculator App')
```

Now run the `calculator.py` program (again if you don't remember how to do that look back at the Number Guess Game chapter).

You should see the message printed out in the Python console. This verifies that the file has been created properly and that you can run the Python code you will define in it.

13.4   The Calculator Operations

We are going to start by defining a set of functions that will implement the add, subtract, multiply and divide operations.

All of these functions take two numbers and return another number. We have also given each function a docstring to illustrate their use, although in practice the functions are so simple and self-describing that the docstring is probably redundant.

The functions are listed below; you can now add them to the `calculator.py` file:

```python
def add(x, y):
    """ Adds two numbers """
    return x + y

def subtract(x, y):
    """ Subtracts two numbers """
    return x - y

def multiply(x, y):
    """ Multiples two numbers """
    return x * y

def divide(x, y):
    """Divides two numbers"""
    return x / y
```

We now have the basic functions needed by the calculator.

13.5   Behaviour of the Calculator

We can no explore what the operation of the calculator program should be.

Essentially, we want to allow the user to be able to select the operation they want to perform, provide the two numbers to use with the operation and then for the program to call the appropriate function. The result of the operation should then be presented to the user.

We then want to ask the user whether they want to continue to use the calculator or to exit the program. This is illustrated below in flow chart form:

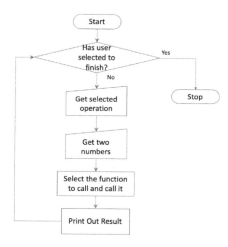

Based on this flowchart we can put in place the skeleton of the logic for the calculator's processing cycle.

We will need a `while` loop to determine whether the user has finished or not and a variable to hold the result and print it out.

The following code provides this skeleton.

```
finished = False
while not finished:
    result = 0
    # Get the operation from the user
    # Get the numbers from the user
    # Select the operation
    print('Result:', result)
    print('==================')
    # Determine if the user has finished

print('Bye')
```

If you try to run this right now then you will find that this code will loop forever as the user is not yet prompted to say if they wish to continue or not. However, it does provide the basic framework; we have

- a variable, finished, with a Boolean flag in it to indicate if the user has finished or not. This is referred to as a flag because it is a Boolean value and because it is being used to determine whether to terminate the main processing loop or not.
- a variable to hold the result of the operation and the two numbers.
- the while loop representing the main processing loop of the calculator.

13.6   Identifying Whether the User Has Finished

We could address several of the remaining areas next; however, we will select the last step—that of determining if the user has finished or not. This will allow us to start to run the application so that we can test out the behaviour.

To do this we need to prompt the user to ask them if they want to continue using the calculator.

At one level this is very straight forward; we could ask the user to input 'y' or 'n' to indicates *yes* I have finished or *no* I want to keep going.

We could therefore use the input function as follows:

```
user_input = input('Do you want to finish (y/n): ')
```

We could then check to see if they have entered a 'y' character and terminate the loop.

However, anytime we take any input from something outside of our program (such as the user) we should verify the input. For example, what should the program do if the user enters 'x' or the number '1'? One option is to treat anything that is not a 'y' as being—*I want to keep going*. However, this is opening up our simple program to bad practices and (in a much larger system) to potential security issues and certainly to potential hacker attacks.

It is a much better idea to verify that the input is what is expected and to reject any input until it is either a 'y' or an 'n'.

This means that the code is more complex than a single input statement; there is for example an implied loop here and as well as some idea of input validation.

This means that this is an ideal candidate for a function that will *encapsulate* this behaviour into a separate operation. We can then test this function which is always a good idea. It also means that where we use the function, we have a level of *abstraction*. That is we can name the function appropriately which will make it easier to see what we intended, instead of having a mass of code in one place.

We will call the function check_if_user_has_finished; this name makes it very clear what the purpose of the function is. It also means that when we use it in our main processing loop its role in that loop will be obvious.

The function is given below:

```python
def check_if_user_has_finished():
    """
    Checks that the user wants to finish or not.
    Performs some verification of the input."""
    ok_to_finish = True
    user_input_accepted = False
    while not user_input_accepted:
        user_input = input('Do you want to finish (y/n): ')
        if user_input == 'y':
            user_input_accepted = True
        elif user_input == 'n':
            ok_to_finish = False
            user_input_accepted = True
        else:
            print('Response must be (y/n), please try again')
    return ok_to_finish
```

Notice the use of two variables that are local to the function:

- the first variable (ok_to_finish) holds the result of the function; whether it is OK to finish or not. It is given a default value of True; this follows the fail closed approach—which suggests that it is always better to fail by closing down an application or connection. In this case it means that if something goes wrong with the code (if it contains a software bug or logic error) the user will not keep looping forever.
- the second variable (user_input_accepted) is used to indicate whether the user has provided an acceptable input or not (i.e. have they entered 'y' or 'n') until they do the loop inside the function will repeat.

The loop itself is interesting as we are looping while the user input has not been accepted; note that we can (almost) read the while loop as plain English text. This is both a feature of Python (it is intended to be easily readable) and also of the use of a meaningful name for the variable itself.

Within the loop we obtain the input from the user; check to see if it is 'y' or 'n'. If it is either of these options, we set the user_input_accepted flag to True. Otherwise the code will print out a message indicating that the only acceptable input is a 'y' or 'n'.

Notice that we only set the ok_to_finish variable to False if the user inputs a 'n'; this is because the ok_to_finish variable by default has a value of True and thus there is no need to reassign True to it if the user select 'n'.

We can now add this function into our main processing loop in place of the last comment:

```
finished = False
while not finished:
    result = 0
    # Get the operation from the user
    # Get the numbers from the user
    # Select the operation
    print('Result:', result)
    print('==================')
    finished = check_if_user_has_finished(()

print('Bye')
```

We can now run the application.

You may wonder why we would do this at this point as it does not yet do any calculations for us; the answer is that we can verify that the overall behaviour of the main loop works and that the check_if_user_has_finished() function operates correctly.

13.7   Selecting the Operation

Next let us implement the function used to obtain the operation to perform.

Again, we want to name this function in such a way as to help with the comprehensibility of our program. In this case we are asking the user to select which operation they want to perform, so let's call the function get_operation_choice.

This time we need to present a list of options to the user and then ask them to make a selection. Again, we want to write our function defensively, so that it makes sure the user only inputs a valid option; if they do not then the function prompts them for another input. This means our function will have a loop and some validation code.

There are four options available to the user: Add, Subtract, Multiply and Divide. We will therefore number then 1 to 4 and ask the user to select an option between 1 and 4.

There are several ways in which we can verify that they have entered a number in this range, including

- converting the string entered into a number and using numerical comparison (but then we need to check that they entered an integer),
- having multiple if and elif statements (but that seems a bit long winded) or
- by checking that the entered character is one of a set of values (which is the approach we will use).

To check that a value is *in* a set of other value (that it is one of the values in the set) you can use the 'in' operator, for example:

```
user_selection in ('1', '2', '3', '4')
```

This will return True if (and only if) user_selection contains one of the strings '1', '2', '3' or '4'.

We can therefore use it in our function to verify that the user entered a valid input.

The get_operation_choice function is shown below:

```
def get_operation_choice():
    input_ok = False
    while not input_ok:
        print('Menu Options are:')
        print('\t1. Add')
        print('\t2. Subtract')
        print('\t3. Multiply')
        print('\t4. Divide')
        print('-----------------')
        user_selection = input('Please make a selection: ')
        if user_selection in ('1', '2', '3', '4'):
            input_ok = True
        else:
            print('Invalid Input (must be 1 - 4)')
    print('-----------------')
    return user_selection
```

Work through this function and make sure you are comfortable with all its elements. The '\t' character is a special character denoting a Tab.

We can now update our main calculator loop with this function:

```
finished = False

while not finished:
    result = 0
    menu_choice = get_operation_choice()

    # Get the numbers from the user
    # Select the operation
    print('Result:', result)
    print('==================')
    finished = check_if_user_has_finished(()

print('Bye')
```

13.8   Obtaining the Input Numbers

Next we need to obtain two numbers from the user to use with the selected operation.

In our introduction to Functions in Python chapter we looked at a function (the `get_integer_input()` function) that could be used to take input from the user and convert it (safely) into an integer; if the user entered a non-number then this function would prompt them to enter an actual number. We can reuse the function here.

However, we need to ask the user for two numbers; we will therefore create a function which uses the `get_integer_input()` function to prompt the user for two numbers and then return both numbers. Both functions are shown here:

```python
def get_numbers_from_user():
    num1 = get_integer_input('Input the first number: ')
    num2 = get_integer_input('Input the second number: ')
    return num1, num2

def get_integer_input(message):
    value_as_string = input(message)
    while not value_as_string.isnumeric():
        print('The input must be an integer')
        value_as_string = input(message)
    return int(value_as_string)
```

Having one function call another function is very common and indeed we have already been doing this; the `input()` function has been used several times, the only difference here is that we have written the `get_integer_input()` function ourselves.

When we can the `get_numbers_from_user()` function we can store the results returned into two variables; one for each result; for example:

```python
n1, n2 = get_numbers_from_user()
```

We can now add this statement to the main calculator loop:

```python
finished = False
while not finished:
    result = 0
    menu_choice = get_operation_choice()
    n1, n2 = get_numbers_from_user()
    # Select the operation
    print('Result:', result)
    print('==================')
    finished = check_if_user_has_finished(()

print('Bye')
```

13.9   Determining the Operation to Execute

We are now almost there and can update our main calculation loop with some logic to determine the actual operation to invoke. To do this we will use an if statement with the optional elif parts. The if statement will be conditional on the operation selected and will then call the appropriate function (such as add, subtract etc.) as shown here:

```
if menu_choice == '1':
    result = add(n1, n2)
elif menu_choice == '2':
    result = subtract(n1, n2)
elif menu_choice == '3':
    result - multiply(n1, n2)
elif menu_choice == '4':
    result = divide(n1, n2)
```

Each part of the if statement calls a different function; but they all store the value returned into the result variable.

We can now add this to the calculation loop to create our fully functional calculator loop:

```
finished = False
while not finished:
    result = 0
    menu_choice = get_operation_choice()
    n1, n2 = get_numbers_from_user()
    if menu_choice == '1':
        result = add(n1, n2)
    elif menu_choice == '2':
        result = subtract(n1, n2)
    elif menu_choice == '3':
        result - multiply(n1, n2)
    elif menu_choice == '4':
        result = divide(n1, n2)
    print('Result:', result)
    print('=================')
    finished = check_if_user_has_finished(()

print('Bye')
```

13.10   Running the Calculator

If you now run the calculator you will be prompted as appropriate for input. You can try and break the calculator by entering characters when numbers are requested, or values out of range for the operations etc. and it should be resilient enough to handle these erroneous inputs, for example:

```
Simple Calculator App
Menu Options are:
  1. Add
  2. Subtract
  3. Multiply
  4. Divide
-----------------
Please make a selection: 5
Invalid Input (must be 1 - 4)
Menu Options are:
  1. Add
  2. Subtract
  3. Multiply
  4. Divide
-----------------
Please make a selection: 1
-----------------
Input the first number: 5
Input the second number: 4
Result: 9
=================
Do you want to finish (y/n): y
Bye
```

13.11   Exercises

For this chapter the exercises relate to extensions to the calculator:

1. Add an option to apply the modulus (%) operator to the two numbers input by the user. This will involve defining an appropriate function and adding this as an option to the menu. You will also need to extend the main calculator control loop to handle this option.
2. Add a power of (**) option to the calculator.
3. Modify the program to take floating point numbers instead of simple integers.
4. Allow the choice of division operator or integer division operator (this have both '/' and '//' available.

Chapter 14
Introduction to Functional Programming

避免藝術所謂的 side effect 所帶來

14.1 Introduction

There has been much hype around Functional Programming in recent years. However, Functional Programming is not a new idea and indeed goes right back to the 1950s and the programming language LISP. However, many people are not clear as to what Functional Programming is and instead jump into code examples and never really understand some of the key ideas associated with Functional Programming such as Referential Transparency.

This chapter introduces Functional Programming (also known as FP) and the key concept of Referential Transparency (or RT).

One idea to be aware of is that Functional Programming is a software coding style or approach and is separate from the concept of a function in Python.

Python Functions can be used to write Functional Programs but can also be used to write procedural style programs; so do not get too hung up on the syntax that might be used or the fact that Python has functions just yet. Instead explore the idea of defining a functional approach to your software design.

14.2 What Is Functional Programming?

Wikipedia describes Functional Programming as:

> … a programming paradigm, a style of building the structure and elements of computer programs, that treats computation as the evaluation of mathematical functions and avoids state and mutable data.

There are a number of points to note about this definition. The first is that it is focussed on the *computational side* of computer programming. This might seem obvious but most of what we have looked at so far in Python would be considered procedural in nature.

© Springer Nature Switzerland AG 2019
J. Hunt, *A Beginners Guide to Python 3 Programming*,
Undergraduate Topics in Computer Science,
https://doi.org/10.1007/978-3-030-20290-3_14

Another thing to note is that the way in which the computations are represented emphasises functions that generate results based purely on the data provided to them. That is these functions only rely on their inputs to generate a new output. They do not generate on any *side effects* and do not depend on the *current state* of the program. As an example of a side effect, if a function stored a running total in a global variable and another function used that total to perform some calculation; then the first function has a side effect of modifying a global variable and the second relies on some global state for its result.

Taking each of these in turn:

1. **Functional Programming aims to avoid side effects**. A function should be replaceable by taking the data it receives and in lining the result generated (this is referred to as referential transparency). This means that there should be no hidden side effects of the function. Hidden side effects make it harder to understand what a program is doing and thus make comprehension, development and maintenance harder. Pure functions have the following attributes:

   • the only observable output is the return value.
   • the only output dependency are the arguments.
   • arguments are fully determined before any output is generated.

2. **Functional Programming avoids concepts such as state**. If some operation is dependent upon the (potentially hidden) state of the program or some element of a program, then its behaviour may differ depending upon that state. This may make it harder to comprehend, implement, test and debug. As all of these impact on the stability and probably reliability of a system, state-based operations may result in less reliable software being developed. As functions do not (should not) rely on any given state (only upon the data they are given) they should as a result be easier to understand, implement, test and debug.

3. **Functional Programming promotes immutable data**. Functional Programming also tends to avoid concepts such as mutable data. Mutable data is data that can change its state. By contrast *Immutability* indicates that once created, data cannot be changed. In Python Strings are immutable. Once you create a new string you cannot modify it. Any functions that apply to a string that might conceptually alter the contents of the string, result in a new String being generated. Many developers take this further by having a presumption of immutability in their code; that means that by default all data holding types are implemented as immutable. This ensures that functions cannot have hidden side effects and thus simplifies programming in general.

4. **Functional Programming promotes declarative programming** which means that programming is oriented around expressions that describe the solution rather than focus on the imperative approach of most procedural programming languages. Imperative languages emphasise aspects of how the solution is derived. For example, an imperative approach to looping through some container and printing out each result in turn would look like this:

```
int sizeOfContainer = container.length
for (int i = 1 to sizeOfContainer) do
   element = container.get(i)
   print(element)
enddo
```

Whereas a functional programming approach would look like:

```
container.foreach(print)
```

Functional Programming has its roots in the lambda calculus, originally developed in the 1930s to explore computability. Many Functional Programming languages can thus be considered as elaborations on this lambda calculus. There have been numerous pure Functional Programming languages including Common Lisp, Clojure and Haskell. Python provides some support for writing in the functional style; particularly where the benefits of it are particularly strong (such as in processing various different types of data).

Indeed, when used judiciously, functional programming can be a huge benefit for, and an enhancement to, the toolkit available to developers.

To summarise then:

- **Imperative Programming** is what is currently perceived as traditional programming. That is, it is the style of programming used in languages such as C, C++, Java and C# etc. In these languages a programmer tells the computer what to do. It is thus oriented around control statements, looping constructs and assignments.
- **Functional Programming** aims to describe the solution, that is *what* the program needs to do (rather than *how* it should be done).

14.3 Advantages to Functional Programming

There are a number of significant advantages to functional programming compared to imperative programming. These include:

1. **Less code**. Typically, a functional programming solution will require less code to write than an equivalent imperative solution. As there is less code to write, there is also less code to understand and to maintain. It is therefore possible that functional programs are not only more elegant to read but easier to update and maintain. This can also lead to enhanced programmer productivity as they spend less time writing reams of code as well as less time reading those reams of code.
2. **Lack of (hidden) side effects (Referential Transparency)**. Programming without side effects is good as it makes it easier to reason about functions (that is

a function is completely described by the data that goes in and the results that come back). This also means that it is safe to reuse these functions in different situations (as they do not have unexpected side effects). It should also be easier to develop, test and maintain such functions.

3. **Recursion is a natural control structure**. Functional languages tend to emphasis recursion as a way of processing structures that would use some form of looping constructs in an imperative language. Although you can typically implement recursion in imperative languages, it is often easier to do in functional languages. It is also worth noting that although recursion is very expressive and a great way for a programmer to write a solution to a problem, it is not as efficient at run time as iteration. However, any expression that can be written as a recursive routine can also be written using looping constructs. Functional programming languages often incorporate *tail end recursive optimisations* to convert recursive routines into iterative ones at runtime. A util end recursive function is one in which the last thing a function does before it returns is to call itself. This means that rather than actually invoking the function and having to set up the context for that function, it should be possible to reuse the current context and to treat it in an iterative manner as a loop around that routine. Thus the programmer benefits from the expressive recursive construct and the runtime benefits of an iterative solution using the same source code. This option is typically not available in imperative languages.

4. **Good for prototyping solutions**. Solutions can be created very quickly for algorithmic or behaviour problems in a functional language. Thus, allowing ideas and concepts to be explored in a rapid application development style.

5. **Modular Functionality**. Functional Programming is modular in terms of functionality (where Object Oriented languages are modular in the dimension of components). They are thus well suited to situations where it is natural to want to reuse or componentise the *behaviour* of a system.

6. **The avoidance of state-based behaviour**. As functions only rely on their inputs and outputs (and avoid accessing any other stored state) they exhibit a cleaner and simpler style of programming. This avoidance of state-based behaviour makes many difficult or challenging areas of programming simpler (such as those in concurrent applications).

7. **Additional control structures**. A strong emphasis on additional control structures such as pattern matching, managing variable scope, tail recursion optimisations etc.

8. **Concurrency and immutable data**. As functional programming systems advocate immutable data structures it is simpler to construct concurrent systems. This is because the data being exchanged and accessed is immutable. Therefore, multiple executing thread or processes cannot affect each other adversely. The Akka Actor model builds on this approach to provide a very clean model for multiple interacting concurrent systems.

9. **Partial Evaluation**. Since functions do not have side effects, it also becomes practical to bind one or more parameters to a function at compile time and to reuse these functions with bound values as new functions that take fewer parameters.

14.4 Disadvantages of Functional Programming

If functional programming has all the advantages previously described, why isn't it the mainstream force that imperative programming languages are? The reality is that functional programming is not without its disadvantages, including:

- **Input-Output is harder in a purely functional language**. Input-Output flows naturally align with stream style processing, which does not neatly fit into the data in, results out, nature of functional systems.
- **Interactive applications are harder to develop**. Interactive applications are constructed via request response cycles initiated by a user action. Again, these do not naturally sit within the purely functional paradigm.
- **Continuously running programs** such as services or controllers may be more difficult to develop, as they are naturally based upon the idea of a continuous loop.
- **Functional programming languages have tended to be less efficient on current hardware platforms**. This is partly because current hardware platforms are not designed with functional programming in mind and also because many of the systems previously available were focussed on the academic community where out and out performance was not the primary focus. However, this has changed to a large extent with modern functional languages such as Scala and Heskell.
- **Not data oriented**. A pure Functional Language does not really align with the needs of the primarily data-oriented nature of many of today's systems. Many (most) commercial systems are oriented around the need to retrieve data from a database, manipulate it in some way and store that data back into a database. Such data can be naturally represented via objects in an Object-Oriented language.
- **Programmers are less familiar** with functional programming concepts and thus find it harder to pick up function-oriented languages.
- **Functional Programming idioms are often less intuitive** to (traditional) procedural programmers than imperative idioms which can make debugging and maintenance harder. Although with the use of a functional approach in many other languages now becoming more popular (including in Python) this trend is changing.
- Many Functional Programming languages have been viewed as **Ivory tower languages** that are only used by academics. This has been true of some older functional languages but is increasingly changing with the advent of languages such as Scala and with the facilities provided in more mainstream programming languages such as Python.

14.5 Referential Transparency

An important concept within the world of functional programming is that of Referential Transparency.

An operation is said to be *Referentially Transparent* if it can be replaced with its corresponding value, without changing the programs behaviour, for a given set of parameters.

For example, let us assume that we have defined the function increment as shown below.

```
def increment(num):
    return num + 1
```

If we use this simple example in an application to increment the value 5:

```
print(increment(5))
print(increment(5))
```

We can say that the function is Referentially Transparent (or RT) if it always returns the same result for the same value (i.e. that increment(5) always returns 6):

```
Run:       parameter-functions ×

  ▶   ↑    /Library/Frameworks/Python.framework/Versions/3.7/bin/python3.7
           6
  ■   ↓    6

  ‖   ⇴    Process finished with exit code 0
```

Any function that references a value which has been captured from its surrounding context and which can be modified cannot be guaranteed to be RT. This can have significant consequences for the maintainability of the resulting code. This can happen if for example the increment function did not add 1 to the parameter but added a global value. If this global value is changed then the function would suddenly start to return different values for the previously entered parameters. For example, the following code is no longer Referentially Transparent:

```
amount = 1
def increment(num):
    return num + amount

print(increment(5))
amount = 2
print(increment(5))
```

The output from this code is 6 and 7—as the value of amount has changed between calls to the increment() function.

A closely related idea is that of *No Side Effects*. That is, a function should not have any side effects, it should base its operation purely on the values it receives, and its only impact should be the result returned. Any hidden side effects again make software harder to maintain.

Of course, within most applications there is a significant need for side effects, for example any logging of the actions performed by a program has a side effect of updating some logged information somewhere (typically in a file), any database updates will have some side effect (i.e. that of updating the database). In addition some behaviour is inherently non RT, for example a function which returns the *current* time can never be Referentially Transparent.

However, for pure functions it is a useful consideration to follow.

14.6   Further Reading

There is a large amount of material on the web that can help you learn more about Functional Programming including:

- https://codeburst.io/a-beginner-friendly-intro-to-functional-programming-4f69aa109569 intended as a friendly introduction to Functional programming.
- https://medium.freecodecamp.org/an-introduction-to-the-basic-principles-of-functional-programming-a2c2a15c84 which provides an introduction to the basic principles of Functional programming.
- https://www.tutorialspoint.com/functional_programming which provides a good grounding in the basic concepts of Functional Programming.
- https://docs.python.org/3/howto/functional.html which is the Python standard library tutorial on Functional Programming.

Chapter 15
Higher Order Functions

15.1 Introduction

In this chapter we will explore the concept of high-order functions. These are functions that take as a parameter, or return (or both), a function. To do this we will first look into how Python represents functions in memory and explore what actually happens when we execute a Python function.

15.2 Recap on Functions in Python

Let us first recap a few things regarding functions in Python:

Functions (mostly) have a name and when invoked (or executed) the body of code associated with the function name is run.

There are some important ideas to remember when considering functions:

- functions can be viewed as named blocks of code and are one of the main ways in which we can organise our programs in Python,
- functions are defined using the keyword `def` and constitute a function header (the function name and the parameters, if any, defined for that function) and the function body (what is executed when the function is run),
- functions are invoked or executed using their name followed by round brackets '()' with or without parameters depending on how the function has been defined.

This means we can write a function such as the following `get_msg` function:

```
def get_msg():
    return 'Hello Python World!'
```

© Springer Nature Switzerland AG 2019
J. Hunt, *A Beginners Guide to Python 3 Programming*,
Undergraduate Topics in Computer Science,
https://doi.org/10.1007/978-3-030-20290-3_15

We can then call it by specifying its name and the round brackets:

```
message = get_msg()
print(message)
```

This of course prints out the string `'Hello Python World!'` which is what you should expect by now.

15.3   Functions as Objects *function が第一級オブジェクト*

A few chapters back we threw in something stating that if you forgot to include the round brackets then you were referencing the function itself rather than trying to execute it!

What exactly does that mean? Let's see what happens if we forgot to include the round brackets:

```
message = get_msg
print(message)
```

The output generated now is:

```
<function get_msg at 0x10ad961e0>
```

which might look very confusing at first sight.

What this is actually telling you is that you have referenced a function called get_msg that is located at a (hexidecimal) address in memory.

It is interesting to note that just as data has to be located in memory so does program code (so that it can be found and run); although typically data and code are located in separate areas of memory (as data tends to be short lived).

Another interesting thing to do is to find out what the *type* of get_msg is—hey it's a function—but what does that mean?

If we issue this statement and run it in Python:

```
print(type(get_msg))
```

Then we will get the following:

```
<class 'function'>
```

This means that it is of the class of things that are functions just as 1 is of the class of things called integers, `'John'` is of the class of things called strings and `42.6` is of the class of things called floating point numbers.

Taking this further it actually means that the *thing* being referenced by
get_msg is a function object (an example or instance of the Function class). This
get_msg is really a type of variable that references (or points at) at the *function
object* in memory which we can execute using the round brackets.

This is illustrated by the following diagram:

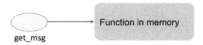

This means that when we run get_msg() what actually happens is we go to
the get_msg variable and following the reference (or pointer) there to the function
and then because we have the round brackets we run that function.

This has two implications:

1. we can pass the reference to a function around,
2. we can make get_msg reference (point) at a different function

Let us look at the first of these implications. If we assign the reference represented by get_msg to something else, then in effect we have an alias for this
function. This is because another variable now also references the same function.
For example, if we write:

```
another_reference = get_msg
print(another_reference())
```

Then the result is that the string 'Hello Python World!' is again printed out.

What this has done is to copy the reference held in get_msg into
another_reference (but it is a copy of that reference and that is the address of
the function in memory). Thus, we now have in memory:

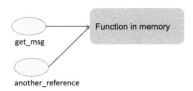

So just to emphasise this—we did not make a copy of the function; only its
address in memory. Thus the same value is held in both get_msg and
another_reference and both these values are references to the same function object
in memory.

What does this mean and why should we care? Well it means that we can pass
references to functions around within our program which can be a very useful
feature that we will look at later in this chapter.

Now let us go back to the second implication mentioned above; we can reassign
another function to get_msg.

For example, let's say we wrote this next:

```
def get_some_other_msg():
    return 'Some other message!!!'

get_msg = get_some_other_msg
print(get_msg())
```

Now `get_msg` no longer references the original functions; it now references the new function defined by `get_some_other_msg`. It means that in memory we now have

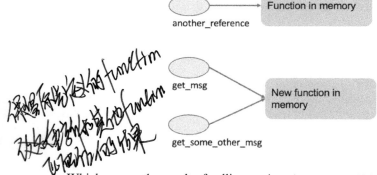

Which means the result of calling `print(get_msg())` will be that the string `'Some other message!!!'` is returned and printed out (rather than the `'Hello Python World!'`).

However, notice that we did not overwrite the original function; it is still being referenced by the `another_reference` variable and indeed can still be called via this variable. For example, the code:

```
print(get_msg())
print(another_reference())
```

now generates the output:

```
Some other message!!!
Hello Python World!
```

This illustrates some of the power but also the potential confusion that comes from how functions are represented and can be manipulated in Python.

15.4   Higher Order Function Concepts

Given that we can assign a reference into a function to a variable; then this might imply that we can also use the same approach to pass a reference to a function as an argument to another function.

This means that one function can take another function as a parameter. Such functions are known as higher-order functions and are one of the key constructs in Functional Programming.

That is, a function that takes another function as a parameter is known as a *higher order function*.

In fact, in Python, Higher-Order Functions are functions that do at least one of the following (and may do both):

- Take one or more functions as a parameter,
- Return as a result a function.

All other functions in Python are *first-order* functions.

Many of the functions found in the Python libraries are higher order functions. It is a common enough pattern that once you are aware of it you will recognise it in many different libraries.

15.4.1 Higher Order Function Example

As an abstract example, consider the following higher order function *apply*. This function (written in pseudo code—not a real programming language) takes an integer and a function. Within the body of the function being defined, the function passed in as a parameter is applied to the integer parameter. The result of the function being defined is then returned:

```
def apply(x, function):
    result = function(x)
    return result
```

The function `apply` is a *higher order* function because its behaviour (and its result) will depend on the behaviour defined by another function—the one passed into it.

We could also define a function that multiplies a number by 10.0, for example:

```
def mult(y):
    return y * 10.0
```

Now we can use the function `mult` with the function apply, for example:

```
apply(5, mult)
```

This would return the value 50.0

15.5   Python Higher Order Functions

As we have already seen when we define a function it actually creates a function object that is referenced by the name of the function. For example, if we create the function `mult_by_two`:

```python
def mult_by_two(num):
    return num * 2
```

Then this has created a function object referenced by the name `multi_by_two` that we can invoke (execute) using the round brackets ' () '.

It is also a one parameter function that takes a number and returns a value which is twice that number

Thus, a parameter that expects to be given a reference to a function that takes a number and returns a number can be given a reference to any function that meets this (implied) contract. This includes our `mult_by_two` function but also any of the following:

```python
def mult_by_five(num):
    return num * 5

def square(num):
    return num * num

def add_one(num):
    return num + 1
```

All of the above could be used with the following higher order function:

```python
def apply(num, func):
    return func(num)
```

For example:

```python
result = apply(10, mult_by_two)
print(result)
```

The output from this code is:

```
20
```

The following listing provides a complete set of the earlier sample functions and how they may be used with the apply function:

```python
print(apply(10, mult_by_five))
print(apply(10, square))
print(apply(10, add_one))
print(apply(10, mult_by_two))
```

The output from this is:

```
50
100
11
20
```

15.5.1 Using Higher Order Functions

Looking at the previous section you may be wondering why you would want to use a higher-order function or indeed why define one. After all, could you not have called one of the functions (multi_by_five, square, add_one or mult_by_two) directly by passing in the integer to used? Yes, we could have, for example we could have done:

```
square(10)
```

And this would have exactly the same effect as calling:

```
apply(10, square)
```

The first approach would seem to be both simpler and more efficient.

The key to why higher-order functions are so powerful is to consider what would happen if we know that some function should be applied to the value 10 but we do not yet know what it is. The actual function will be provided at some point in the future. Now we are creating a reusable piece of code that will be able to apply an appropriate function to the data we have when that function is known.

For example, let us assume that we want to calculate the amount of tax someone should pay based on their salary. However, we do not know how to calculate the tax that this person must pay as it is dependent on external factors. The calculate_tax function could take an appropriate function that performs that calculation and provides the appropriate tax value.

The following listing implements this approach. The function calculate_tax does not know how to calculate the actual tax to be paid, instead a function must be provided as a parameter to the calculate_tax function. The function passed in takes a number and returns the result of performing the calculation. It is used with the salary parameter also passed into the calculate_tax function.

```python
import math

def simple_tax_calculator(amount):
    return math.ceil(amount * 0.3)

def calculate_tax(salary, func):
    return func(salary)

print(calculate_tax(45000.0, simple_tax_calculator))
```

The `simple_tax_calculator` function defines a function that takes a number and multiplies it by `0.3` and then uses the `math.ceil` function (imported from the `math` library/module) to round it up to a whole number. A call is then made to the `calculate_tax` function passing in the float `45000.0` as the salary and a *reference* to the `simple_tax_calculator` function. Finally, it prints out the tax calculated. The result of running this program is:

```
Run:        higher_order_examples
   ▶   ↑   /Library/Frameworks/Python.framework/Versions/3.7/bin/python3.7
           13500
   ■   ↓
           Process finished with exit code 0
   ‖   ⇥
```

Thus, the function `calculate_tax` is a reusable function that can have different tax calculation strategies defined for it.

15.5.2 Functions Returning Functions

In Python as well as passing a function into another function; functions can be returned from a function. This can be used to select amongst a number of different options or to create a new function based on the parameters.

For example, the following code creates a function that can be used to check whether a number is even, odd or negative based on the string passed into it:

```
def make_checker(s):
    if s == 'even':
        return lambda n: n%2 == 0
    elif s == 'positive':
        return lambda n: n >= 0
    elif s == 'negative':
        return lambda n: n < 0
    else:
        raise ValueError('Unknown request')
```

Note the use of the raise `Value Error`; for the moment we will just say that this is a way of showing that there is a problem in the code which may occur if this function is called with an in appropriate parameter value for 's'.

This function is a *factory* for functions that can be created to perform specific operations. It is used below to create three functions that can be used to validate what type a number is:

```
f1 = make_checker('even')
f2 = make_checker('positive')
f3 = make_checker('negative')
print(f1(3))
print(f2(3))
print(f3(3))
```

Of course, it is not only anonymous functions that can be returned from a function; it is also possible to return a named function. This is done by returning just the name of the function (i.e. without the round brackets).

In the following example, a named function is defined within an outer function (although it could have been defined elsewhere in the code). It is then returned from the function:

```python
def make_function():
    def adder(x, y):
        return x + y

    return adder
```

We can then use this `make_function` to create the `adder` function and store it into another variable. We can now use this function in our code, for example:

```python
f1 = make_function()
print(f1(3, 2))
print(f1(3, 3))
print(f1(3, 1))
```

Which produces the output

```
5
6
4
```

15.6   Online Resources

Further information on higher order functions in Python can be found using the following online resources:

- https://en.wikipedia.org/wiki/Higher-order_function Wikipedia page on Higher Order functions.
- https://docs.python.org/3.1/library/functools.html a module to support the creation and use of higher order functions.
- https://www.tutorialspoint.com/functional_programming/functional_programming_higher_order_functions.htm A tutorial on higher order functions.

15.7   Exercises

The aim of this exercise is to explore higher order functions.

You should write a higher order function function called `my_higher_order_function(i, func)`. This function takes a parameter and a second function to apply to the parameter.

Now you should write a sample program that uses the higher order function you just created to perform. An example of the sort of thing you might implement is given below:

```
print(my_higher_order_function(2, double))
print(my_higher_order_function(2, triple))
print(my_higher_order_function(16, square_root))
print(my_higher_order_function(2, is_prime))
print(my_higher_order_function(4, is_prime))
print(my_higher_order_function('2', is_integer))
print(my_higher_order_function('A', is_integer))
print(my_higher_order_function('A', is_letter))
print(my_higher_order_function('1', is_letter))
```

If you are using the above code as your test application then you should write each of the supporting functions; each should take a single parameter.

Sample output from this code snippet is:

```
4
8
4.0
True
False
True
False
True
False
```

Note a simple way to find the square root of a number is to use the exponent (or power of) operator and multiply by 0.5.

Chapter 16
Curried Functions

16.1 Introduction

Currying is a technique which allows new functions to be created from existing functions by *binding* one or more parameters to a specific value. It is a major source of reuse of functions in Python which means that functionality can be written once, in one place and then reused in multiple other situations.

The name Currying may seem obscure, but the technique is named after Haskell Curry (for whom the Haskell programming language is also named).

This chapter introduces the core ideas behind currying and explores how currying can be implemented in Python. The chapter also introduces the concept of closures and how they affect curried functions.

16.2 Currying Concepts

At an abstract level, consider having a function that takes two parameters. These two parameters, x and y are used within the function body with the multiply operator in the form x * y. For example, we might have:

```
operation(x, y): return x * y
```

This function operation() might then be used as follows

```
total = operation(2, 5)
```

Which would result in 5 being multiplied by 2 to give 10. Or it could be used:

© Springer Nature Switzerland AG 2019
J. Hunt, *A Beginners Guide to Python 3 Programming*,
Undergraduate Topics in Computer Science,
https://doi.org/10.1007/978-3-030-20290-3_16

```
total = operation(10, 5)
```

Which would result in 5 being multiplied by 10 to give 50.

If we needed to double a number, we could thus reuse the `operation()` function many times, for example:

```
operation(2, 5)
operation(2, 10)
operation(2, 6)
operation(2, 151)
```

All of the above would double the second number. However, we have had to remember to provide the 2 so that the number can be doubled. However, the number 2 has not changed between any of the invocations of the `operation()` function. What if we fixed the first parameter to always be 2, this would mean that we could create a new function that apparently only takes one parameter (the number to double). For example, let us say we could write something like:

```
double = operation(2, *)
```

Such that we could now write:

```
double(5)
double(151)
```

In essence `double()` is an alias for `operation()`, but an alias that provides the value 2 for the first parameter and leaves the second parameter to be filled in by the future invocation of the `double` function.

16.3   Python and Curried Functions

A curried function in Python is a function where one or more of its parameters have been *applied or bound* to a value, resulting in the creation of a new function with one fewer parameters than the original. For example, let us create a function that multiplies two numbers together:

```
def multiply(a, b):
    return a * b
```

This is a general function that does exactly what it says; it multiplies any two numbers together. These numbers could be any two integers or floating-point numbers etc.

We can thus invoke it in the normal manner:

```
print(multiply(2, 5))
```

The result of executing this statement is:

```
10
```

We could now define a new method that takes a function and a number and returns a new (anonymous) function that takes one *new* parameter and calls the function passed in with the number passed in and the new parameter:

```
def multby(func, num):
    return lambda y: func(num, y)
```

Look carefully at this function; it has used or *bound* the number passed into the multby function to the invocation of the function passed in, but it has also defined a new variable 'y' that will have to be provided when this new anonymous function is invoked. It then returns a reference to the anonymous function as the result of multby.

The multby function can now be used to bind the first parameter of the multiply function to anything we want. For example, we could bind it to 2 so that it will always double the second parameter and store the resulting function reference into a property double:

```
double = multby(multiply, 2)
```

We could also bind the value 3 to the first parameter of multiple to make a function that will triple any value:

```
triple = multby(multiply, 3)
```

Which means we can now write:

```
print(double(5))
print(triple(5))
```

which produces the output

```
10
15
```

You are not limited to just binding one parameter; you can bind any number of parameters in this way.

Curried functions are therefore very useful for creating new functions from existing functions.

16.4 Closures

One question that might well be on your mind now is what happens when a function references some data that is in scope where it is defined but is no longer available when it is evaluated? This question is answered by the implementation of a concept known as *closure*.

Within Computer Science (and programming languages in particular) a closure (or a lexical closure or function closure) is a function (or more strictly a reference to a function) together with a referencing environment. This referencing environment records the context within which the function was originally defined and if necessary, a reference to each of the non-local variables used by that function. These non-local or free variables allow the function body to reference variables that are external to the function, but which are utilised by that function. This referencing environment is one of the distinguishing features between a functional language and a language that supports function pointers (such as C).

The general concept of a lexical closure was first developed during the 1960s but was first fully implemented in the language Scheme in the 1970s. It has since been used within many functional programming languages including LISP and Scala.

At the conceptual level, a closure allows a function to reference a variable available in the scope where the function was originally defined, but not available by default in the scope where it is executed.

For example, in the following simple programme, the variable more is defined outside the body of the function named increase. This is permissible as the variable is a *global* variable. Thus, the variable more is *within scope* at the point of definition.

```
more = 100

def increase(num):
    return num + more

print(increase(10))
more = 50
print(increase(10))
```

Within our program we invoke the increase function by passing in the value
10. This is done twice with the variable more being reset to 50 between the two.
The output from this program is shown below:

```
110
60
```

Note that it is the *current* value of more that is being used when the function
executes and not the value of more present at the point that the function was
defined. Hence the output is 110 and 60 that is 100 + 10 and then 50 + 10.

This might seem obvious as the variable more is still in scope within the same
function as the invocations of the function referenced by increase.

However, consider the following example:

```
def increment(num):
    return num + 1

def reset_function():
    global increment
    addition = 50
    increment = lambda num: num + addition

print(increment(5))
reset_function()
print(increment(5))
```

In the above listing the function increment initially adds 1 to whatever value
has been passed to it. Then in the program this function is called with the value 5
and the result returned by the function is printed. This will be the value 6.

However, after this a second function, reset_function() is invoked. This
function has a variable that is *local* to the function. That is, *normally* it would only
be available within the function reset_function. This variable is called
addition and has the value 50.

The variable `addition` is however, used within the function body of a new anonymous function definition. This function takes a number and adds the value of `addition` to that number and returns this as the result of the function. This new function is then assigned to the name `increment`. Note that to ensure we reference the *global* name `increment` we must use the keyword `global` (otherwise we will create a local variable that just happens to have the same name as the function).

Now, when the second invocation of `increment` occurs, the `reset_function()` method has terminated and *normally* the variable `addition` would no longer even be in existence. However, when this program runs the value `55` is printed out from the second invocation of `increment`. That is the function being referenced by the name `increment`, when it is called the second time, is the one defined within `reset_function()` and which uses the variable `addition`.

The actual output is shown below:

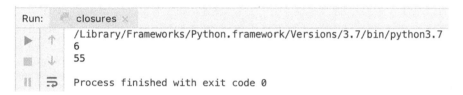

So, what has happened here? It should be noted that the value `50` was not copied into the second function body. Rather it is a concrete example of the use of a reference environment with the closure concept. Python ensures that the variable `addition` is available to the function, even if the invocation of the function is somewhere different to where it was defined by binding any free variables (those defined outside the scope of the function) and storing them so that they can be accessed by the function's context (in effect moving the variable from being a *local* variable to one which is available to the function anywhere; but only to the function).

16.5   Online Resources

Further information on currying see:

- https://en.wikipedia.org/wiki/Currying Wikipedia page on currying.
- https://wiki.haskell.org/Currying A page introducing currying (based on the Haskell language but still a useful reference).
- https://www.python-course.eu/currying_in_python.php A tutorial on currying in Python.

16.6   Exercises

This exercise is about creating a set of functions to perform currency conversions based on specified rates using currying to create those functions.

Write a function that will curry another function and a parameter in a similar manner to `multby` in this chapter—call this function `curry()`.

Now define a function that can be used to convert an amount into another amount based on a rate. The definition of this conversion function is very straight forward and just involves multiplying the number by the rate.

Now create a set of functions that can be used to convert a value in one currency into another currency based on a specific rate. We do not want to have to remember the rate, only the name of the function. For example:

```
dollars_to_sterling = curry(convert, 0.77)
print(dollars_to_sterling(5))

euro_to_sterling = curry(convert, 0.88)
print(euro_to_sterling(15))

sterling_to_dollars = curry(convert, 1.3)
print(sterling_to_dollars(7))

sterling_to_euro = curry(convert, 1.14)
print(sterling_to_euro(9))
```

If the above code is run the output would be:

```
3.85
13.2
9.1
10.26
```

Chapter 17
Introduction to Object Orientation

17.1 Introduction

This chapter introduces the core concepts in Object Orientation. It defines the terminology used and attempts to clarify issues associated with objects. It also discusses some of the perceived strengths and weaknesses of the object-oriented approach. It then offers some guidance on the approach to take in learning about objects.

17.2 Classes

A class is one of the basic building blocks of Python. It is also a core concept in a style of programming known as Object Oriented Programming (or OOP). OOP provides an approach to structuring programs/applications so that the data held, and the operations performed on that data, are bundled together into classes and accessed via objects.

As an example, in an OOP style program, employees might be represented by a class Employee where each employee has an id, a name, a department and a desk_number etc. They might also have operations associated with them such as take_a_holiday() or get_paid().

In many cases classes are used to represent real world entities (such as employees) but they do not need to, they can also represent more abstract concepts such as a transaction between one person and another (for example an agreement to buy a meal).

Classes act as *templates* which are used to construct instances or examples of a class of things. Each example of the class Person might have a name, an age, an

© Springer Nature Switzerland AG 2019
J. Hunt, *A Beginners Guide to Python 3 Programming*,
Undergraduate Topics in Computer Science,
https://doi.org/10.1007/978-3-030-20290-3_17

address etc., but they have their own values for their name, age and address. For example, to represent the people in a family we might create an example of the class Person with the name Paul, the age 52 and the address set to London. We may also create another Person object (instance) with the name Fiona, the age 48 and the address also of London and so on.

An instance or object is therefore an example of a class. All instances/objects of a class possess the same data variables but contain their own data values. Each instance of a class responds to the same set of requests and has the same behaviour.

Classes allow programmers to specify the *structure* of an object (i.e. its attributes or fields, etc.) and the its behaviour separately from the objects themselves.

This is important, as it would be extremely time-consuming (as well as inefficient) for programmers to define each object individually. Instead, they define classes and create *instances* or *objects* of those classes.

They can then store related data together in a named concept which makes it much easier to structure and maintain code.

17.3   What Are Classes for?

We have already seen several types of data in Python such as integer, string, boolean etc. Each of these allowed us to hold a single item of data (such as the integer 42 or the string 'John' and the value True). However, how might we represent a Person, a Student or an Employee of a firm? One way we can do this is to use a class to represent them.

As indicated above, we might represent any type of (more complex) data item using a combination of attributes (or fields) and behaviours. These attributes will use existing data types, these might be integers, strings, Booleans, floating-point numbers or other classes.

For example, when defining the class Person we might give it:

- a field or attribute for the person's name,
- a field or attribute for their age,
- a field or attribute for their email,
- some behaviour to give them a birthday (which will increment their age),
- some behaviour to allow us to send them a message via their email,
- etc.

In Python classes are used:

- as a template to create instances (or objects) of that class,
- define instance methods or common behaviour for a class of objects,
- define attributes or fields to hold data within the objects,
- be sent messages.

Objects (or instances), on the other hand, can:

- be created from a class,
- hold their own values for instance variables,
- be sent messages,
- execute instance methods,
- may have many copies in the system (all with their own data).

17.3.1   What Should a Class Do?

A class should accomplish one specific purpose; it should capture only one idea. If more than one idea is encapsulated in a class, you may reduce the chances for reuse, as well as contravene the laws of encapsulation in object-oriented systems. For example, you may have merged two concepts together so that one can directly access the data of another. This is rarely desirable.

The following guidelines may help you to decide whether to split the class with which you are working. Look at the comment describing the class (if there is no class comment, this is a bad sign in itself). Consider the following points:

- Is the description of the class short and clear? If not, is this a reflection on the class? Consider how the comment can be broken down into a series of short clear comments. Base the new classes around those comments.
- If the comment is short and clear, do the class and instance variables make sense within the context of the comment? If they do not, then the class needs to be re-evaluated. It may be that the comment is inappropriate, or the class and instance variables inappropriate.
- Look at how and where the attributes of the class are used. Is their use in line with the class comment? If not, then you should take appropriate action.

17.3.2   Class Terminology

The following terms are used in Python (and other languages that support object orientation):

- *Class* A class defines a combination of data and behaviour that operates on that data. A class acts as a template when creating new instances.
- *Instance or object* An instance also known as an object is an example of a class. All instances of a class possess the same data fields/attributes but contain their own data values. Each instance of a class responds to the same set of requests.
- *Attribute/field/instance variable* The data held by an object is represented by its attributes (also sometimes known as a field or an instance variable). The "state" of an object at any particular moment relates to the current values held by its attributes.

- *Method* A method is a procedure defined within an object.
- *Message* A message is sent to an object requesting some operation to be performed or some attribute to be accessed. It is a request to the object to do something or return something. However, it is up to the object to determine how to execute that request. A message may be considered akin to a procedure call in other languages.

17.4   How Is an OO System Constructed?

At this point you may be wondering how a system can be built from classes and objects instantiated from those classes? What would such an application look like? It is clear it is different to writing functions and free-standing application code that calls those functions?

Let's use a real world (physical) system to explore what an OOP application might look like.

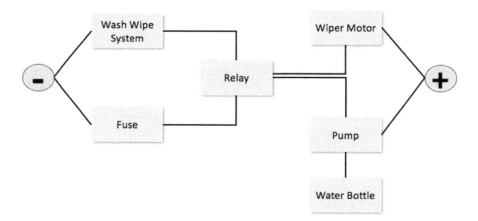

This system aims to provide a diagnosis tutor for the equipment illustrated above. Rather than use the wash–wipe system from a real car, students on a car mechanics diagnosis course use this software simulation. The software system mimics the actual system, so the behaviour of the pump depends on information provided by the relay and the water bottle.

The operation of the wash–wipe system is controlled by a switch which can be in one of five positions: off, intermittent, slow, fast and wash. Each of these settings places the system into a different state:

Switch setting	System state
Off	The system is inactive
Intermittent	The blades wipe the windscreen every few seconds
Slow	The wiper blades wipe the windscreen continuously
Fast	The wiper blades wipe the windscreen continuously and quickly
Wash	The pump draws water from the water bottle and sprays it onto the windscreen

For the pump and the wiper motor to work correctly, the relay must function correctly. In turn, the relay must be supplied with an electrical circuit. This electrical circuit is negatively fused and thus the fuse must be intact for the circuit to be made. Cars are negatively switched as this reduces the chances of short circuits leading to unintentional switching of circuits.

17.4.1   Where Do We Start?

This is often a very difficult point for those new to object-oriented systems. That is, they have read the basics and understand simple diagrams, but do not know where to start. It is the old chestnut, "I understand the example but don't know how to apply the concepts myself". This is not unusual and, in the case of object orientation, is probably normal.

The answer to the question "where do I start?" may at first seem somewhat obscure; you should start with the data. Remember that objects are things that exchange messages with each other. The things possess the data that is held by the system and the messages request actions that relate to the data. Thus, an object-oriented system is fundamentally concerned with data items.

Before we go on to consider the object-oriented view of the system, let us stop and think for a while. Ask yourself where could I start; it might be that you think about starting "with some form of functional decomposition" (breaking the problem down in terms of the functions it provides) as this might well be the view the user has of the system. As a natural part of this exercise, you would identify the data required to support the desired functionality. Notice that the emphasis would be on the system functionality.

Let us take this further and consider the functions we might identify for the example presented above:

Function	Description
Wash	Pump water from the water bottle to the windscreen
Wipe	Move the windscreen wipers across the windscreen

We would then identify important system variables and sub-functions to support the above functions.

Now let us go back to the object-oriented view of the world. In this view, we place a great deal more emphasis on the data items involved and consider the operations associated with them (effectively, the reverse of the functional decomposition view). This means that we start by attempting to identify the primary data items in the system; next, we look to see what operations are applied to, or performed on, the data items; finally, we group the data items and operations together to form objects. In identifying the operations, we may well have to consider additional data items, which may be separate objects or attributes of the current object. Identifying them is mostly a matter of skill and experience.

The object-oriented design approach considers the operations far less important than the data and their relationships. In the next section we examine the objects that might exist in our simulation system.

17.4.2   Identifying the Objects

We look at the system as a whole and ask what indicates the state of the system. We might say that the position of the switch or the status of the pump is significant. This results in the data items shown below

Data item	States
switch setting	Is the switch set to off, intermittent, wipe, fast wipe or wash?
wiper motor	Is the motor working or not?
pump state	Is the pump working or not?
fuse condition	Has the fuse blown or not?
water bottle level	The current water level
relay status	Is current flowing or not?

The identification of the data items is considered in greater detail later. At this point, merely notice that we have not yet mentioned the functionality of the system or how it might fit together, we have only mentioned the significant items. As this is such a simple system, we can assume that each of these elements is an object and illustrate it in a simple object diagram:

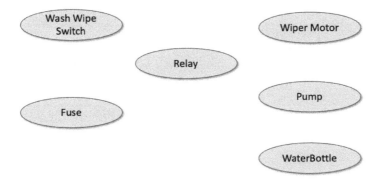

Notice that we have named each object after the element associated with the data item (e.g. the element associated with the fuse condition is the fuse itself) and that the actual data (e.g. the condition of the fuse) is an instance variable of the object. This is a very common way of naming objects and their instance variables. We now have the basic objects required for our application.

17.4.3   Identifying the Services or Methods

At the moment, we have a set of objects each of which can hold some data. For example, the water bottle can hold an integer indicating the current water level. Although object-oriented systems are structured around the data, we still need some procedural content to change the state of an object or to make the system achieve some goal. Therefore, we also need to consider the operations a user of each object might require. Notice that the emphasis here is on the user of the object and what they require of the object, rather than what operations are performed on the data.

Let us start with the switch object. The switch state can take a number of values. As we do not want other objects to have direct access to this variable, we must identify the services that the switch should offer. As a user of a switch we want to be able to move it between its various settings. As these settings are essentially an enumerated type, we can have the concept of incrementing or decrementing the switch position. A switch must therefore provide a move_up and a move_down interface. Exactly how this is done depends on the programming language; for now, we concentrate on specifying the required facilities.

If we examine each object in our system and identify the required services, we may end up with the following table:

Object	Service	Description
switch	move_up	Increment switch value
	move_down	Decrement switch value
	State?	Return a value indicating the current switch state
fuse	working?	Indicate if the fuse has blown or not
wiper motor	working?	Indicate whether the wipers are working or not
relay	working?	Indicate whether the relay is active or not
pump	working?	Indicate whether the pump is active or not
water bottle	fill	Fill the water bottle with water
	extract	Remove some water from the water bottle
	empty	Empty the water bottle

We generated this table by examining each of the objects in isolation to identify the services that might reasonably be required. We may well identify further services when we attempt to put it all together.

Each of these services should relate to a method within the object. For example, the moveUp and moveDown services should relate to methods that change the state instance variable within the object. Using a generic pseudo-code, the move_up method, within the switch object, might contain the following code:

```
def move_up(self):
    if self.state == "off" then
        self.tate = "wash"
    else if self.state == "wash" then
        self.state = "wipe"
```

This method changes the value of the state variable in switch. The new value of the instance variable depends on its previous value. You can define moveDown in a similar manner. Notice that the reference to the instance variable illustrates that it is global to the object. The moveUp method requires no parameters. In object-oriented systems, it is common for few parameters to be passed between methods (particularly of the same object), as it is the object that holds the data.

17.4.4   Refining the Objects

If we look back to able table, we can see that fuse, wiper motor, relay and pump all possess a service called working?. This is a hint that these objects may have something in common. Each of them presents the same interface to the outside world. If we then consider their attributes, they all possess a common instance variable. At this point, it is too early to say whether fuse, wiper motor, relay and pump are all instances of the same class of object (e.g. a Component class) or whether they are all instances of classes which inherit from some common super-class (see below). However, this is something we must bear in mind later.

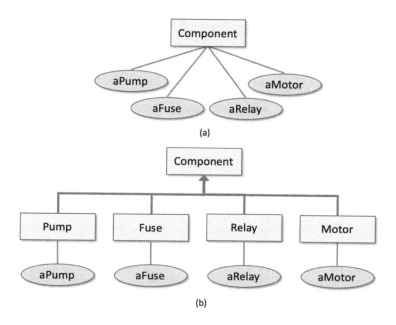

(a)

(b)

17.4.5   Bringing It All Together

So far, we have identified the primary objects in our system and the basic set of services they should present. These services were based solely on the data the objects hold. We must now consider how to make our system function. To do this, we need to consider how it might be used. The system is part of a very simple diagnosis tutor; a student uses the system to learn about the effects of various faults on the operation of a real wiper system, without the need for expensive electronics. We therefore wish to allow a user of the system to carry out the following operations:

- change the state of a component device
- ask the motor what its new state is

The `move_up` and `move_down` operations on the switch change the switch's state. Similar operations can be provided for the fuse, the water bottle and the relay. For the fuse and the relay, we might provide a `change_state` interface using the following algorithm:

```
define change_state(self)
      if self.state == "working" then
            self.tate = "notWorking"
      else
            self.state = "working"
```

Discovering the state of the motor is more complicated. We have encountered a situation where one object's state (the value of its instance variable) is dependent on information provided by other objects. If we write down procedurally how the value of other objects affect the status of the pump, we might get the following pseudo-code:

```
if fuse is working then
      if switch is not off then
            if relay is working then
                  pump status = "working"
```

This algorithm says that the pump status depends on the relay status, the switch setting and the fuse status. This is the sort of algorithm you might expect to find in your application. It links the sub-functions together and processes the data.

In an object-oriented system, well-mannered objects pass messages to one another. How then do we achieve the same effect as the above algorithm? The answer is that we must get the objects to pass messages requesting the appropriate information. One way to do that is to define a method in the pump object that gets the required information from the other objects and determines the motor's state. However, this requires the pump to have links to all the other objects so that it can send them messages. This is a little contrived and loses the structure of the underlying system. It also loses any modularity in the system. That is, if we want to add new components then we have to change the pump object, even if the new components only affect the switch. This approach also indicates that the developer is thinking too procedurally and not really in terms of objects.

In an object-oriented view of the system, the pump object only needs to know the state of the relay. It should therefore request this information from the relay. In turn, the relay must request information from the switches and the fuse.

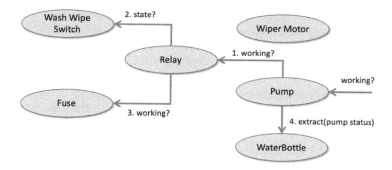

The above illustrates the chain of messages initiated by the pump object:

1. pump sends a working? message to the relay,
2. relay sends a state? message to the switch, the switch replies to the relay,
3. relay sends a second working? message to the fuse:

   - The fuse replies to the relay
   - the relay replies to the motor
   - If the pump is working, then the pump object sends the final message to the water bottle

4. pump sends a message extract to the water bottle

In step four, a parameter is passed with the message because, unlike the previous messages that merely requested state information, this message requests a change in state. The parameter indicates the rate at which the pump draws water from the water bottle.

The water bottle should not record the value of the pump's status as it does not own this value. If it needs the motor's status in the future, it should request it from the pump rather than using the (potentially obsolete) value passed to it previously.

In the above figure we assumed that the pump provided the service working? which allows the process to start. For completeness, the pseudo-code of the working? method for the pump object is:

```
def working?(self)
        self.status = relay.working().
        if self.status == "working" then
            water_bottle.extract(self.status)
```

This method is a lot simpler than the procedural program presented earlier. At no point do we change the value of any variables that are not part of the pump, although they may have been changed as a result of the messages being sent. Also, it only shows us the part of the story that is directly relevant to the pump. This means that it can be much more difficult to deduce the operation of an object-oriented system merely by reading the source code. Some Python environments (such as the PyCharm IDE) alleviate this problem, to some extent, through the use of sophisticated browsers.

17.5   Where Is the Structure in an OO Program?

People new to object orientation may be confused because they have lost one of the key elements that they use to help them understand and structure a software system: the main program body. This is because the objects and the interactions between them are the cornerstone of the system. In many ways, the following figure shows the object-oriented equivalent of a main program. This also highlights an important feature of most object-oriented approaches: graphical illustrations. Many aspects of object technology, for example object structure, class inheritance and message chains, are most easily explained graphically.

Let us now consider the structure of our object-oriented system. It is dictated by the messages that are sent between objects. That is, an object must possess a reference to another object in order to send it a message. The resulting system structure is illustrated below.

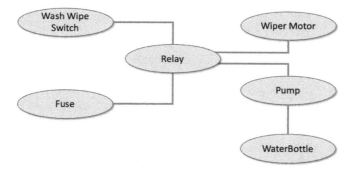

In Python, this structure is achieved by making instance variables reference the appropriate objects. This is the structure which exists between the instances in the system and does not relate to the classes, which act as templates for the instances.

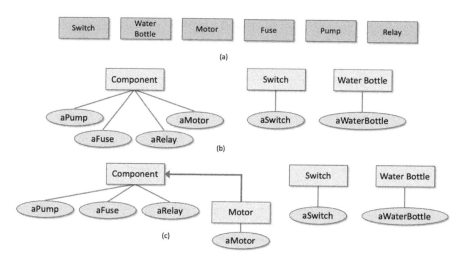

We now consider the classes that create the instances. We could assume that each object is an instance of an equivalent class (see above (a)). However, as has already been noted, some of the classes bear a very strong resemblance. In particular, the fuse, the relay, the motor and the pump share a number of common features. Table following table compares the features (instance variables and services) of these objects.

	fuse	relay	motor	pump
instance variable	state	state	state	state
services	working?	working?	working?	working?

From this table, the objects differ only in name. This suggests that they are all instances of a common class such as Component. This class would possess an additional instance variable, to simplify object identification.

If they are all instances of a common class, they must all behave in exactly the same way. However, we want the pump to start the analysis process when it receives the message working?, so it must possess a different definition of working? from fuse and relay. In other ways it is very similar to fuse and relay, so they can be instances of a class (say Component) and pump and motor can be instances of classes that inherit from Component (but redefine working?). This is illustrated in the previous figure (c). The full class diagram is presented in the Figure below.

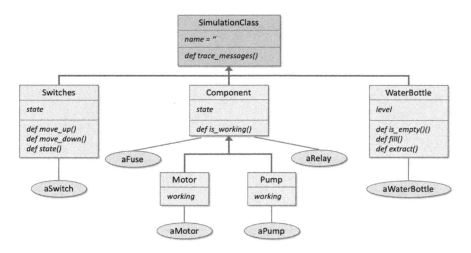

17.6   Further Reading

If you want to explore some of the ideas presented in this chapter in more detail here are sone online references:

- https://en.wikipedia.org/wiki/Object-oriented_programming This is the wikipedia entry for Object Oriented Programming and thus provides a quick reference to much of the terminology and history of the subject and acts asa jumping off point for other references.
- https://dev.to/charanrajgolla/beginners-guide—object-oriented-programming which provides a light hearted look at the four concepts within object orientations namely abstraction, inheritance, polymorphism and Encapsulation.
- https://www.tutorialspoint.com/python/python_classes_objects.htm A Tutorials Point course on Object Oriented Programming and Python.

Chapter 18
Python Classes

18.1 Introduction

In Python everything is an object and as such is an example of a type or class of things. For example, integers are an example of the int class, real numbers are examples of the float class etc. This is illustrated below for a number of different types within Python:

```
print(type(4))
print(type(5.6))
print(type(True))
print(type('Ewan'))
print(type([1, 2, 3, 4]))
```

This prints out a list of classes that define what it is to be an int, or a float or a bool etc. in Python:

```
<class 'int'>
<class 'float'>
<class 'bool'>
<class 'str'>
<class 'list'>
```

However, you are not just restricted to the built-in types (aka classes); it is also possible to define user defined types (classes). These can be used to create your own data structures, your own data types, your own applications etc.

This chapter considers the constructs in Python used to create user defined classes.

© Springer Nature Switzerland AG 2019
J. Hunt, *A Beginners Guide to Python 3 Programming*,
Undergraduate Topics in Computer Science,
https://doi.org/10.1007/978-3-030-20290-3_18

18.2   Class Definitions

In Python, a class definition has the following format

```
class nameOfClass(SuperClass):
    __init__
    attributes
    methods
```

Although you should note that you can mix the order of the definition of attributes, and methods as required within a single class.

The following code is an example of a class definition:

```
class Person:
    def __init__(self, name, age):
        self.name = name
        self.age = age
```

Although this is not a hard and fast rule, it is common to define a class in a file named after that class. For example, the above code would be stored in a file called Person.py; this makes it easier to find the code associated with a class. This is shown below using the PyCharm IDE:

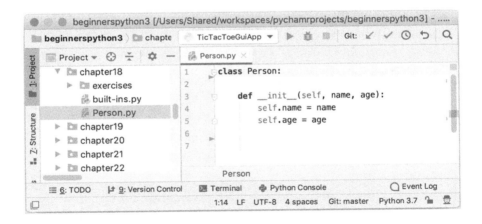

The Person class possesses two *attributes* (or instance variables) called name and age.

There is also a special method defined called __init__. This is an initialiser (also known as a constructor) for the class. It indicates what data must be supplied when an instance of the Person class is created and how that data is stored internally.

In this case a name and an age must be supplied when an instance of the Person class is created.

The values supplied will then be stored within an instance of the class (represented by the *special* variable self) in instance variables/attributes self.name and self.age. Note that the parameters to the __init__ method are *local* variables and will disappear when the method terminates, but self.name and self.age are instance variables and will exist for as long as the object is available.

Let us look for a moment at the special variable *self*. This is the first parameter passed into any method. However, when a method is called we do not pass a value for this parameter ourselves; Python does. It is used to represent the object within which the method is executing. This provides the context within which the method runs and allows the method to access the data held by the object. Thus *self* is the object itself.

You may also be wondering about that term *method*. A method is the name given to behaviour that is linked directly to the Person class; it is not a free-standing function rather it is part of the definition of the class Person.

Historically, it comes from the language Smalltalk; this language was first used to simulate a production plant and a method represented some behaviour that could be used to simulate a change in the production line; it therefore represented a *method* for making a change.

18.3 Creating Examples of the Class Person

New instances/objects (examples) of the class Person can be created by using the name of the class and passing in the values to be used for the parameters of the initialisation method (with the exception of the first parameter *self* which is provided automatically by Python).

For example, the following creates two instances of the class Person:

```
p1 = Person('John', 36)
p2 = Person('Phoebe', 21)
```

The variable p1 holds a reference to the *instance* or *object* of the class Person whose attributes hold the values 'John' (for the name attribute) and 36 (for the age attribute). In turn the variable p2 references an instance of the class Person whose name and age attributes hold the values 'Phoebe' and 21. Thus in memory we have:

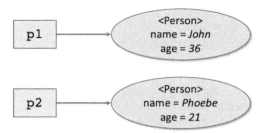

The two variables reference separate *instances* or examples of the class Person. They therefore respond to the same set of methods/operations and have the same set of attributes (such as name and age); however, they have their own values for those attributes (such as 'John' and 'Phoebe').

Each instance also has its own unique identifier—that shows that even if the attribute values happen to be the same between two objects (for example there happen to be two people called John who are both 36); they are still separate instances of the given class. This identifier can be accessed using the id() function, for example:

```
print('id(p1):', id(p1))
print('id(p2):', id(p2))
```

When this code is run p1 and p2 will generate different identifiers, for example:

```
id(p1): 4547191808
id(p2): 4547191864
```

Note that actual number generated may vary from that above but should still be unique (within your program).

18.4   Be Careful with Assignment

Given that in the above example, p1 and p2 reference different instances of the class Person; what happens when p1 or p2 are assigned to another variable? That is, what happens in this case:

```
p1 = Person('John', 36)
px = p1
```

What does px reference? Actually, it makes a complete copy of the value held by p1; however, p1 does not hold the instance of the class Person; it holds the address of the object. It thus copies the address held in p1 into the variable px. This means that both p1 and px now reference (point at) the same instance in memory; we there have this:

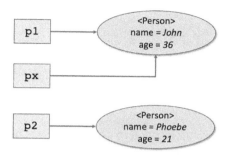

This may not be obvious when you print p1 and px:

```
print(p1)
print(px)
```

As this could just imply that the object has been copied:

```
John is 36
John is 36
```

However, if we print the unique identifier for what is referenced by p1 and px then it becomes clear that it is the same instance of class Person:

```
print('id(p1):', id(p1))
print('id(px):', id(px))
```

which prints out

```
id(p1): 4326491864
id(px): 4326491864
```

As can be seen the unique identifier is the same.

Of course, if p1 is subsequently assigned a different object (for example if we ran p1 = p2) then this would have no effect on the value held in px; indeed, we would now have:

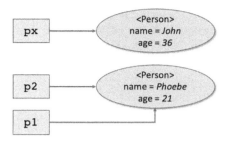

18.5   Printing Out Objects

If we now use the print() function to print the objects held by p1 and p2, we will get what might at first glance appear to be a slightly odd result:

```
print(p1)
print(p2)
```

The output generated is

```
<__main__.Person object at 0x10f08a400>
<__main__.Person object at 0x10f08a438>
```

What this is showing is the name of the class (in this case Person) and a hexadecimal number indicates where it is held in memory. Neither of which is particularly useful and certainly doesn't help us in knowing what information p1 and p2 are holding.

18.5.1   Accessing Object Attributes

We can access the attributes held by p1 and p2 using what is known as the *dot* notation. This notation allows us to follow the variable holding the object with a dot ('.') and the attribute we are interested in access. For example, to access the name of a person object we can use p1.name or for their age we can use p1.age:

```
print(p1.name, 'is', p1.age)
print(p2.name, 'is', p2.age)
```

The result of this is that we output

```
John is 36
Phoebe is 21
```

Which is rather more meaningful.

In fact, we can also update the attributes of an object directly, for example we can write:

```
p1.name = 'Bob'
p1.age = 54
```

If we now run

```
print(p1.name, 'is', p1.age)
```

then we will get

```
Bob is 54
```

We will see in a later chapter (Python Properties) that we can restrict access to these attributes by making them into *properties*.

18.5.2   *Defining a Default String Representation*

In the previous section we printed out information from the instances of class Person by accessing the attributes name and age.

However, we now needed to know the internal structure of the class Person to print out its details. That is, we need to know that there are attributes called name and age available on this class.

It would be much more convenient if the object itself knew how to convert its self into a string to be printed out!

In fact we can make the class Person do this by defining a method that can be used to convert an object into a string for printing purposes.

This method is the __str__ method. The method is expected to return a string which can be used to represent appropriate information about a class.

The signature of the method is

```
def __str__(self)
```

Methods that start with a double underbar ('__') are by convention considered special in Python and we will see several of these methods later on in the book. For the moment we will focus only on the __str__() method.

We can add this method to our class `Person` and see how that affects the output generated when using the `print()` function.

We will return a string from the __str__ method that provides and the `name` and `age` of the person:

```
class Person:
    def __init__(self, name, age):
        self.name = name
        self.age = age

    def __str__(self):
        return self.name + ' is ' + str(self.age)
```

Note that in the __str__ method we access the name and age attributes using the `self` parameter passed into the method by Python. Also note that it is necessary to convert the `age` number attribute into a string. This is because the '+' operator will do string *concatenation* unless one of the operands (one of the sides of the '+') is a number; in which case it will try and do arithmetic addition which of course will not work if the other operand is a string!

If we now try to print out p1 and p2:

```
print(p1)
print(p2)
```

The output generated is:

```
John is 36
Phoebe is 21
```

Which is much more useful.

18.6   Providing a Class Comment

It is common to provide a comment for a class defining what that class does, its purpose and any important points to note about the class.

This can be done by providing a *docstring* for the class just after the class declaration header; you can use the triple quotes string (''' '' ''...'' '' '') to create multiple line *docstrings*, for example:

```
class Person:
    """ An example class to hold a
        persons name and age"""

    def __init__(self, name, age):
        self.name = name
        self.age = age

    def __str__(self):
        return self.name + ' is ' + str(self.age)
```

The *docstring* is accessible through the __doc__ attribute of the class. The intention is to make information available to users of the class, even at runtime. It can also be used by IDEs to provide information on a class.

18.7   Adding a Birthday Method

Let us now add some behaviour to the class Person. In the following example, we define a *method* called birthday() that takes no parameters and increments the age attribute by 1:

```
class Person:
    """ An example class to hold a persons name and age"""

    def __init__(self, name, age):
        self.name = name
        self.age = age

    def __str__(self):
        return self.name + ' is ' + str(self.age)

    def birthday(self):
        print ('Happy birthday you were', self.age)
        self.age += 1
        print('You are now', self.age)
```

Note that again the first parameter passed into the method birthday is self. This represents the instance (the example of the class Person) that this method will be used with.

If we now create an instance of the class Person and call birthday() on it, the age will be incremented by 1, for example:

```
p3 = Person('Adam', 19)
print(p3)
p3.birthday()
print(p3)
```

When we run this code, we get

```
Adam is 19
Happy birthday you were 19
You are now 20
Adam is 20
```

As you can see Adam is initially 19; but after his birthday he is now 20.

18.8   Defining Instance Methods

The birthday() method presented above is an example of what is known as an instance method; that is, it is tied to an instance of the class. In that case the method did not take any parameters, nor did it return any parameters; however, instance methods can do both.

For example, let us assume that the Person class will also be used to calculate how much someone should be paid. Let us also assume that the rate is £7.50 if you are under 21 but that there is a supplement of 2.50 if you are 21 or over.

We could define an instance method that will take as input the number of hours worked and return the amount someone should be paid:

```python
class Person:
    """ An example class to hold a persons name and age"""
    # ...
    def calculate_pay(self, hours_worked):
        rate_of_pay = 7.50
        if self.age >= 21:
            rate_of_pay += 2.50
        return hours_worked * rate_of_pay
```

We can invoke this method again using the *dot* notation, for example:

```python
pay = p2.calculate_pay(40)
print('Pay', p2.name, pay)
pay = p3.calculate_pay(40)
print('Pay', p3.name, pay)
```

Running this shows that Phoebe (who is 21) will be paid £400 while Adam who is only 19 will be paid only £300:

```
Pay Phoebe 400.0
Pay Adam 300.0
```

Another example of an instance method defined on the class `Person` is the `is_teenager()` method. This method does not take a parameter, but it does return a Boolean value depending upon the `age` attribute:

```
class Person:
    """ An example class to hold a persons name and age"""
    #...
    def is_teenager(self):
        return self.age < 20
```

Note that the *implicitly* provided parameter 'self' is still provided even when a method does not take a parameter.

18.9 Person Class Recap

Let us bring together the concepts that we have looked at so far in the final version of the class `Person`.

```
class Person:
    """ An example class to hold a persons name and age"""

    def __init__(self, name, age):
        self.name = name
        self.age = age

    def __str__(self):
        return self.name + ' is ' + str(self.age)

    def birthday(self):
        print ('Happy birthday you were', self.age)
        self.age += 1
        print('You are now', self.age)

    def calculate_pay(self, hours_worked):
        rate_of_pay = 7.50
        if self.age >= 21:
            rate_of_pay += 2.50
        return hours_worked * rate_of_pay

    def is_teenager(self):
        return self.age < 20
```

This class exhibits several features we have seen already and expands a few others:

- The class has a two parameter initialiser that takes a `String` and an `Integer`.
- It defines two attributes held by each of the instances of the class; `name` and `age`.
- It defines a `__str__` method so that the details of the `Person` object can be easily printed.
- It defines three methods `birthday()`, `calculate_pay()` and `is_teenager()`.
- The method `birthday()` does not return anything (i.e. it does not return a value) and is comprised of three statements, two print statements and an assignment.
- `is_teenager()` returns a `Boolean` value (i.e. one that returns `True` or `False`).

An example application using this class is given below:

```
p1 = Person('John', 36)
print(p1)
print(p1.name, 'is', p1.age)
print('p1.is_teenager', p1.is_teenager())
p1.birthday()
print(p1)
p1.age = 18
print(p1)
```

This application creates an instance of the `Person` class using the values 'John' and 36. It then prints out `p1` using `print` (which will automatically call the `__str__()` method on the instances passed to it). It then accesses the values of `name` and `age` properties and prints these. Following this it calls the `is_teenager()` method and prints the result returned. It then calls the `birthday()` method. Finally, it assigns a new value to the `age` attribute. The output from this application is given below:

```
John is 36
John is 36
p1.is_teenager False
Happy birthday you were 36
You are now 37
John is 37
John is 18
```

18.10   The del Keyword

Having at one point created an object of some type (whether that is a `bool`, an `int` or a user defined type such as `Person`) it may later be necessary to delete that object. This can be done using the keyword `del`. This keyword is used to delete objects which allows the memory they are using to be reclaimed and used by other parts of your program.

For example, we can write

```
p1 = Person('John', 36)
print(p1)
del p1
```

After the `del` statement the object held by `p1` will no longer be available and any attempt to reference it will generate an error.

You do not need to use `del` as setting `p1` above to the `None` value (representing nothingness) will have the same effect. In addition, if the above code was defined within a function or a method then `p1` will cease to exist once the function or method terminates and this will again have the same effect as deleting the object and freeing up the memory.

18.11   Automatic Memory Management

The creation and deletion of objects (and their associated memory) is managed by the Python Memory Manager. Indeed, the provision of a memory manager (also known as automatic memory management) is one of Python's advantages when compared to languages such as C and C++. It is not uncommon to hear C++ programmers complaining about spending many hours attempting to track down a particularly awkward bug only to find it was a problem associated with memory allocation or pointer manipulation. Similarly, a regular problem for C++ developers is that of memory creep, which occurs when memory is allocated but is not freed up. The application either uses all available memory or runs out of space and produces a run time error.

Most of the problems associated with memory allocation in languages such as C ++ occur because programmers must not only concentrate on the (often complex) application logic but also on memory management. They must ensure that they allocate only the memory which is required and deallocate it when it is no longer required. This may sound simple, but it is no mean feat in a large complex application.

An interesting question to ask is "why do programmers have to manage memory allocation?". There are few programmers today who would expect to have to manage the registers being used by their programs, although 30 or 40 years ago the situation was very different. One answer to the memory management question, often cited by those who like to manage their own memory, is that "it is more efficient, you have more control, it is faster and leads to more compact code". Of course, if you wish to take these comments to their extreme, then we should all be programming in assembler. This would enable us all to produce faster, more efficient and more compact code than that produced by Python or languages such as Java.

The point about high level languages, however, is that they are more productive, introduce fewer errors, are more expressive and are efficient enough (given modern computers and compiler technology). The memory management issue is somewhat similar. If the system automatically handles the allocation and deallocation of memory, then the programmer can concentrate on the application logic. This makes the programmer more productive, removes problems due to poor memory management and, when implemented efficiently, can still provide acceptable performance.

Python therefore provides automatic memory management. Essentially, it allocates a portion of memory as and when required. When memory is short, it looks for areas which are no longer referenced. These areas of memory are then freed up (deallocated) so that they can be reallocated. This process is often referred to as *Garbage Collection*.

18.12   Intrinsic Attributes

Every class (and every object) in Python has a set of *intrinsic* attributes set up by the Python runtime system. Some of these intrinsic attributes are given below for classes and objects.

Classes have the following intrinsic attributes:

- __name__ the name of the class
- __module__ the module (or library) from which it was loaded
- __bases__ a collection of its base classes (see inheritance later in this book)
- __dict__ a dictionary (a set of key-value pairs) containing all the attributes (including methods)
- __doc__ the documentation string.

   For objects:

- __class__ the name of the class of the object
- __dict__ a dictionary containing all the object's attributes.

Notice that these intrinsic attributes all start and end with a double underbar—this indicates their special status within Python.

An example of printing these attributes out for the class Person and a instance of the class are shown below:

```
print('Class attributes')
print(Person.__name__)
print(Person.__module__)
print(Person.__doc__)
print(Person.__dict__)
print('Object attributes')
print(p1.__class__)
print(p1.__dict__)
```

The output from this is:

```
Class attributes
Person
__main__
 An example class to hold a persons name and age
{'__module__': '__main__', '__doc__': ' An example class to
hold a persons name and age', 'instance_count': 4,
'increment_instance_count': <classmethod object at
0x105955588>, 'static_function': <staticmethod object at
0x1059555c0>, '__init__': <function Person.__init__ at
0x10595d268>, '__str__': <function Person.__str__ at
0x10595d2f0>, 'birthday': <function Person.birthday at
0x10595d378>, 'calculate_pay': <function Person.calculate_pay
at 0x10595d400>, 'is_teenager': <function Person.is_teenager at
0x10595d488>, '__dict__': <attribute '__dict__' of 'Person'
objects>, '__weakref__': <attribute '__weakref__' of 'Person'
objects>}
Object attributes
<class '__main__.Person'>
{'name': 'John', 'age': 36}
```

18.13   Online Resources

See the following for further information on Python classes:

- https://docs.python.org/3/tutorial/classes.html The Python Standard library Class tutorial.
- https://www.tutorialspoint.com/python3/python_classes_objects.htm The tutorials point tutorial on Python 3 classes.

18.14   Exercises

The aim of this exercise is to create a new class called Account.

1. Define a new class to represent a type of bank account.
2. When the class is instantiated you should provide the account number, the name of the account holder, an opening balance and the type of account (which can be a string representing 'current', 'deposit' or 'investment' etc.). This means that there must be an __init__ method and you will need to store the data within the object.

3. Provide three instance methods for the `Account`; `deposit(amount)`, `withdraw(amount)` and `get_balance()`. The behaviour of these methods should be as expected, deposit will increase the balance, withdraw will decrease the balance and `get_balance()` returns the current balance.
4. Define a simple test application to verify the behaviour of your `Account` class.

It can be helpful to see how your class `Account` is expected to be used. For this reason a simple test application for the `Account` is given below:

```
acc1 = Account('123', 'John', 10.05, 'current')
acc2 = Account('345', 'John', 23.55, 'savings')
acc3 = Account('567', 'Phoebe', 12.45, 'investment')

print(acc1)
print(acc2)
print(acc3)

acc1.deposit(23.45)
acc1.withdraw(12.33)
print('balance:', acc1.get_balance())
```

The following output illustrates what the result of running this test application might look like:

```
Account[123] - John, current account = 10.05
Account[345] - John, savings account = 23.55
Account[567] - Phoebe, investment account = 12.45
balance: 21.17
```

Chapter 19
Class Side and Static Behaviour

19.1 Introduction

Python classes can hold data and behaviour that is not part of an instance or object; instead they are part of the class.

This chapter introduces class side data, behaviour and static behaviour.

19.2 Class Side Data

In Python classes can also have attributes; these are referred to as *class* variables or attributes (as opposed to instance variables or attributes).

In Python variables defined within the scope of the class, but outside of any methods, are tied to the class rather than to any instance and are thus class variables.

For example, we can update the class Person to keep a count of how many instances of the class are created:

```
class Person:
    """ An example class to hold a persons name and age"""

    instance_count = 0

    def __init__(self, name, age):
        Person.instance_count += 1
        self.name = name
        self.age = age
```

The variable instance_count is not part of an individual object, rather it is part of the class and all instances of the class can access that shared variable by prefixing it with the class name.

© Springer Nature Switzerland AG 2019
J. Hunt, *A Beginners Guide to Python 3 Programming*,
Undergraduate Topics in Computer Science,
https://doi.org/10.1007/978-3-030-20290-3_19

Now each time a new instance of the class is created, the instance_count is incremented, thus if we write:

```
p1 = Person('Jason', 36)
p2 = Person('Carol', 21)
p3 = Person('James', 19)
p4 = Person('Tom', 31)
print(Person.instance_count)
```

The output will be:

4

This is because 4 instances have been created and thus __init__() has been run 4 times and instance_count has been incremented four times.

19.3   Class Side Methods

It is also possible to define behaviour that is linked to the *class* rather than an individual object; this behaviour is defined in a class method.

Class methods are written in a similar manner to any other method but are *decorated* with @classmethod and take a first parameter which represents the class rather than an individual instance. This decoration is written before the method declaration.

An example of a class method is shown below:

```
class Person:
    """ An example class to hold a persons name and age"""
    instance_count = 0

    @classmethod
    def increment_instance_count(cls):
        cls.instance_count += 1

    def __init__(self, name, age):
        Person.increment_instance_count()
        self.name = name
        self.age = age
```

In this case the class method increments the instance_count variable; note that the instance_count variable is accessed via the cls parameter passed into the increment_instance_count method by Python. As this is a class method you do not need to prefix the class attribute with the name of class; instead the first parameter to the class method, cls, represents the class itself.

The class method can be accessed by *prefixing* it with the name of the class and using the *dot* notation to indicate which method to call. This is illustrated in the body of the __init__() method.

19.3.1   Why Class-Side Methods?

It may at first seem unclear what should normally go in an instance method as opposed to what should go in a class method. After all, they are both defined in the class. However, it is important to remember that

- Instance methods define the behaviour of the instance or object.
- Class methods define the behaviour of the class.

Class-side methods should only perform one of the following roles:

- *Instance creation* This role is very important as it is how you can use a class as a factory for objects and can help hide a whole load of set up and instantiation work.
- *Answering enquiries about the class* This role can provide generally useful objects, frequently derived from class variables. For example, they may return the number of instances of this class that have been created.
- *Instance management* In this role, class-side methods control the number of instances created. For example, a class may only allow a single instance of the class to be created; this is termed a singleton class. Instance management methods may also be used to access an instance (e.g. randomly or in a given state).
- *Examples* Occasionally, class methods are used to provide helpful examples which explain the operation of a class. This can be very good practice.
- *Testing* Class-side methods can be used to support the testing of an instance of a class. You can use them to create an instance, perform an operation and compare the result with a known value. If the values are different, the method can report an error. This is a very useful way of providing regression tests.
- *Support* for one of the above roles.

Any other tasks should be performed by an instance method.

19.4   Static Methods

There is one more type of method that can be defined on a class; these are *static* methods.

Static methods are defined within a class but are not tied to either the class nor any instance of the class; they do not receive the special first parameter representing either the class (cls for class methods) or the instances (self for instance methods).

They are in effect, the same as *free standing functions* but are defined within a class often for convenience or to provide a way to group such functions together.

A *static* method is a method that is decorated with the @staticmethod decorator. An example of a static method is given below:

```
class Person:

    @staticmethod
    def static_function():
        print('Static method')
```

Static methods are invoked via the name of the class they are defined in, for example:

```
Person.static_function()
```

A note for Java and C# programmers; in both Java and C# the term class side and static are used interchangeably (not helped by the use of the keyword static for these methods). However, in both cases those methods are the equivalent of class side methods in Python. In Python *class* methods and *static* methods are two very, very different things—do not use these terms interchangeably.

19.5   Hints

There are a range of special methods available in Python on a class.

All of these special methods start and end with a double underbars ('__').

In general, in Python anything that starts and ends with these double underbars is considered special and so care should be taken when using them.

You should never name one of your own methods or functions __<some-thing>__ unless you intend to (re)define some default behaviour.

19.6   Online Resources

There is surprisingly little information available on Python's static and class methods (which in part explains why many developers are confused by them), however the following are available:

- https://python-reference.readthedocs.io/en/latest/docs/functions/staticmethod. html documentation on static methods.
- https://python-reference.readthedocs.io/en/latest/docs/functions/classmethod. html?highlight=classmethod documentation on class methods.
- https://www.tutorialspoint.com/class-method-vs-static-method-in-python   tutorial on class methods versus static methods.

19.7 Exercises

The aim of this exercise is to add housekeeping style methods to the `Account` class. You should follow these steps:

1. We want to allow the `Account` class from the last chapter to keep track of the number of instances of the class that have been created.
2. Print out a message each time a new instance of the `Account` class is created.
3. Print out the number of accounts created at the end of the previous test program. For example add the following two statements to the end of the program:

```
print('Number of Account instances created:',
Account.instance_count)
```

Chapter 20
Class Inheritance

20.1 Introduction

Inheritance is a core feature of Object-Oriented Programming. It allows one class to *inherit* data or behaviour from another class and is one of the key ways in which reuse is enabled within classes.

This chapter introduces inheritance between classes in Python.

20.2 What Is Inheritance?

Inheritance allows features defined in one class to be *inherited* and reused in the definition of another class. For example, a `Person` class might have the attributes `name` and `age`. It might also have behaviour associated with a `Person` such as `birthday()`.

We might then decide that we want to have another class `Employee` and that employees also have a `name` and an `age` and will have birthdays. However, in addition an `Employee` may have an employee `Id` attribute and a `calculate_pay()` behaviour.

At this point we could duplicate the definition of the `name` and `age` attributes and the `birthday()` behaviour in the class `Employee` (for example by cutting and pasting the code between the two classes).

However, this is not only inefficient; it may also cause problems in the future. For example we may realise that there is a problem or bug in the implementation of `birthday()` and may correct it in the class `Person`; however, we may forget to apply the same fix to the class `Employee`.

In general, in software design and development it is considered best practice to define something once and to reuse that something when required.

© Springer Nature Switzerland AG 2019
J. Hunt, *A Beginners Guide to Python 3 Programming*,
Undergraduate Topics in Computer Science,
https://doi.org/10.1007/978-3-030-20290-3_20

In an object-oriented system we can achieve the reuse of data or behaviour via inheritance. That is one class (in this case the `Employee` class) can *inherit* features from another class (in this case `Person`). This is shown pictorially below:

In this diagram the `Employee` class is shown as inheriting from the `Person` class. This means that the `Employee` class obtains all the data and behaviour of the `Person` class. It is therefore as though the `Employee` class has defined three attributes `name`, `age` and `id` and two methods `birthday()` and `calculate_pay()`.

A class that is defined as extending a parent class has the following syntax:

```
class SubClassName(BaseClassName):
    class-body
```

Note that the parent class is specified by providing the name of that class in round brackets after the name of the new (child) class.

We can define the class `Person` in Python as before:

```
class Person:
    def __init__(self, name, age):
        self.name = name
        self.age = age

    def birthday(self):
        print('Happy birthday you were', self.age)
        self.age += 1
        print('You are now', self.age)
```

We could now define the class `Employee` as being a class whose definition builds on (or inherits from) the class `Person`:

```
class Employee(Person):
    def __init__(self, name, age, id):
        super().__init__(name, age)
        self.id = id

    def calculate_pay(self, hours_worked):
        rate_of_pay = 7.50
        if self.age >= 21:
            rate_of_pay += 2.50
        return hours_worked * rate_of_pay
```

Here we do several things:

1. The class is called `Employee` but it extends `Person`. This is indicated by including the name of the class being inherited in parentheses after the name of the class being defined (e.g. `Employee(Person)`) in the class declaration.
2. Inside the `__init__` method we reference the `__init__()` method defined in the class `Person` and used to initialise instances of that class (via the `super().__init__()` reference. This allows whatever initialisation is required for `Person` to happen. This is called from within the `Employee` class's `__init__()` which then allows any initialisation required by the `Employee` to occur. Note that the call to the `super().__init__()` initialiser can come anywhere within the `Employee.__init__()` method; but by convention it comes first to ensure that whatever the `Person` class does during initialisation does not over write what happens in the `Employee` class.
3. All instances of the class `Person` have a name, and age and have the behaviour `birthday()`.
4. All instances of the class `Employee` have a name, and age and an id and have the behaviours `birthday()` and `calculate_pay(house_worked)`.
5. The method `calculate_pay()` defined in the `Employee` class can access the attributes name and age just as it can access the attribute id. In fact, it uses the employee's age to determine the rate of pay to apply.

We can go further, and we can subclass `Employee`, for example with the class `SalesPerson`:

```
class SalesPerson(Employee):
    def __init__(self, name, age, id, region, sales):
        super().__init__(name, age, id)
        self.region = region
        self.sales = sales

    def bonus(self):
        return self.sales * 0.5
```

Now we can say that the class `SalesPerson` has a name, an age and an `id` as well as a `region` and a `sales total`. It also has the methods `birthday()`, `calculate_pay(hourse_worked)` and `bonus()`.

In this case the `SalesPerson.__init__()` method calls the `Employee.__init__()` method as that is the next class up the hierarchy and thus we want to run that classes initialisation behaviour before we set up the `SalesPerson` class (which of course in turn runs the `Person` classes initialisation behaviour).

We can now write code such as:

```
print('Person')
p = Person('John', 54)
print(p)
print('-' * 25)

print('Employee')
e = Employee('Denise', 51, 7468)
e.birthday()
print('e.calculate_pay(40):', e.calculate_pay(40))
print('-' * 25)

print('SalesPerson')
s = SalesPerson('Phoebe', 21, 4712, 'UK', 30000.0)
s.birthday()
print('s.calculate_pay(40):', s.calculate_pay(40))
print('s.bonus():', s.bonus())
```

With the output being:

```
Person
John is 54
-------------------------
Employee
Happy birthday you were 51
You are now 52
e.calculate_pay(40): 400.0
-------------------------
SalesPerson
Happy birthday you were 21
You are now 22
s.calculate_pay(40): 400.0
s.bonus(): 15000.0
```

It is important to note that we have not done anything to the class `Person` by defining `Employee` and `SalesPerson`; that is it is not affected by those class definitions. Thus, a `Person` *does not* have an employee id. Similarly, neither an `Employee` nor a `Person` have a `region` or a `sales` total.

In terms of behaviour, instances of all three classes can run the method `birthday()`, but

- only `Employee` and `SalesPerson` objects can run the method `calcul-cate_pay()` and
- only `SalesPerson` objects can run the method `bonus()`.

20.3   Terminology Around Inheritance

The following terminology is commonly used with inheritance in most object oriented languages including Python:

Class A class defines a combination of data and procedures that operate on that data.

Subclass A subclass is a class that inherits from another class. For example, an `Employee` might inherit from a class `Person`. Subclasses are, of course, classes in their own right. Any class can have any number of subclasses.

Superclass A superclass is the parent of a class. It is the class from which the current class inherits. For example, `Person` might be the superclass of `Employee`. In Python, a class can have any number of superclasses.

Single or multiple inheritance Single and multiple inheritance refer to the number of super classes from which a class can inherit. For example, Java is a single inheritance system, in which a class can only inherit from one class. Python by contrast is a multiple inheritance system in which a class can inherit from one or more classes.

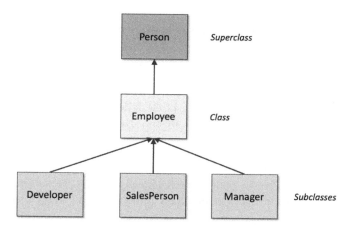

Note that a set of classes, involved in an inheritance hierarchy, such as those shown above, are often named after the class at the root (top) of the hierarchy; in this case it would make these classes part of the *Person* class hierarchy.

Types of Hierarchy

In most object-oriented systems there are two types of hierarchy; one refers to *inheritance* (whether single or multiple) and the other refers to *instantiation*. The inheritance hierarchy has already been described. It is the way in which one class inherits features from a superclass.

The instantiation hierarchy relates to instances or objects rather than classes and is important during the execution of the object.

There are two types of instance relationships: one indicates a *part-of* relationship, while the other relates to a *using* relationship (it is referred to as an *is-a* relationship). This is illustrated below:

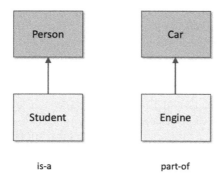

The difference between an *is-a* relationship and a *part-of* relationship is often confusing for new programmers (and sometimes for those who are experienced in non object oriented languages). The above figure illustrates that a Student *is-a* type of Person whereas an Engine is *part-of* a Car. It does not make sense to say that a student is part-of a person or that an engine is-a type of car!

In Python, *inheritance* relationships are implemented by the sub-classing mechanism. In contrast, part-of relationships are implemented using instance attributes in Python.

The problem with classes, inheritance and is-a relationships is that on the surface they appear to capture a similar concept. In the following figure the hierarchies all capture some aspect of the use of the phrase *is-a*. However, they are all intended to capture a different relationship.

The confusion is due to the fact that in modern English we tend to overuse the term *is-a*. For example, in English we can say that an Employee is a type of Person or that Andrew is a Person; both are semantically correct. However, in Python classes such as Employee and Person and an object such as Andrew are different things. We can distinguish between the different types of relationship by being more precise about our definitions in terms of a programming language, such as Python.

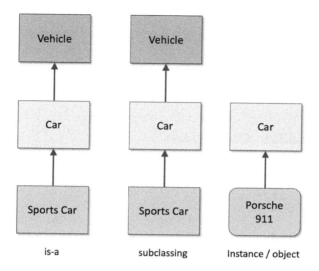

20.4   The Class Object and Inheritance

Every class in Python extends one or more superclasses. This is true even of the class Person shown below:

```
class Person:
    def __init__(self, name, age):
     self.name = name
     self.age = age
```

This is because if you do not specify a superclass explicitly Python automatically adds in the class object as a parent class. Thus the above is exactly the same as the following listing which explicitly lists the class object as the superclass of Person:

```
class Person(object):
    def __init__(self, name, age):
        self.name = name
        self.age = age
```

Both listings above define a class called Person that extends the class object. In fact, between Python 2.2 and Python 3 it was required to use the long hand form to ensure that the *new style* classes were being used (as opposed to an older way in which classes were defined pre Python 2.2). As such it is common to find that Python developers still use the long hand (explicit) form when defining classes that directly extend `object`.

The fact that all class eventually inherit from the class `object` means that behaviour defined in object is available for all classes everywhere.

20.5   The Built-in Object Class

The class object is the base (root) class for all classes in Python. It has methods that are therefore available in all Python objects. It defines a common set of *special* methods and *intrinsic* attributes. The methods include the special methods `__str__()`, `__init()__`, `__eq__()` (equals) and `__hash__()` (hash method). It also defines attributes such as `__class__`, `__dict__`, `__doc__` and `__module__`.

20.6   Purpose of Subclasses

Subclasses are used to refine the behaviour and data structures of a superclass.

A parent class may define some generic/shared attributes and methods; these can then be inherited and reused by several other (sub) classes which add subclass specific attributes and behaviour.

In fact, there are only a small number of things that a subclass should do relative to its parent or super class. If a proposed subclass does not do any of these then your selected parent class is not the most appropriate super class to use.

A subclass should modify the behaviour of its parent class or extend the data held by its parent class. This modification should refine the class in one or more of these ways:

- Changes to the external protocol or interface of the class, that is it should extend the set of methods or attributes provided by the class.
- Changes in the implementation of the methods; i.e. the way in which the behaviour provided by the class are implemented.
- Additional behaviour that references inherited behaviour.

If a subclass does not provide one or more of the above, then it is incorrectly placed. For example, if a subclass implements a set of new methods, but does not refer to the attributes or methods of the parent class, then the class is not really a subclass of the parent (it does not extend it).

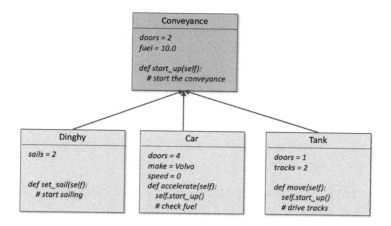

As an example, consider the class hierarchy illustrated above. A generic root class has been defined. This class defines a Conveyance which has doors, fuel (both with default values) and a method, start_up(), that starts the engine of the conveyance. Three subclasses of Conveyance have also been defined: Dinghy, Car and Tank. Two of these subclasses are appropriate, but one should probably not inherit from Conveyance. We shall consider each in turn to determine their suitability.

- The class Tank overrides the number of doors inherited, uses the start_up method within the method move, and provides a new attribute. It therefore matches all three of our criteria.
- Similarly, the class Car overrides the number of doors and uses the method start_up(). It also uses the instance variable fuel within a new method accelerate(). It also, therefore, matches our criteria.
- The class Dinghy defines a new attribute sails and a new method set_sail(). As such, it does not use any of the features inherited from Conveyance. However, we might say that it has extended Conveyance by providing this attribute and method. We must then consider the features provided by Conveyance. We can ask ourselves whether they make sense within the context of Dinghy. If we assume that a dinghy is a small sail-powered boat, with no cabin and no engine, then nothing inherited from Conveyance is useful. In this case, it is likely that Conveyance is misnamed, as it defines some sort of a *motor vehicle*, and the Dinghy class should not have extended it.

20.7 Overriding Methods

Overriding occurs when a method is defined in a class (for example, Person) and also in one of its subclasses (for example, Employee). It means that instances of Person and Employee both respond to requests for this method to be run but each has their own implementation of the method.

For example, let us assume that we define the method __str__() in these classes (so that we have a string representation of these objects to use with the print function). The pseudo code definition of this in Person might be:

```
def __str__(self):
    return 'Person ' + self.name + ' is ' + str(self.age)
```

In Employee, it might be defined as:

```
def __str__(self):
    return 'Employee(' + str(self.id) + ')'
```

The method in Employee replaces the version in Person for all instances of Employee. If we ask an instance of Employee for the result of __str__(), we get the string 'Employee(<some_id>)'. If you are confused, think of it this way:

> If you ask an object to perform some operation, then, to determine which version of the method is run, look in the class used to create the instance. If the method is not defined there, look in the class's parent. Keep doing this until you find a method which implements the operation requested. This is the version which is used.

As a concrete example, see the classes Person and Employee below; in which the __str__() method in Person is overridden in Employee.

```
class Person:
    def __init__(self, name, age):
        self.name = name
        self.age = age
    def __str__(self):
        return self.name + ' is ' + str(self.age)

class Employee(Person):
    def __init__(self, name, age, id):
        super().__init__(name, age)
        self.id = id
    def __str__(self):
        return self.name + ' is ' + str(self.age) + ' - i
str(self.id) + ')'
```

Instances of these classes will both be convertible to a string using __str__() but the version used by instances of Employee will differ from that used with instances of Person, for example:

```
p = Person('John', 54)
print(p)
e = Employee('Denise', 51, 1234)
print(e)
```

Generates as output:

```
John is 54
Denise is 51 - id(1234)
```

As can be seen from this the Employee class prints the name, age and id of the Employee while the Person class only prints the name and age.

20.8   Extending Superclass Methods

However, in the previous section we had to duplicated the code in Person down in Employee so that we could convert the name and age attributes into strings.

However we can avoid this duplication by invoking the parent class's method from within the child class version (as we in fact did for the __init__() initialiser).

For example:

```
class Person:
    def __init__(self, name, age):
        self.name = name
        self.age = age

    def __str__(self):
        return self.name + ' is ' + str(self.age)

class Employee(Person):
    def __init__(self, name, age, id):
        super().__init__(name, age)
        self.id = id

    def __str__(self):
        return super().__str__() + '-id(' + str(self.id) + ')'
```

In this version of the code the Employee classes version of the __str__() method first calls the parent classes version of this method and then adds the location information to the string returned from that. This means that we only have one location that converts name and age into a string.

The output from the code

```
p = Person('John', 54)
print(p)
e = Employee('Denise', 51, 1234)
print(e)
```

remains exactly the same:

```
John is 54
Denise is 51 - id(1234)
```

20.9   Inheritance Oriented Naming Conventions

There are two naming conventions to be aware of with respect to Python classes and inheritance. These are that

- *Single underbar convention*. Methods or instance variables/attributes (those accessed via `self`) whose names start with a single under bar are considered to be *protected* that is they are private to the class but can be accessed from any subclass. Their scope is thus the class and any subclasses (either direct subclasses or any level of sub subclass).
- *Double underbar convention*. Method or instance variables/attributes (those accessed via `self`) whose names start with a double under bar should be considered *private* to that class and should not be called from outside of the class. This includes any subclasses; private means private to the class and only to that class.

Any identifier of the form __somename (at least two leading underscores and at most one trailing underscore) is textually replaced with _classname__somename, where classname is the current class name with leading underscore(s) stripped.

Python does what is called *name mangling* to provide some support for methods that start with a double under bar. This mangling is done without regard to the syntactic position of the identifier, so it can be used to define class-private instance and class variables, methods, variables stored in globals, and even variables stored in instances.

20.10   Python and Multiple Inheritance

Python supports the idea of multiple inheritance; that is a class can inherit from one or more other classes (many object-oriented languages limit inheritance to a single class such as Java and C#).

This idea is illustrated by the following diagram:

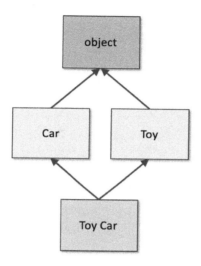

In this case the class `ToyCar` inherits from the class `Car` and the class `Toy`. In turn the `Car` and `Toy` classes inherit from the (default) base class `object`.

The syntax for defining multiple inheritance in Python allows multiple super-classes to be listed in the parent class list (defined by the brackets following the class name). Each parent class is separated by a comma. The syntax is thus:

```
class SubClassName(BaseClassName1, BaseClassName2, …
BaseClassNameN):
    class-body
```

For example:

```
class Car:
    """ Car """

class Toy:
    """ Toy """

class ToyCar(Car, Toy):
    """ A Toy Car """
```

We can say that the class `ToyCar` inherits all the attributes (data) and methods (behaviour) defined in classes `Car`, `Toy` and `object`.

One of the fundamental questions that this raises is how is inheritance of behaviour managed within a multiple inheritance hierarchy. The challenge that multiple inheritance possesses is illustrated by adding a couple of methods to the class hierarchy we are looking at. In this example we have added the method `move()` to both the class `Car` and the class `Toy`:

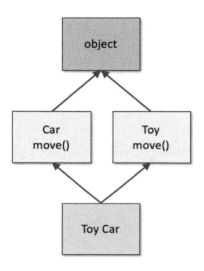

The question here is which version of the method `move()` will be run when an instance of the `ToyCar` class is instantiated and we call `toy_car.move()`?

This illustrates (a simple version of) the so-called "diamond inheritance" problem.

The issue is that with multiple base classes from which attributes or methods may be inherited, there is often ambiguity that must be resolved. Here, when we create an instance of the class `ToyCar`, and call the `move()` method, does this invoke the one inherited from the `Car` base class or from the `Toy` base class?

The answer is that in Python 3, a *breadth first* search is used to find methods defined in parent classes; this means that when the method `move()` is called on `ToyCar`, it would first look in `Car`; it would then only look in `Toy` if it could not find a method `move()` in `Car`. If it cannot find the method in either `Car` or `Toy` it would then look in the class `object`.

As a result, it will find the version in `Car` first and use that version.

This is shown below:

```
class Car:
    def move(self):
        print('Car - move()')

class Toy:
    def move(self):
        print('Toy - move()')

class ToyCar(Car, Toy):
    """ A Toy Car """

tc = ToyCar()
tc.move()
```

The output of this is

```
Car - move()
```

However, if we alter the order in which the `ToyCar` inherits from the parent classes such that we swap `Toy` and `Car` around:

```
class ToyCar(Toy, Car):
    """ A Toy Car """
```

Then the `Toy` class is searched first and the output is changed to `Toy – move()`.

This shows that the order in which a class inherits from multiple classes *is significant* In Python.

20.11   Multiple Inheritance Considered Harmful

At first sight multiple inheritance in Python might appear to be particularly useful; after all it allows you to mix together multiple concepts into a single class very easily and quickly. This is certainly true and it can be a very flexible feature if used with care. However, the word *care* is used here and should be noted.

Multiple inheritance can also be very dangerous and is quiet a contentious topic for programmers and for those designing programming languages. Few things in programming are inherently bad but multiple inheritance can result in a level of complexity (and unexpected behaviour) that can tie developers in knots.

Part of the problem highlighted by those protesting against multiple inheritance is down to the increased complexity and ambiguity that can occur with multiple inheritance trees that may interconnect between the different classes. One way to think of this is that if a class inherits from multiple classes, then that class may have the same classes in the class hierarchy multiple times, this can make it hard to determine which version of a method may execute and this may allow bugs to go untouched or indeed introduce expected issues due to different interactions between methods. This is exacerbated when inherited methods call super() using the same method name such as:

```
def get_data(self):
    return super().get_data() + 'FData'
```

The following diagram presents a somewhat convoluted multiple inheritance example where the class names A-X have been used so that there is no semantic meaning attributable to the inherited classes. Different classes define several common methods (print_info() and get_data()).

All the classes in the hierarchy define a __str__() method that returns the class name; if the class extends a class other than object, then the super version of __str__() is also invoked:

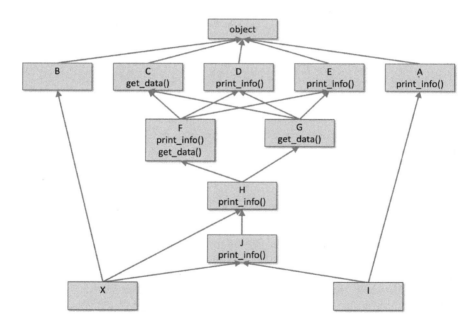

The code for this class hierarchy is given at the end of the section to avoid breaking up the flow.

We can now use the X class in a simple Python program:

```
x = X()
print('print(x):', x)
print('-' * 25)
x.print_info()
```

The question now is what is the output from this program?

What is the string printed to represent X? What is printed out as a result of calling the method `print_info()`?

The output from this simple code is:

```
print(x): CGFHJX
-------------------------
HCDataGDataFData
```

However, if we change the order of inheritance for the class 'H' from (F, G) to (G, F) then the output changes:

```
print(x): CFGHJX
-------------------------
HCDataFDataGData
```

This is of course because the search order, back up through the class hierarchy, is now different.

Note that this change came about not because of a modification we made to the class we instantiated (that is the class X), but from the order of the classes that one of its parents inherited from. This can be one of the unintended consequences of multiple inheritance; changing something in the multiple class hierarchy at one level can break some behaviour further down the hierarchy in a class that is unknown to the developer.

Also note that the class inheritance diagram we presented earlier did not state what order the parent classes were listed in for any specific class (this was left to the discretion of the programmer).

Of course Python is not ambiguous nor does it get confused; it is the human developer that can get confused and be surprised with the behaviour that is then presented. Indeed, if you try and define a class hierarchy which Python cannot resolve into a consistent structure it will tell you so, for example:

```
Traceback (most recent call last):
  File "multiple_inheritance_example.py", line 65, in <mc
    class Z(H, J):
TypeError: Cannot create a consistent method resolution
order (MRO) for bases F, G
```

What can be confusing is that Python's ability to produce a consistent structure can also be dependent on the order of inheritance. For example, if we modify the classes that 'X' inherits from such that the order is I and J:

```
class X(I, J):
    def __str__(self):
        return super().__str__() + 'X'
```

Then this compiles and can be used with the previous code (albeit with different output):

```
print(x): AIX
--------------------------
A
```

However, if we change the order of the parent classes such that we swap I and J:

```
class X(J, I):
    def __str__(self):
        return super().__str__() + 'X'
```

We now get a TypeError exception raised:

```
Traceback (most recent call last):
  File "multiple_inheritance_example.py", line 73, in <module>
    class X(J, I):
TypeError: Cannot create a consistent method resolution
order (MRO) for bases J, I
```

Therefore, in general care needs to be taken when utilising multiple inheritance; but that is not to say that such situations are not useful. In some cases you want a class to inherit from parents that have complete different hierarchies and are completely separate from each other; in such situations multiple inheritance can be very useful—these so called *orthogonal behaviours* are one of the best uses of multiple inheritance and should not be ignored merely due to concerns of increased complexity.

The class definitions used for the multiple inheritance class hierarchy are given below:

```python
class A:
    def __str__(self):
        return 'A'
    def print_info(self):
        print('A')

class B:
    def __str__(self):
        return 'B'

class C:
    def __str__(self):
        return 'C'
    def get_data(self):
        return 'CData'

class D:
    def __str__(self):
        return 'D'
    def print_info(self):
        print('D')

class E:
    def __str__(self):
        return 'E'
    def print_info(self):
        print('E')

class F(C, D, E):
    def __str__(self):
        return super().__str__() + 'F'
    def get_data(self):
        return super().get_data() + 'FData'
    def print_info(self):
        print('F' + self.get_data())

class G(C, D, E):
    def __str__(self):
        return super().__str__() + 'G'
    def get_data(self):
        return super().get_data() + 'GData'

class H(F, G):
    def __str__(self):
        return super().__str__() + 'H'
    def print_info(self):
        print('H' + self.get_data())
```

```
class J(H):
    def __str__(self):
        return super().__str__() + 'J'

class I(A, J):
    def __str__(self):
        return super().__str__() + 'I'

class X(J, H, B):
    def __str__(self):
        return super().__str__() + 'X'
```

20.12   Summary

To recap on the concept of inheritance. Inheritance is supported between classes in Python. For example, a class can extend (subclass) another class or a set of classes. A subclass inherits all the methods and attributes defined for the parent class(es) but may override these in the subclass.

In terms of the inheritance we say:

- A subclass inherits from a super class.
- A subclass obtains all code and attributes from the super class.
- A subclass can add new code and attributes.
- A subclass can override inherited code and attributes.
- A subclass can invoke inherited behaviour or access inherited attributes.

20.13   Online Resources

There are many resources available online relating to class inheritance including:

- https://docs.python.org/3/tutorial/classes.html#inheritance The Python software foundation tutorial on class inheritance.
- https://en.wikipedia.org/wiki/Multiple_inheritance which provides a discussion on multiple inheritance and the potential challenges it can introduce.

20.14 Exercises

The aim of these exercises is to extend the Account class you have been developing from the last two chapters by providing DepositAccount, CurrentAccount and InvestmentAccount subclasses.

Each of the classes should extend the Account class by:

- CurrentAccount adding an overdraft limit as well as redefining the withdraw method.
- DepositAccount by adding an interest rate.
- InvestmentAccount by adding an investment type attribute.

These features are discussed below:

The CurrentAccount class can have an overdraft_limit attribute. This can be set when an instance of a class is created and altered during the lifetime of the object. The overdraft limit should be included in the __str__() method used to convert the account into a string.

The CurrentAccount withdraw() method should verify that the balance never goes below the overdraft limit. If it does then the withdraw() method should not reduce the balance instead it should print out a warning message.

The DepositAccount should have an interest rate associated with it which is included when the account is converted to a string.

The InvestmentAccount will have a investment_type attribute which can hold a string such as 'safe' or 'high risk'.

This also means that it is no longer necessary to pass the type of account as a parameter—it is implicit in the type of class being created.

For example, given this code snippet:

```
#  CurrentAccount(account_number, account_holder,
#                 opening_balance, overdraft_limit)
acc1 = CurrentAccount('123', 'John', 10.05, 100.0)
#  DepositAccount(account_number, account_holder,
opening_balance,
#                 interest_rate)
acc2 = DepositAccount('345', 'John', 23.55, 0.5)
# InvestmentAccount(account_number, account_holder,
opening_balance,
#                   investment_type)
acc3 = InvestmentAccount('567', 'Phoebe', 12.45, 'high risk')

acc1.deposit(23.45)
acc1.withdraw(12.33)

print('balance:', acc1.get_balance())
acc1.withdraw(300.00)
print('balance:', acc1.get_balance())
```

Then the output might be:

```
balance: 21.17
Withdrawal would exceed your overdraft limit
balance: 21.17
```

Chapter 21
Why Bother with Object Orientation?

21.1 Introduction

The pervious four chapters have introduced the basic concepts behind object orientation, the terminology and explored some of the motivation. This chapter looks at how object orientation addresses some of the issues that have been raised with procedural languages. To do this it looks at how a small extract of a program might be written in a language such as C, considers the problems faced by the C developer and then looks at how the same functionality might be achieved in an object-oriented language such as Python. Do not worry too much about the syntax you will be presented with; it is mostly a form of pseudo code and it should not detract from the legibility of the examples.

21.2 The Procedural Approach

Consider the following example:

```
record Date {
    int day
    int month
    int year
}
```

This defines a data structure for recording dates. There are similar structures in many procedural languages such as C, Ada and Pascal.

So, what is wrong with a structure such as this? Nothing, apart from the issue of visibility? That is, what can see this structure and what can update the contents of

© Springer Nature Switzerland AG 2019
J. Hunt, *A Beginners Guide to Python 3 Programming*,
Undergraduate Topics in Computer Science,
https://doi.org/10.1007/978-3-030-20290-3_21

the structure? Any code can directly access and modify its contents. Is this problem? It could be, for example, some code could set the day to −1, the month to 13 and the year to 9999.

As far as the structure is concerned the information it now holds is fine (that is day = 01, month = 13, year = 9999). This is because the structure only knows it is supposed to hold integers; it knows nothing about dates per se. This is not surprising, it is only data.

21.2.1 Procedures for the Data Structure

This data is associated with procedures that perform operations on it. These operations might be to

- test whether the date represents a date at a weekend or part of the working week.
- change the date (in which case the procedure may also check to see that the date is a valid one).

For example:

```
is_day_of_week(date)
in_month(date, 2)
next_day(date)
set_day(date, 9, 3, 1946)
```

How do we know that these procedures are related to the date structure we have just looked at? By the naming conventions of the procedures and by the fact that one of the parameters is a data (record).

The problem is that these procedures are not limited in what they can do to the data (for example the setDay procedure might have been implemented by a Brit who assumes that the data order is day, month and year. However, it may be used by an American who assumes that date order is month, day, year. Thus the mean of set_day(date, 9, 3, 1946) will be interpreted very differently. The American views this as the 3rd of September 1946, while the Brit views this as the 9th of March, 1946. In either case, there is nothing to stop the date record being updated with both versions. Obviously the set_day() procedure might check the new date to see it was legal, but then again it might not. The problem is that the data is naked and has no defense against what these procedures do to it. Indeed, it has no defense against what any procedures that can access it, may do to it.

21.2.2   Packages

One possibility is of course to use a package construct. In languages such as Ada, packages are common place and are used as a way of organising code and restricting visibility. For example,

```
package Dates is
    type Date is ....
    function is_day_of_week(d: Date) return Boolean;
    function in_month(d: Date, m: Integer) return
                                    Boolean;
...
```

The package construct provides some ring fencing of the data structure and a grouping of the data structure with the associated procedures. In order to use this package a developer must import the package. They can then access the procedures and work with data of the specified type (in this case Date).

There can even be data that is hidden from the user within a private part. This therefore increases the ability to encapsulate the data (hide the data) from unwelcome attention.

21.3   Does Object Orientation Do Any Better?

This is an important question "*Does object orientation do any better?*" than the procedural approach described above? We will first consider clases then inheritance.

21.3.1   Packages Versus Classes

It has been argued (to me at least) that an Ada package is just like a class. It provides a template from which you can create executable code, it provides a wall around your data with well-defined gateways etc. However, there are a number of very significant differences between packages and classes.

Firstly, packages tend to be larger (at least conceptually) units than classes. For example, the TextIO package in Ada is essentially a library of textual IO facilities, rather than a single concept such as the class string in Python. Thus packages are not used to encapsulate a single small concept such as string or Date, but rather a whole set of related concepts (as indeed they are used in Python). Thus, a class is a finer level of granularity than a package.

Secondly, packages still provide a relatively loose association between the data and the procedures. An Ada package may actually deal with very many data structures with a wide range of methods. The data and the methods are related primarily via the related set of concepts represented by the package. In contrast a class tends to closely relate data and methods in a single concept. Indeed, one of the guidelines relating to good class design is that if a class represents more than one concept, then you should split it into two classes.

Thus, this close association between data and code means that the resulting concept is more than just a data structure (it is closer to a concrete realisation of concept). For example:

```python
class Date:

    def __init__(self, day, month, year):
        self.day = day
        self.month = month
        self.year = year

    def is_day_of_week(self):
        """Check if date is a week day"""
        # ... To be defined

    def in_month(self, month_index):
        """Check if month is in month_index"""
        return self.month == month_index
```

Anyone using an instance of Date now gets an object which can tell you whether it is a day of the week or not and can hold the appropriate data. Note that the is_day_of_week() method takes no parameters other than self, it doesn't need to as it and the date information are part of the same thing. This means that a user of a Date object will never need to get their hands on the actual data holding the date (i.e. the integers day, month and year). Instead, they should go via the methods. This may only seem a small step, but it is a significant one, nothing outside the object should need to access the data within the object. In contrast the data structure in the procedural version, is not only held separately to the procedures, the values for day, month or year it must also be modified directly.

For example, compare the differences between an excerpt from a program to manipulate dates (using a procedural programming language):

```
d: Date;
setDay(d, 28);
setMonth(d, 2);
setYear(d, 1998);
isDayOfWeek(d);
inMonth(d, 2);
```

Note that it was necessary to first create the data and then to set the fields in the data structure. Here we have been good and have used the interface procedures to do this. Once we had the data set up we could then call methods such as IsDayOfWeek and InMonth on that data.

In contrast the Python code uses a constructor to pass in the appropriate initialisation information. How this is initialised internally is hidden from the user of the class Date. We then call method such as is_day_of_week() and is_month(12) directly on the object date.

The thing to think about here is where would code be defined?

```
date = Date(12, 2, 1998)
date.is_day_of_week()
date.in_month(12)
```

21.3.2 Inheritance

Inheritance is a key element in an object-oriented language allowing one class to inherit data and methods from another.

One of the most important features of inheritance (ironically) is that it allows the developer to get inside the encapsulation bubble in limited and controlled ways.

This allows the sub-class to take advantage of internal data structures and methods, without compromising the encapsulation afforded to objects. For example, let us define a subclass of the class Date:

```
class Birthday(Date):
    name = ''
    age = 0
    def is_birthday():
        # ... Check to see if it is their birthday
```

The method is_birthday() could check to see if the current date, matched the birthday represented by an instance of Birthday and return true if it does and false if it does not.

Note however, that the interesting thing here is that not only have we not had to define integers to represent the date, nor have we had to define methods to access such dates. These have both been inherited from the parent class Date.

In addition, we can now treat an instance of Birthday as either a Date or as a Birthday depending on what we want to do!

What would you do in languages such as C, Pascal or Ada? One possibility is that you could define a new package Birthday, but that package would not extend Dates, it would have to import Dates and add interfaces to it etc? However, you certainly couldn't treat a Birthday package as a Dates package.

In languages such as Python, because of polymorphism, you can do exactly that. You can reuse existing code that only knew about Date, for example:

```python
birthday = Birthday(12, 3, 1974)

def test(date):
    # Do something that works with a date

t.test(birthday)
```

This is because birthday is indeed a type of Date as well as being a type of Birthday.

You can also use all of the features defined for Date on Birthdays:

```python
birthday.is_day_of_week()
```

Indeed, you don't actually know where the method is defined. This method could be defined in the class Birthday (where it would override that defined in the class Date). However, it could be defined in the class Date (if no such method is defined in Birthday); without looking at the source code there is no way of knowing!

Of course, you can also use the new methods defined in the class Birthday on instance (objects) of this class. For example:

```python
birthday.is_birthday()
```

21.4   Summary

Classes in an object-oriented language provide a number of features that are not present in procedural languages. To summarise, the main points to be noted from this chapter on object orientation are:

- Classes provide for inheritance.
- Inheritance provides for reuse.
- Inheritance provides for extension of a data type.
- Inheritance allows for polymorphism.
- Inheritance is a unique feature of object orientation.

Chapter 22
Operator Overloading

22.1 Introduction

We will explore Operator Overloading in this chapter; what it is, how it works and why we want it.

22.2 Operator Overloading

22.2.1 Why Have Operator Overloading?

Operator overloading allows user defined *classes* to appear to have a natural way of using operators such as +, −, <, > or == as well as logical operators such as & (and) and | (or).

This leads to more succinct and readable code as it is possible to write code such as:

```
q1 = Quantity(5)
q2 = Quantity(10)
q3 = q1 + q2
```

It feels more natural for both developers and those reading the code. The alternative would be to create methods such as add and write code such as

```
q1 = Quantity(5)
q2 = Quantity(10)
q3 = q1.add(q2)
```

Which semantically might mean the same thing but feel less *natural* to most people.

© Springer Nature Switzerland AG 2019
J. Hunt, *A Beginners Guide to Python 3 Programming*,
Undergraduate Topics in Computer Science,
https://doi.org/10.1007/978-3-030-20290-3_22

22.2.2   Why Not Have Operator Overloading?

If operator overloading is such a good idea, why don't all programming languages support it? Interestingly Java, a very widely used programming language, does not support operator overloading!

One answer is because it can be abused! For example, what is the meaning of the following code:

```
p1 = Person('John')
p2 = Person('Denise')
p3 = p1 + p2
```

It is not clear what '+' means in this context; in what way is Denise being added to John; does it imply they are getting married? If so, what is the result that is held in p3?

The problem here is that from a design perspective (which in this case may be purely intuitive but in other cases may relate to the intention of an application) the plus operator does not make sense for the type Person. However, there is nothing in the Python language to indicate this and thus anyone can code any operator into any class!

As a general design principle; developers should follow the semantics of built in types and thus should only implement those operators which are appropriate for the type being developed. For example, for arithmetic value types such as Quantity it makes perfect sense to provide a plus operator but for domain specific data-oriented types such as Person it does not.

22.2.3   Implementing Operator Overloading

To implement operators such as '+' in a user defined class it is necessary to implement specific methods that are then mapped to the arithmetic or logical operators used by users of the class.

These methods are considered *special* in that they start with and end with a double underscore ('__'). Such methods are considered private and usually restricted for Python oriented implementations (we have seen these already with methods such as __init__() and __str__()).

As an example, let us assume that we want to implement the '+' and '−' operators for our Quantity type. We also want our Quantity type to hold an actual value and be able to be converted into a string for printing purposes.

To implement the '+' and '−' operators we need to provide two special methods one will provide the implementation of the '+' operator and one will provide the implementation of the '−' operator:

- '+' operator is implemented by a method with the signature **def** __add__ (self, other):
- '−' operator is implemented by a method with the signature **def** __sub__ (self, other):

Where other represents another Quantity or other suitable type which will be either added to, or subtracted from, the current Quantity object.

The methods will be mapped by Python to the operators '+' and '−'; such that if someone attempts to add to quantities together then the __add__() method will be called etc.

The definition of the class Quantity is given below; note that the class actually just wraps a number held in the attribute value.

```
class Quantity:
    def __init__(self, value=0):
        self.value = value
    def __add__(self, other):
        new_value = self.value + other.value
        return Quantity(new_value)
    def __sub__(self, other):
        new_value = self.value - other.value
        return Quantity(new_value)
    def __str__(self):
        return 'Quantity[' + str(self.value) + ']'
```

Using this class definition, we can create two instances of the type Quantity and add them together:

```
q1 = Quantity(5)
q2 = Quantity(10)
print('q1 =', q1, ', q2 =', q2)

q3 = q1 + q2
print('q3 =', q3)
```

If we run this code snippet we get:

```
q1 = Quantity[5] , q2 = Quantity[10]
q3 = Quantity[15]
```

Note that we have made the class `Quantity` *immutable*; that is once a `Quantity` instance has been created its value cannot be changed (it is fixed).

This means that when two quantities are added tougher a new instance of the class `Quantity` is created. This is analogous to how integers work, if you add together 2 + 3 then you get 5; neither 2 or 3 are modified however; instead a new integer 5 is generated—this is an example of the general design principle; developers should follow the semantics of built in types; `Quantity` objects act like number objects.

22.3   Numerical Operators

There are nine different numerical operators that can be implemented by special methods; these operators are listed in the following table:

Operator	Expression	Method
Addition	q1 + q2	__add__(self, q2)
Subtraction	q1 − q2	__sub__(self, q2)
Multiplication	q1 * q2	__mul__(self, q2)
Power	q1 ** q2	__pow__(self, q2)
Division	q1 / q2	__truediv__(self, q2)
Floor Division	q1 // q2	__floordiv__(self, q2)
Modulo (Remainder)	q1 % q2	__mod__(self, q2)
Bitwise Left Shift	q1 ≪ q2	__lshift__(self, q2)
Bitwise Right Shift	q1 ≫ q2	__rshift__(self, q2)

We have already seen examples of add and subtract; this table indicates how we can also provide operators for multiplication and division etc.

The above table also presents Bitwise shift operators (both left and right). These operate at the bit level used to represent numbers under the hood and can be a very efficient way of manipulating numeric values; however, we do not want to support these operators for our `Quantity` class therefore we will only implement the core numeric operators of multiplication, division and power.

Also note that the names of the division methods are not div but `__truediv__()` and `__floordiv__()` indicating the difference in behaviour between '/' and '//'.

The updated `Quantity` class is given below:

```
class Quantity:
    def __init__(self, value=0):
        self.value = value

    def __add__(self, other):
        new_value = self.value + other.value
        return Quantity(new_value)

    def __sub__(self, other):
        new_value = self.value - other.value
        return Quantity(new_value)

    def __mul__(self, other):
        new_value = self.value * other.value
        return Quantity(new_value)

    def __pow__(self, other):
        new_value = self.value ** other.value
        return Quantity(new_value)

    def __truediv__(self, other):
        new_value = self.value / other.value
        return Quantity(new_value)

    def __floordiv__(self, other):
        new_value = self.value // other.value
        return Quantity(new_value)

    def __mod__(self, other):
        new_value = self.value % other.value
        return Quantity(new_value)

    def __str__(self):
        return 'Quantity[' + str(self.value) + ']'
```

This means that we can now extend our simple application that uses the Quantity class to include some of these additional numerical operators:

```
q1 = Quantity(5)
q2 = Quantity(10)
print('q1 =', q1, ', q2 =', q2)

q3 = q1 + q2
print('q3 =', q3)
print('q2 - q1 =', q2 - q1)

print('q1 * q2 =', q1 * q2)
print('q1 / q2 =', q1 / q2)
```

The output from this is now:

```
q1 = Quantity[5] ,q2 = Quantity[10]
q3 = Quantity[15]
q2 - q1 = Quantity[5]
q1 * q2 = Quantity[50]
q1 / q2 = Quantity[0.5]
```

One interesting point to note is that the multiple and divide style methods, we might want to multiple a Quantity by an integer or divide a Quantity by an integer. There is nothing to stop us doing this and indeed this might be a very useful behaviour. This would allow a Quantity to be multiplied by 2 or divided by 2, for example:

```
print('q1 * 2', q1 * 2)
print('q2 / 2', q2 / 2)
```

At the moment if we tried to run the above code we would generate an error telling us that an int does not have a value attribute. However, we can test to see if the argument passed into the __mult__() and __truediv__() methods is an int or not using the isinstance function. This function takes a variable and the name of a class and returns True if the contents of the variable is an instance of the named class, for example:

```
class Quantity:
    # Code ommitted for brevity

    def __mul__(self, other):
        if isinstance(other, int):
            new_value = self.value * other
        else:
            new_value = self.value * other.value
        return Quantity(new_value)

    def __truediv__(self, other):
        if isinstance(other, int):
            new_value = self.value / other
        else:
            new_value = self.value / other.value
        return Quantity(new_value)
```

Now when we run the earlier print statements we generate the output:

```
q1 * 2 Quantity[10]
q2 / 2 Quantity[5.0]
```

22.4 Comparison Operators

Numerical types (such as integers and real numbers) also support comparison operators such as equals, not equals, greater than, less than as well as greater than or equal to and less than or equal to.

Python allows these comparison operators to be defined for user defined types/classes as well.

Just as numerical operators such as '+' and '−' are implemented by special methods so are comparison operators. For example the '<' operator is implemented by a method called __lt__(self, other).

The complete list of comparison operators and the associated special methods is given in the following table:

Operator	Expression	Method
Less than	q1 < q2	__lt__(q1, q2)
Less than or equal to	q1 <= q2	__le__(q1, q2)
Equal to	q1 == q2	__eq__(q1, q2)
Not Equal to	q1 != q2	__ne__(q1, q2)
Greater than	q1 > q2	__gt__(q1, q2)
Greater than or equal to	q1 >= q2	__ge__(q1, q2)

We can add these definitions to our Quantity class to provide a more complete type that can be used in comparison style tests (such as if statements).

The updated Quantity class is given below (with some of the numerical operators omitted for brevity):

```python
class Quantity:
    def __init__(self, value=0):
        self.value = value
    def __add__(self, other):
        new_value = self.value + other.value
        return Quantity(new_value)

    # remaining numerical operators omitted for brevity ...

    def __eq__(self, other):
        return self.value == other.value

    def __ne__(self, other):
        return self.value != other.value

    def __ge__(self, other):
        return self.value >= other.value

    def __gt__(self, other):
        return self.value > other.value

    def __lt__(self, other):
        return self.value < other.value

    def __le__(self, other):
        return self.value <= other.value

    def __str__(self):
        return 'Quantity[' + str(self.value) + ']'
```

This now means that we can update out sample application to take advantage of these comparison operators:

```python
q1 = Quantity(5)
q2 = Quantity(10)
print('q1 =', q1, ',q2 =', q2)
q3 = q1 + q2
print('q3 =', q3)
print('q1 < q2: ', q1 < q2)
print('q3 > q2: ', q3 > q2)
print('q3 == q1: ', q3 == q1)
```

The output from this is now:

```
q1 = Quantity[5] ,q2 = Quantity[10]
q3 = Quantity[15]
q1 < q2:   True
q3 > q2:   True
q3 == q1:  False
```

22.5   Logical Operators

The final category of operators that can be defined on a class are Logical operators. These are operators that can be used with and/or type tests; they typically return the values True or False.

As with the numerical operators and the comparison operators; the logical operators are implemented by a set of special methods.

The following table summarises the logical operators and the methods used to implement them:

Operator	Expression	Method
AND	q1 & q2	__and__(q1, q2)
OR	q1 | q2	__or__(q1, q2)
XOR	q1 ^ q2	__xor__(q1, q2)
NOT	~q1	__invert__()

As these operators do not really make sense for the Quantity type, we will not define them. For example, what would it mean to say:

```
q1 | q2
```

In what way is q1 an alternative to q2?

22.6   Summary

Only use operators when they make sense and only implement those operators that work with the type you are defining. In general, this means

- Arithmetic operators should only be used for values types with a numeric property.

- Comparison operators typically only make sense for classes that can be ordered.
- Logical operators typically work for types that are similar in nature to Booleans.

22.7   Online Resources

Some online resources on operator overloading include:

- https://docs.python.org/3/reference/datamodel.html for information on operator overloading in Python.
- https://pythonprogramming.net/operator-overloading-intermediate-python-tutorial/ Tutorial on operator overloading.
- http://cafe.elharo.com/programming/operator-overloading-considered-harmful/ An article on why operagoer overloading may be harmful to good programming style.

22.8   Exercises

The aim of this exercise is to create a new numeric style class.

You should create a new user defined class called Distance. It will be very similar to Quantity.

You should be able to add two distances together, subtract one distance from another, divide a distance by an integer, multiply a distance by an integer etc.

You should therefore be able to support the following program:

```
d1 = Distance(6)
d2 = Distance(3)

print( d1 + d2)
print (d1 - d2)
print (d1 / 2)
print(d2 // 2)
print(d2 * 2)
```

Note that the division and multiplication operators work with a distance and an integer; you will therefore need to think about how to implement the special methods for these operators.

The output from this might be:

```
Distance[9]
Distance[3]
Distance[3.0]
Distance[1]
Distance[6]
```

Chapter 23
Python Properties

23.1 Introduction

Many object-oriented languages have the explicit concept of encapsulation; that is the ability to hide data within an object and only to provide specific gateways into that data. These gateways are methods defined to *get* or *set* the value of an attribute (often referred to as getters and setters). This allows more control over access to the data; for example, it is possible to check that only a positive integer above zero, but below 120, is used for a person's age etc.

In many languages such as Java and C# attributes can be hidden from external access using specific keywords (such as private) that indicate the data should be made private to the object.

Python does not explicitly have the concept of encapsulation; instead it relies on two things; a standard convention used to indicate that an attribute should be considered private and a concept called a property which allows setters and getters to be defined for an attribute.

23.2 Python Attributes

All object attributes are publicly available in Python; that is, they are all visible to any code using the object.

For example, given the following definition of the class Person both name and age are part of the public interface of the class Person;

© Springer Nature Switzerland AG 2019
J. Hunt, *A Beginners Guide to Python 3 Programming*,
Undergraduate Topics in Computer Science,
https://doi.org/10.1007/978-3-030-20290-3_23

```
class Person:
    def __init__(self, name, age):
        self.name = name
        self.age = age

    def __str__(self):
        return 'Person[' + str(self.name) + '] is ' +
                        str(self.age)
```

Because name and age are part of the class's public interface it means that we can write:

```
person = Person('John', 54)
person.name = 42
person.age = -1
print(person)
```

Which is of course a bit bizarre as the person now has the name '42' and an age of −1, thus the output from this is:

```
Person[42] is -1
```

We can indicate that we want to treat age and name as being private to the object by prefixing the attribute names with an underbar ('_') as shown below:

```
class Person:
    def __init__(self, name, age):
        self._name = name
        self._age = age

    def __str__(self):
        return 'Person[' + str(self._name) +'] is ' + s
                        str(self._age)
```

This tells Python programmers that we want to consider _name and _age as being *private*. However, it should be noted that this is only a *convention*; albeit a *very strongly* adhered to convention. There is still nothing here that would stop someone writing:

```
person = Person('John', 54)
person._age = -1
print(person)
```

However, the developer of the class Person is at liberty to change the internals of the class (such as _age) without notice and most would consider that anyone who had ignored the convention and now had a problem had only themselves to blame.

23.3 Setter and Getter Style Methods

This of course raises the question; how should we now get hold of a Persons' name and age in an acceptable way?

The answer is that a developer should provide *getter* methods and *setter* methods that can be used to access the values.

We can update the Person class with some getter methods and a single setter method:

```
class Person:
    def __init__(self, name, age):
        self._name = name
        self._age = age

    def get_age(self):
        return self._age

    def set_age(self, new_age):
        if isinstance(new_age, int) & new_age > 0 &
new_age < 120:
            self._age = new_age

    def get_name(self):
        return self._name

    def __str__(self):
        return 'Person[' + str(self._name) +'] is ' +
str(self._age)
```

The two getter methods have the format of get_ followed by the name of the attribute they are getting. Thus, we have get_age and get_name. Typically, all that getters do is to return the attribute being used (as is the case here).

The single setter method is a little different; it validates the data that has been provided to check that it is appropriate (i.e. that it is an Integer using isinstance (new_age, int) and that it is a value over Zero but under 120). Only if the data passes these checks is it used as the new value of the person's age, for example if we try to set a persons age to −1:

```
person = Person('John', 54)
person.set_age(-1)
print(person)
```

Then this is ignored, and the person's age remains as it was, thus the output of this is:

```
Person[John] is 54
```

It should be noted that this might be considered *silent failure*; that is we tried to set the age and it failed but no one knows this. In many cases rather than fail silently we would prefer to notify someone of the error by throwing some form of Error object; this will be discussed in the next chapter on Error and Exception handling.

You might well ask at this point where is the setter for the _name attribute? The answer is that we want to make the _name attribute a *read only* attribute and therefore we have not provided a setter style method. This is a common idiom followed in Python—you can have read-write attributes and read-only attributes depending on whether they have getter and setter methods or not. It is also possible to a *write-only* attribute, but this is very rare and only has a few use cases.

23.4 Public Interface to Properties

Although we now have a more formal interface to the attributes held by an instance of the class Person; it is rather ungainly:

```
person = Person('John', 54)
print(person)
print(person.get_age())
print(person.get_name())
```

We end up having to write more code and although there is an argument that it makes the code more obvious (i.e. person.get_age() can be read as get the age of the person object); it is somewhat verbose and you have to remember to include the parentheses (()').

To get around this a concept known as Properties was introduced in Python 2.2. In the original syntax for this it was possible to add an addition line of code to the class that told Python that you wanted to provide a new property and that specific methods were to be used to set and get the values of this property.

The syntax for defining a property in this way is:

```
<property_name> = property(fget=None, fset=None,
  fdel=None, doc=None)
```

Where `fget` indicates the getter function, `fset` the setter function `fdel` the function to be used to delete a value and `doc` provides documentation on the property (all of which are optional).

We can modify our `Person` class so that `age` is now a property (note a common convention is that if the attribute is named _age, the methods are named `get_age` and `set_age` and the property will be called `age`):

```
class Person:
    def __init__(self, name, age):
        self._name = name
        self._age = age

    def get_age(self):
        return self._age
    def set_age(self, new_age):
        if isinstance(new_age,int) & new_age > 0 &
new_age < 120:
            self._age = new_age

    age = property(get_age, set_age, doc="An age property")

    def get_name(self):
        return self._name

    name = property(get_name, doc="A name property")

    def __str__(self):
        return 'Person[' + str(self._name) +'] is ' +
                        str(self._age)
```

We can now write:

```
person = Person('John', 54)
print(person)
print(person.age)
print(person.name)
person.age = 21
print(person)
```

Notice how we can now write person.age and person.age = 21; in both these cases we are accessing the *property* age that results in the method get_age() and set_age() being executed respectively. Thus, the setter is still protecting the update to the underlying _age attribute that is actually used to hold the actual value.

Also note that if a method is not provided for one of the fget, fset, fdel methods then this is not an error; it merely indicates that the property does not support that type of accessor. Thus, the name property is a *read_only* property as it does not define a setter method.

A delete method can be used to release the memory associated with an attribute; in the case of an int it is not required but it may be required for a more complex, user defined type.

We could therefore write:

```
def del_name(self):
        del self._name
name = property(get_name, fdel=del_name, doc="A name
property")
```

Note that we are using a keyword reference for the delete method as we have skipped the setter and cannot therefore rely on positional arguments.

23.5   More Concise Property Definitions

The example shown in the previous section works but it is still quite verbose itself; while this is on the class writers' side it still seems somewhat heavyweight.

To overcome this a more concise option has been available since Python 2.4. This approach uses what are known as decorators. Decorators represent meta data (that is information about your code that the Python interpreter can use to work out what you want it to do with certain things).

Python 2.4 introduced three new decorators @property, @<property-name>.setter and @<propertyname>.deleter. These decorators are added to the start of a method definition to indicate that the method should be used to provide access to a property (and define that property), define a setter for the property or a deleter for the property.

We will now update our Person class to use the decorators:

```
class Person:
    def __init__(self, name, age):
        self._name = name
        self._age = age

    @property
    def age(self):
        """ The docstring for the age property """
        print('In age method')
        return self._age

    @age.setter
    def age(self, value):
        print('In set_age method')
        if isinstance(value, int) & value > 0 & value < 120:
            self._age = value

    @property
    def name(self):
        print('In name')
        return self._name

    @name.deleter
    def name(self):
        del self._name

    def __str__(self):
        return 'Person[' + str(self._name) +'] is ' +
str(self._age)
```

Notice three important things about this example:

- The name of the methods is no longer a `set_age` and `get_age`; instead both methods are now just `age` and the decorator distinguishes their role. Also notice that we no longer have a separate statement that declares the property—it is now implicit in the use of the `@property` decorator and the name of the associated method.
- The `@property` decorator is used to define the name of the property (in this case age) and to define further decorators which will be named after the property with a `.setter` or `.deleter` element e.g. `@age.setter`.
- The documentation string is now defined in the method associated with the `@property` decorator (providing this documentation string is usually considered good practice).

However, we do not need to change the program that used the class `Person`, as the interface to the class remained the same.

23.6 Online Resources

Some online resources on properties are:

- https://www.python-course.eu/python3_properties.php a discussion on Python properties versus getters and setters.
- https://www.journaldev.com/14893/python-property-decorator a short introduction to the @property decorator.

23.7 Exercises

In this exercise you will add *properties* to an existing class.

Return to the Account class that you created several chapters ago; convert the balance into a read only property using decorators, then verify that the following program functions correctly:

```
acc1 = CurrentAccount('123', 'John', 10.05, 100.0)
acc2 = DepositAccount('345', 'John', 23.55, 0.5)
acc3 = acc3 = InvestmentAccount('567', 'Phoebe', 12.45,
'high risk')

print(acc1)
print(acc2)
print(acc3)

acc1.deposit(23.45)
acc1.withdraw(12.33)
print('balance:', acc1.balance)

print('Number of Account instances created:',
Account.instance_count)

print('balance:', acc1.balance)
acc1.withdraw(300.00)
print('balance:', acc1.balance)
```

The output from this might be:

```
Creating new Account
Creating new Account
Creating new Account
Account[123] - John, current account = 10.05overdraft
limit: -100.0
Account[345] - John, savings account = 23.55interest
rate: 0.5
Account[567] - Phoebe, investment account = 12.45
balance: 21.17
Number of Account instances created: 3
balance: 21.17
Withdrawal would exceed your overdraft limit
balance: 21.17
```

Chapter 24
Error and Exception Handling

24.1 Introduction

This chapter considers exception and error handling and how it is implemented in Python. You are introduced to the object model of exception handling, to the throwing and catching of exceptions, and how to define new exceptions and exception-specific constructs.

24.2 Errors and Exceptions

When something goes wrong in a computer program someone needs to know about it. One way of informing other parts of a program (and potentially those running a program) is by generating an error object and propagating that through the code until either something *handles* the error and sorts thing out or the point at which the program is entered is found.

If the Error propagates out of the program, then the user who ran the program needs to know that something has gone wrong. They are notified of a problem via a short report on the Error that occurred and a stack trace of where that error can be found.

You may have already seen these yourself when writing your own programs. For example, the following screen dump illustrates a programming *error* where someone has tried to concatenate a string and a number together using the '+'

© Springer Nature Switzerland AG 2019
J. Hunt, *A Beginners Guide to Python 3 Programming*,
Undergraduate Topics in Computer Science,
https://doi.org/10.1007/978-3-030-20290-3_24

operator. This *error* has propagated out of the program and a stack trace of the code that was called is presented (in this case the function print used the __str__() method of the class `Person`). Note the line numbers are included which helps with *debugging* the problem.

```
Run:    properties
        /Users/Shared/workspaces/pycharm/venv/bin/python /Users/Shared/workspaces/pycharm/pythonintro/properties/properties.py
        Traceback (most recent call last):
          File "/Users/Shared/workspaces/pycharm/pythonintro/properties/properties.py", line 32, in <module>
            print(person)
          File "/Users/Shared/workspaces/pycharm/pythonintro/properties/properties.py", line 28, in __str__
            return 'Person[' + str(self._name) +'] is ' + self._age
        TypeError: Can't convert 'int' object to str implicitly

        Process finished with exit code 1
```

In Python the terms Error and Exception are used inter-changeably; although from a style point of view Exceptions might be used to represent issues with operations such as arithmetic exceptions and errors might be associated with functional issues such as a file not being found.

24.3   What Is an Exception?

In Python, everything is a type of object, including integers, strings, booleans and indeed Exceptions and Errors. In Python the Exception/Error types are defined in a class hierarchy with the root of this hierarchy being the `BaseException` type. All built-in errors and exceptions eventually extend from the `BaseException` type. It has a subclass `Exception` which is the root of all user defined exceptions (as well as many built-in exceptions). In turn `ArithmeticException` is the base class for all built-in exceptions associated with arithmetic errors.

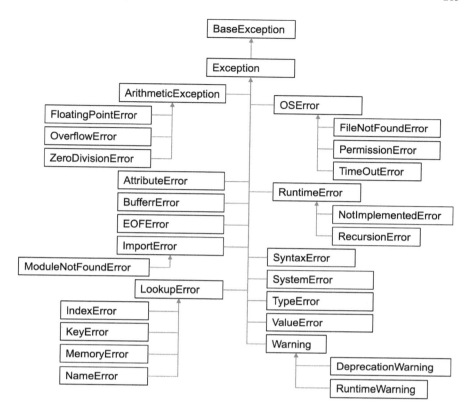

The above diagram illustrates the class hierarchy for some of the common types of errors and exceptions.

When an exception occurs, this is known as *raising* an exception and when it is passed to code to handle this is known as *throwing* an exception. These are terms that will become more obvious as this chapter progresses.

24.4   What Is Exception Handling?

An exception moves the flow of control from one place to another. In most situations, this is because a problem occurs which cannot be handled locally but that can be handled in another part of the system.

The problem is usually some sort of error (such as dividing by zero), although it can be any problem (for example, identifying that the postcode specified with an address does not match). The purpose of an exception, therefore, is to handle an error condition when it happens at run time.

It is worth considering why you should wish to handle an exception; after all the system does not allow an error to go unnoticed. For example, if we try to divide by zero, then the system generates an error for you. This may mean that the user has entered an incorrect value, and we do not want users to be presented with a dialog suggesting that they enter the system debugger. We can therefore use exceptions to force the user to correct the mistake and rerun the calculation.

The following table illustrates terminology typically used with exception/error handling in Python.

Exception	An error which is generated at runtime
Raising an exception	Generating a new exception
Throwing an exception	Triggering a generated exception
Handling an exception	Processing code that deals with the error
Handler	The code that deals with the error (referred to as the catch block)
Signal	A particular type of exception (such as *out of bounds* or *divide by zero*)

Different types of error produce different types of exception. For example, if the error is caused by dividing an integer by zero, then the exception is a *arithmetic* exception. The type of exception is identified by objects and can be caught and processed by exception handlers. Each handler can deal with exceptions associated with its class of error or exception (and its subclasses).

An exception is instantiated when it is raised. The system searches back up the execution stack (the set of functions or methods that have been invoked in reverse order) until it finds a handler which can deal with the exception. The associated handler then processes the exception. This may involve performing some remedial action or terminating the current execution in a controlled manner. In some cases, it may be possible to restart executing the code.

As a handler can only deal with an exception of a specified class (or subclass), an exception may pass through a number of handler blocks before it finds one that can process it.

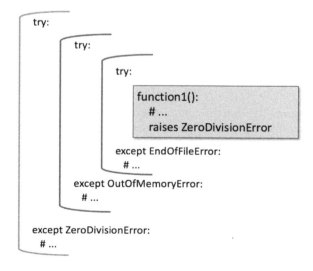

The above figure illustrates a situation in which a divide by zero exception called ZeroDivisionError is raised. This exception is passed up the execution stack where it encounters an exception handler defined for an End of File exception. This handler cannot handle the ZeroDivisionError and so it is passed further up the execution stack. It then encounters a handler for an out of memory exception. Again, it cannot deal with a ZeroDivisionError and the exception is passed further up the execution stack until it finds a handler defined for the ZeroDivisionError. This handler then processes the exception.

24.5   Handling an Exception

You can catch an exception by implementing the try—except construct. This construct is broken into three parts:

- try block. The try block indicates the code which is to be monitored for the exceptions listed in the except expressions.
- except clause. You can use an optional except clause to indicate what to do when certain classes of exception/error occur (e.g. resolve the problem or generate a warning message). There can be any number of except clauses in sequence checking for different types of error/exceptions.
- else clause. This is an optional clause which will be run if and only if no exception was thrown in the try block. It is useful for code that must be executed if the try clause does not raise an exception.
- finally clause. The optional finally clause runs after the try block exits (whether or not this is due to an exception being raised). You can use it to clean up any resources, close files, etc.

This language construct may at first seem confusing, however once you have worked with it for a while you will find it less daunting.

As an example, consider the following function which divides a number by zero; this will raise the ZeroDivisionError when it is run for any number:

```
def runcalc(x):
    x / 0
```

If we now call this function, we will get the error trackback in the standard output:

```
runcalc(6)
```

This is shown below:

```
/Library/Frameworks/Python.framework/Versions/3.7/bin/python3.7 /Users/Shared/workspaces/pycharm/python
Traceback (most recent call last):
  File "/Users/Shared/workspaces/pycharm/pythonintro/exceptions/exceptions.py", line 67, in <module>
    main()
  File "/Users/Shared/workspaces/pycharm/pythonintro/exceptions/exceptions.py", line 39, in main
    runcalc(0)
  File "/Users/Shared/workspaces/pycharm/pythonintro/exceptions/exceptions.py", line 2, in runcalc
    x / 0
ZeroDivisionError: division by zero
```

However, we can handle this by wrapping the call to `runcalc` within a `try` statement and providing an `except` clause. The syntax for a `try` statement with an `except` clause is:

```
try:
    <code to monitor>
except <type of exception to monitor for>:
    <code to call if exception is found>
```

A concrete example of this is given below for a `try` statement that will be used to monitor a call to `runcalc`:

```
try:
    runcalc(6)
except ZeroDivisionError:
    print('oops')
```

which now results in the string 'oops' being printed out. This is because when `runcalc` is called the '/' operator throws the `ZeroDivisionError` which is passed back to the calling code which has an `except` clause specifying this type of exception. This *catches* the exception and runs the associated code block which in this case prints out the string 'oops'.

In fact, we don't have to be as precise as this; the `except` clause can be given a class of exception to look for and it will match any exception that is of that type or is an instance of a subclass of the exception. We therefore can also write:

```
try:
    runcalc(6)
except Exception:
    print('oops')
```

The `Exception` class is a grandparent of the `ZeroDivisionError` thus any ZeroDivisionError object is also a type of `Exception` and thus the `except` block matches the exception passed. This means that you can write one `except` clause and that clause can handle a whole range of exceptions.

However, if you don't want to have a common block of code handling your exceptions, you can define different behaviours for different types of exception. This is done by having a series of except clauses; each monitoring a different type of exception:

```
try:
    runcalc(6)
except ZeroDivisionError:
    print('oops')
except IndexError:
    print('arrgh')
except FileNotFoundError:
    print('huh!')
except Exception:
    print('Duh!')
```

In this case the first except monitors for a ZeroDivisionError but the other excepts monitor for other types of exception. Note that the except Exception is the last except clause in the list as ZeroDivisionError, IndexError and FileNotFoundError are all eventual subclasses of Exception and thus this clause would catch any of these types of exception. As only one except clause is allowed to run; if this except handler came fist the other except handers would never ever be run.

24.5.1 Accessing the Exception Object

It is possible to gain access to the exception object being caught by the except clause using the as keyword. This follows the exception type being monitored and can be used to bind the exception object to a variable, for example:

```
try:
    runcalc(6)
except ZeroDivisionError as exp:
    print(exp)
    print('oops')
```

Which produces:

```
division by zero
oops
```

If there are multiple except clauses, each except clause can decide whether to bind the exception object to a variable or not (and each variable can have a different name):

```
try:
    runcalc(6)
except ZeroDivisionError as exp:
    print(exp)
    print('oops')
except IndexError as e:
    print(e)
    print('arrgh')
except FileNotFoundError:
    print('huh!')
except Exception as exception:
    print(exception)
    print('Duh!')
```

In the above example three of the four except clauses bind the exception to a
variable (each with a different name—although they could all have the same name)
but one, the FileNotFoundError except clause does not bind the exception to a
variable.

24.5.2   *Jumping to Exception Handlers*

One of the interesting features of Exception handling in Python is that when an
Error or an Exception is raised it is immediately *thrown* to the exception handlers
(the except clauses). Any statements that follow the point at which the exception
is raised are not run. This means that a function may be terminated early and further
statements in the calling code may not be run.

As an example, consider the following code. This code defines a function
my_function() that prints out a string, performs a division operation which will
cause a ZeroDivisionError to be raised if the y value is Zero and then it has a
further print statement. This function is called from within a try statement.
Notice that there is a print statement each side of the call to my_function().
There is also a handler for the ZeroDivisionError.

```
def my_function(x, y):
    print('my_function in')
    result = x / y
    print('my_function out')
    return result


print('Starting')

try:
    print('Before my_function')
    my_function(6, 2)
    print('After my_function')
except ZeroDivisionError as exp:
    print('oops')

print('Done')
```

When we run this the output is

```
Starting
Before my_function
my_function in
my_function out
After my_function
Done
```

Which is what would probably be expected; we have run every statement with the exception of the except clause as the ZeroDivisionError was not raised.

If we now change the call to my_function() to pass in 6 and 0 we will raise the ZeroDivisionError.

```
print('Starting')

try:
    print('Before my_function')
    my_function(6, 0)
    print('After my_function')
except ZeroDivisionError as exp:
    print('oops')

print('Done'
```

Now the output is

```
Starting
Before my_function
my_function in
oops
Done
```

The difference is that the second print statement in my_function() has not been run; instead after print 'my_function in' and then raising the error we have jumped straight to the except clause and run the print statement in the associated block of code.

This is partly why the term *throwing* is used with respect to error and exception handling; because the error or exception is raised in one place and thrown to the point where it is handled, or it is thrown out of the application if no except clause is found to handle the error/exception.

24.5.3   Catch Any Exception

It is also possible to specify an except clause that can be used to catch any type of error or exception, for example:

```
try:
    my_function(6, 0)
except IndexError as e:
    print(e)
except:
    print('Something went wrong')
```

This must be the last except clause as it omits the exception type and thus acts as a wildcard. It can be used to ensure that you get notified that an error did occur—although you do not know what type of error it actually was; therefore, use this feature with caution.

24.5.4   The Else Clause

The try statement also has an optional else clause. If this is present, then it must come after all except clauses. The else clause is executed if and only if no exceptions were raised. If any exception was raised the else clause will not be run. An example of the else clause is shown below:

```
try:
    my_function(6, 2)
except ZeroDivisionError as e:
    print(e)
else:
    print('Everything worked OK')
```

In this case the output is:

```
my_function in
my_function out
Everything worked OK
```

As you can see the `print` statement in the `else` clause has been executed, however if we change the `my_function()` call to pass in a zero as the second parameter (which will cause the function to raise a `ZeroDivisionError`), then the output is:

```
my_function in
division by zero
```

As you can see the `else` clause was not run but the `except` handler was executed.

24.5.5 The Finally Clause

An optional finally clause can also be provided with the `try` statement. This clause is the last clause in the statement and must come after any `except` classes as well as the `else` clause.

It is used for code that you want to run whether an exception occurred or not. For example, in the following code snippet:

```
try:
    my_function(6, 2)
except ZeroDivisionError as e:
    print(e)
else:
    print('Everything worked OK')
finally:
    print('Always runs')
```

The `try` block will run, if no error is raised then the `else` clause will be executed and last of all the finally code will run, we will therefore have as output:

```
my_function in
my_function out
Everything worked OK
Always runs
```

If however we pass in 6 and 0 to `my_function()`:

```
try:
    my_function(6, 0)
except ZeroDivisionError as e:
    print(e)
else:
    print('Everything worked OK')
finally:
    print('Always runs')
```

We will now raise an exception in `my_function()` which means that the `try` block will execute, then the `ZeroDivisionError` will be raised, it will be handled by the `except` clause and then the `finally` clause will run. The output is now:

```
my_function in
division by zero
Always runs
```

As you can see in both cases the `finally` clause is executed.

The `finally` clause can be very useful for general housekeeping type activities such as shutting down or closing any resources that your code might be using, even if an error has occurred.

24.6   Raising an Exception

An error or exception is raised using the keyword `raise`. The syntax of this is

```
raise <Exception/Error type to raise>()
```

For example:

```
def function_bang():
    print('function_bang in')
    raise ValueError('Bang!')
    print('function_bang')
```

In the above function the second statement in the function body will create a new instance of the `ValueError` class and then raise it so that it is thrown allowing it to be caught by any exception handlers that have been defined.

We can handle this exception by writing a `try` block with an `except` clause for the `ValueError` class. For example:

```
try:
    function_bang()
except ValueError as ve:
    print(ve)
```

This generates the output

```
function_bang in
Bang!
```

Note that if you just want to raise an exception without providing any constructor arguments, then you can just provide the name of the exception class to the
raise keyword:

```
raise ValueError # short hand for raise ValueError()
```

You can also *re-raise* an error or an exception; this can be useful if you merely
want to note that an error has occurred and then re throw it so that it can be handled
further up in your application:

```
try:
    function_bang()
except ValueError:
    print('oops')
    raise
```

This will re raise the ValueError caught by the except clause. Note here we
did not even bind it to a variable; however, we could have done this if required.

```
try:
    function_bang()
except ValueError as ve:
    print(ve)
    raise
```

24.7   Defining an Custom Exception

You can define your own Errors and Exceptions, which can give you more control
over what happens in particular circumstances. To define an exception, you create a
subclass of the Exception class or one of its subclasses.

For example, to define a InvalidAgeException, we can extend the
Exception class and generate an appropriate message:

```
class InvalidAgeException(Exception):
    """ Valid Ages must be between 0 and 120 """
```

This class can be used to explicitly represent an issue when an age is set on a
Person which is not within the acceptable age range.

We can use this with the class Person that we defined earlier in the book; this version of the Person class defined age as a property and attempted to validate that an appropriate age was being set:

```python
class Person:
    def __init__(self, name, age):
        self._name = name
        self._age = age

    @property
    def age(self):
        """ The docstring for the age property """
        print('In age method')
        return self._age

    @age.setter
    def age(self, value):
        print('In set_age method(', value, ')')
        if isinstance(value, int) & (value > 0 & value < 120):
            self._age = value
        else:
            raise InvalidAgeException(value)

    @property
    def name(self):
        print('In name')
        return self._name

    @name.deleter
    def name(self):
        del self._name

    def __str__(self):
        return 'Person[' + str(self._name) + '] is ' +
self._age
```

Note that the age setter method now throws an InvalidAgeException, so if we write:

```python
try:
    p = Person('Adam', 21)
    p.age = -1
except InvalidAgeException:
    print('In here')
```

We can capture the fact that an invalid age has been specified.

However, in the exception handler we don't know what the invalid age was. We can of course provide this information by including it in the data held by the InvalidAgeException.

If we now modify the class definition such that we provide an initialiser to allow parameters to be passed into the new instance of the `InvalidAgeException`:

```python
class InvalidAgeException(Exception):
    """ Valid Ages must be between 0 and 120 """

    def __init__(self, value):
        self.value = value

    def __str__(self):
        return 'InvalidAgeException(' + str(self.value) + ')'
```

We have also defined a suitable `__str__()` method to convert the exception into a string for printing purposes.

We do of course need to update the setter to provide the value that has caused the problem:

```python
@age.setter
def age(self, value):
    print('In set_age method(', value, ')')
    if isinstance(value, int) & (value > 0 & value < 120):
        self._age = value
    else:
        raise InvalidAgeException(value)
```

We can now write:

```python
try:
    p = Person('Adam', 21)
    p.age = -1
except InvalidAgeException as e:
    print(e)
```

Now if the exception is raised a message will be printed out giving the actual value that caused the problem:

```
In set_age method( -1 )
InvalidAgeException(-1)
```

24.8 Chaining Exceptions

One final feature that can be useful when creating your own exceptions is to chain them to a generic underlying exception. This can be useful when a generic exception is raised, for example, by some library or by the Python system itself, and you want to convert it into a more meaningful application exception.

For example, let us say that we want to create an exception to represent a specific issue with the parameters passed to a function divide, but we don't want to use the generic ZeroDivisionException, instead we want to use our own DivideByYWhenZeroException. This new exception could be defined as

```python
class DivideByYWhenZeroException(Exception):
    """ Sample Exception class"""
```

And we can use it in a function divide:

```python
def divide(x, y):
    try:
        result = x /y
    except Exception as e:
        raise DivideByYWhenZeroException from e
```

We have used the raise and from keywords when we are instantiating the DivideByYWhenZeroException. This chains our exception to the original exception that indicates the underling problem.

We can now call the divide method as below:

```python
def main():
    divide(6, 0)
```

This produces a Traceback as given below:

```
Traceback (most recent call last):
  File
"/Users/Shared/workspaces/pycharm/pythonintro/exceptions/exce
ptions.py", line 43, in divide
    result = x /y
ZeroDivisionError: division by zero
The above exception was the direct cause of the following
exception:
Traceback (most recent call last):
  File
"/Users/Shared/workspaces/pycharm/pythonintro/exceptions/exce
ptions.py", line 136, in <module>
    main()
  File
"/Users/Shared/workspaces/pycharm/pythonintro/exceptions/exce
ptions.py", line 79, in main
    divide(6, 0)
  File
"/Users/Shared/workspaces/pycharm/pythonintro/exceptions/exce
ptions.py", line 45, in divide
    raise DivideByYWhenZeroException from e
__main__.DivideByYWhenZeroException
```

As can be seen you get information about both the (application specific) `DivideByYWhenZeroException` and the original `ZeroDivisionError`—the two are linked together. This can be very useful when defining such application specific exceptions (but where the actual underlying exception must still be understood).

24.9   Online Resources

For more information on Pythons errors and exceptions sets:

- https://docs.python.org/3/library/exceptions.html The Standard Library documentation for built-in exceptions.
- https://docs.python.org/3/tutorial/errors.html The Standard Python documentation tutorial on errors and exceptions.
- https://www.tutorialspoint.com/python/python_exceptions.htm An alternative tutorial on Python exception handling.

24.10   Exercises

This exercise involves adding error handling support to the `CurrentAccount` class.

In the `CurrentAccount` class it should not be possible to withdraw or deposit a negative amount.

Define an exception/error class called `AmountError`. The `AmountError` should take the account involved and an error message as parameters.

Next update the `deposit()` and `withdraw()` methods on the `Account` and `CurrentAccount` class to raise an `AmountError` if the amount supplied is negative.

You should be able to test this using:

```
try:
    acc1.deposit(-1)
except AmountError as e:
    print(e)
```

This should result in the exception 'e' being printed out, for example:

```
AmountError (Cannot deposit negative amounts) on Account[123] -
John, current account = 21.17overdraft limit: -100.0
```

Next modify the class such that if an attempt is made to withdraw money which will take the balance below the over draft limit threshold an Error is raised.

The Error should be a `BalanceError` that you define yourself. The `BalanceError` exception should hold information on the account that generated the error.

Test your code by creating instances of `CurrentAccount` and taking the balance below the overdraft limit.

Write code that will use `try` and `except` blocks to catch the exception you have defined.

You should be able to add the following to your test application:

```python
try:
    print('balance:', acc1.balance)
    acc1.withdraw(300.00)
    print('balance:', acc1.balance)
except BalanceError as e:
    print('Handling Exception')
    print(e)
```

Chapter 25
Python Modules and Packages

25.1 Introduction

Modules and packages are two constructs used in Python to organise larger programs. This chapter introduces modules in Python, how they are accessed, how they are define and how Python finds modules etc. It also explores Python packages and sub-packages.

25.2 Modules

A module allows you to group together related functions, classes and code in general. You can think of a module as being like a library of code (although in fact many libraries are themselves composed of several modules as for example, a library may have optional or extensions to the core functionality).

It is useful to organise your code into modules when the code either becomes large or when you want to reuse some elements of the code base in multiple projects.

Breaking up a large body of code from a single file helps with simplifying code maintenance and comprehensibility of code, testing, reuse and scoping code. These are explored below:

- *Simplicity*—Focussing on a subset of an overall problem helps us to develop solutions that work for the subset and can be combined together to solve the overall problem. This means that individual modules can be simpler than the overall solution.
- *Maintenance*—Modules typically make it easier to define logical boundaries between one body of code and another. This means it is easier to see what comprises a module and to verify that the module works appropriately even

© Springer Nature Switzerland AG 2019
J. Hunt, *A Beginners Guide to Python 3 Programming*,
Undergraduate Topics in Computer Science,
https://doi.org/10.1007/978-3-030-20290-3_25

when modified. It also helps to distinguish one body of code from another so makes it easier to work out where changes should go.

- *Testing*—As one module can be made independent of another module there are less dependencies and cross overs. This means that a module can be tested in isolation and even before other modules, and the overall application, have been written.
- *Reusability*—Defining a function or class on one module means that it is easier to reuse that function or class in another module, as the boundaries between the one module and another are clear.
- *Scoping*—Modules typically also define a namespace, that is a scope within which each function or class is unique. Think of a namespace a bit like a surname; within a classroom there may be several people with the first name 'John', but we can distinguish each person by using their full name, for example 'John Hunt', 'John Jones', 'John Smith' and 'John Brown'; each surname in this example provides a namespace which ensures each John is unique (and can be referenced uniquely).

25.3   Python Modules

In Python a module equates to a file containing Python code. A module can contain

- Functions
- Classes
- Variables
- Executable code
- Attributes associated with the module such as its name.

The name of a module is the name of the file that it is defined in (minus the suffix '.py'). For example, the following diagram illustrates a function and a class defined within a file called utils.py:

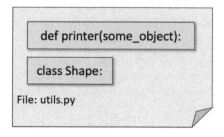

Thus, the printer() function and the class Shape are defined in the utils module. They can be referenced via the name of the utils module.

As an example, let us look at a definition for our `utils` module defined in the file `util.py`:

```python
"""This is a test module"""
print('Hello I am the utils module')

def printer(some_object):
    print('printer')
    print(some_object)
    print('done')

class Shape:
    def __init__(self, id):
        self._id = id

    def __str__(self):
        return 'Shape - ' + self._id

    @property
    def id(self):
        """ The docstring for the id property """

        print('In id method')
        return self._id

    @id.setter
    def id(self, value):
        print('In set_age method')
        self._id = id

default_shape = Shape('square')
```

The module has a comment which is at the start of the file—this is useful documentation for anyone working with the module. In some cases, the comment at the start of the module can provide extensive documentation on the module such as what it provides, how to use the features in the module and examples that can be used as a reference.

The module also has some executable code (the `print` statement just after the comment) that will be run when the module is loaded/initialised by Python. This will happen when the module is first referenced in an application.

A variable `default_shape` is also initialised when the module is loaded and can also be referenced outside the module in a similar manner to the module's function and class. Such variables can be useful in setting up defaults or predefined data that can be used by developers working with the module.

25.4 Importing Python Modules

25.4.1 Importing a Module

A user defined module is *not* automatically accessible to another file or script; it is necessary to `import` the module. Importing a module makes the functions, classes and variables defined in the module visible to the file they are imported into.

For example, to import all the contents of the `utils` module into a file called `my_app.py` we can use:

```
import utils
```

Note that we do not give the file name (i.e. `utils.py`) instead we give the module name to import (which does not include the `.py`).

The result is as shown below:

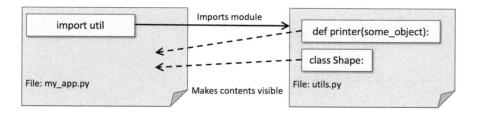

Once the definitions within the `utils` module are visible inside `my_app.py` we can use them as if they had been defined in the current file. Note that due to scoping the function, class and variable defined within the `utils` module will be prefixed by the name of the module; i.e. `utils.printer` and `utils.Shape` etc.:

```
import utils

utils.printer(utils.default_shape)
shape = utils.Shape('circle')
utils.printer(shape)
```

When we run the `my_app.py` file we will produce the following output:

```
Hello I am the utils module
printer
Shape - square
done
printer
Shape - circle
```

Notice that the first line of the output is the output from the `print` statement in the `utils` module (i.e. the line `print('Hello I am the utils module')`) this illustrates the ability in Python to define behaviour that will be run when a module is loaded; typically this might execute some housekeeping code or set up behaviour required by the module. It should be noted that the module is only initialised the first time that it is loaded and thus the executable statements are only run once.

If we forgot to include the `import` statement at the start of the file, then Python would not know to use the `utils` module. We would thus generate an error indicating that the `utils` element is not known: `NameError: name 'utils' is not defined`.

There can be any number of modules imported into a file; these can be both user defined modules and system provided modules. The modules can be imported via separate import statements or by supplying a comma separated list of modules:

```
import utils
import support
import module1, module2, module3
```

A common convention is to place all import statements at the start of a file; however, this is only a convention and `import` statements can be placed anywhere in a file prior to where the imported module's features are required. It is a common enough convention however, that tools such as PyCharm will indicate a style issue if you do not put the imports at the start of the file.

25.4.2   *Importing from a Module*

One issue with the previous example is that we have had to keep referring to the facilities provided by the `utils` module as `utils.<thing of interest>`; which while making it very clear that these features come from the `utils` module, is a little tedious. It is the equivalent of referring to a person via their full name every time we speak to them. However, if they are the only other person in the room then we don't usually need to be so formal; we could just use their first name.

A variant of the import statement allows us to import *everything* from a particular module and remove the need to prefix the modules functions or classes with the module name, for example:

```
from <module name> import *
```

Which can be read as *from <module name> import everything* in that module and make it directly available.

```
from utils import *
printer(default_shape)
shape = Shape('circle')
printer(shape)
```

As this shows we can reference default_shape, the printer() function and the Shape class directly. Note the '*' here is often referred to as a wildcard; meaning that it represents everything in the module.

The problem with this form of import is that it can result in name clashes as it brings into scope all the elements defined in the utils module. However, we may only actually be interested in the Shape class; in which case we can choose to only bring that feature in, for example:

```
from utils import Shape
s = Shape('rectangle')
print(s)
```

Now only the Shape class has been imported into the file and made directly available.

You can even give an alias for an element being imported from a module using the import statement. For example, you can alias the whole package:

```
import <module_name> as <alternative_module_name>
```

for example:

```
import utils as utilities
utilities.printer(utilities.default_shape)
```

In this example, instead of referring to the module we are importing as utils, we have given it an alias and called it utilities.

We can also alias individual elements of a module, for example a function can be given an alias, as can a variable or a class. The syntax for this is

```
from <module_name> import <element> as <alias>
```

For example:

```
from utils import printer as myfunc
```

In this case the printer function in the utils module is being aliased to myfunc and will thus be known as myfunc in the current file.

We can even combine multiple from imports together with some of the elements being imported having aliases:

```
from utils import Shape, printer as myfunc
s = Shape('oval')
myfunc(s)
```

25.4.3 Hiding Some Elements of a Module

By default, any element in a module whose name starts with an underbar ('_') is hidden when a wildcard import of the contents of a module is performed.

In this way certain named items can be hidden unless they are explicitly imported. Thus, if our utils module now included a function:

```
"""This is a test module"""
print('Hello I am the utils module')

# as before

def _special_function():
    print('Special function')
```

And then we tried to import the whole module using the wildcard import and access _special_function:

```
from utils import *
_special_function()
```

We will get an error:

```
NameError: name '_special_function' is not defined
```

However, if we explicitly import the function then we can still reference it:

```
from utils import _special_function
_special_function()
```

Now the code works:

```
Hello I am the utils module
Special function
```

This can be used to hide features that are either not intended to be used externally from a module (developers then use them at their own peril) or to make advanced features only available to those who really want them.

25.4.4   Importing Within a Function

In some cases, it may be useful to limit the scope of an import to a function; thus, avoiding any unnecessary use of, or name clashes with, local features.

To do this you merely add an import into the body of a function, for example:

```
def my_func():
    from util import Shape
    s = Shape('line')
```

In this case the Shape class is only accessible within the body of my_func().

25.5   Module Properties

Every module has a set of properties that can be used to find what features it provides, what its name is, what (if any) its documentation string is etc.

These properties are considered special as they all start, and end, with a double underbar ('__'). These are:

- __name__ the name of the module
- __doc__ the doctoring for the module
- __file__ the file in which the module was defined.

You can also obtain a list of the contents of a module once it has been imported using the `dir(<module-name>)` function. For example:

```
import utils
print(utils.__name__)
print(utils.__doc__)
print(utils.__file__)
print(dir(utils))
```

Which produces:

```
Hello I am the utils module
utils
This is a test module
utils.py
['Shape', '__builtins__', '__cached__', '__doc__', '__file__',
'__loader__', '__name__', '__package__', '__spec__',
'_special_function', 'default_shape', 'printer']
```

Note that the executable `print` statement is still executed as this is run when the module is loaded into Python's current runtime; even though all we do it then access some of the module's properties.

Mostly module properties are used by tools to help developers; but they can be a useful reference when you are first encountering a new module.

25.6   Standard Modules

Python comes with many built-in modules as well as many more available from third parties.

Of particular use is the `sys` module, which contains a number of data items and functions that relate to the execution platform on which a program is running.

Some of the `sys` module's features are shown below, including `sys.path()`, which lists the directories that are searched to resolve a module when an `import` statement is used. This is a writable value, allowing a program to add directories (and hence modules) before attempting an import.

```
import sys
print('sys.version: ', sys.version)
print('sys.maxsize: ', sys.maxsize)
print('sys.path: ', sys.path)
print('sys.platform: ', sys.platform)
```

Which produces the following output on a Mac:

```
[Clang 6.0 (clang-600.0.57)]
sys.maxsize:  9223372036854775807
sys.path:  ['/pythonintro/modules', '/workspaces/pycharm', '/
Library/Frameworks/Python.framework/Versions/3.7/lib/
python37.zip', '/Library/Frameworks/Python.framework/Versions/
3.7/lib/python3.7', '/Library/Frameworks/Python.framework/
Versions/3.7/lib/python3.7/lib-dynload', '/Library/Frameworks/
Python.framework/Versions/3.7/lib/python3.7/site-packages']
sys.platform:  Darwin
```

A common module management tool is known as *Anaconda*. Anaconda (which is widely used particularly within the Data Science and Data Analytics field) is shipped with a large number of common third party Python libraries/modules. Using Anaconda avoids the need to download separate modules; instead Anaconda acts as a repository of (most) modules and means that accessing these modules is as simple as importing them into your code.

You can download Anaconda from https://www.anaconda.com/download.

To see the available Python libraries in Anaconda use the Anaconda Navigator:

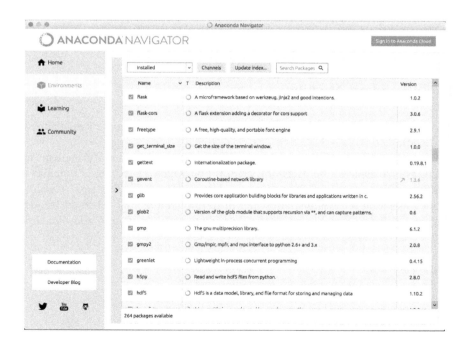

25.7   Python Module Search Path

One point that we have glossed over so far is how does Python find these modules? The answer is that it uses a special environment variable called the PYTHONPATH. This is a variable that can be set up prior to running Python that tells it where to look for to find any named modules.

It is hinted at in the previous section where the sys module's path variable is printed out. On the machine that this code was run on the output of this variable was:

```
sys.path:   ['/pycharm/pythonintro/modules', '/workspaces/
pycharm', '/Library/Frameworks/Python.framework/Versions/3.7/
lib/python37.zip', '/Library/Frameworks/Python.framework/
Versions/3.7/lib/python3.7', '/Library/Frameworks/
Python.framework/Versions/3.7/lib/python3.7/lib-dynload', '/
Library/Frameworks/Python.framework/Versions/3.7/lib/python3.7/
site-packages']
```

This is actually a list of the locations that Python would look into find a module; these include the PyCharm project holding the modules related to the examples used in this book (which is the current directory), then a top level PyCharm location and a series of Python locations (where locations equal directories on the host machine).

Python will search though each of these locations in turn to find the named module; it will use the first module it finds. The actual search algorithm is:

- The current directory.
- If the module isn't found, Python then searches each directory in the shell variable PYTHONPATH.
- If all else fails, Python checks the default path. On Unix/Linux this default path is normally /usr/local/lib/python/.

One point to note about this search order is that it is possible to hide a system provided module by creating a user defined one and giving it the same name as the system module; this is because your own module will be found first and will hide the system provided one.

In this case the PYTHONPATH will be used to find built in Python modules under the Python installation, while our own user defined modules will be found within the PyCharm project workspace directories.

It is also possible to override the default PYTHONPATH variable. It is what is known as an environment variable and so it can be set as a Unix/Linux or Windows operating system environment variable which can then be picked up by your Python environment. The syntax used to set the PYTHONPATH depends on whether you are using Windows or Unix/Linux as it is set at the operating system level:

Here is a typical PYTHONPATH from a Windows system:

```
set PYTHONPATH = c:\python30\lib;
```

And here is a typical PYTHONPATH from a Unix/Linux system:

```
set PYTHONPATH = /usr/local/lib/python
```

25.8   Modules as Scripts

Any Python file is not only a module but also a Python script or program. This means that it can be executed directly if required. For example, the following is the contents of a file called module1.py:

```
"""This is a test module"""
print('Hello I am module 1')

def f1():
    print('f1[1]')

def f2():
    print('f2[1]')

x = 1 + 2
print('x is', x)
f1()
f2()
```

When this file is run directly, or loaded into the Python REPL, then the free-standing code will be executed and the output generated will be:

```
Hello I am module 1
x is 3
f1[1]
f2[1]
```

This looks fine until you try to use module1 with your own code; the free-standing code will still execute this if we now write:

```
import module1
module1.f1()
```

Where you might expect only to see the result of running the f1() function from module1 you actually get:

```
Hello I am module 1
x is 3
f1[1]
f2[1]
f1[1]
```

The first 4 lines are run when module1 is loaded as they are free standing executable statements within the module.

We can of course remove the free-standing code; but what if we sometimes want to run module1 as a script/program and sometimes use it as a module imported into other modules?

In Python we can distinguish between when a file is loaded as a module and when it is being run as a standalone script/program. This is because Python sets the module property __name__ to the name of the module when it is being loaded as a module; but if a file is being run as a standalone script (or the entry point of an application) then the __name__ is set to the string __main__. This is partly because historically main() has been the entry point for applications in numerous other languages such as C, C++, Java and C#.

We can now determine whether a module is being loaded or run as a script/main application by checking the __name__ property of the module (which is directly accessible from within a module). If the module is the __main__ entry point then run some code; if it is not then do something else.

For example,

```python
"""This is a test module"""
print('Hello I am module 1')

def f1():
    print('f1[1]')

def f2():
    print('f2[1]')

if __name__ == '__main__':
    x = 1 + 2
    print('x is', x)
    f1()
    f2()
```

Now the code within the `if` statement will only be executed when this module is loaded as the starting point for an application/script. Note that the `print` statement at the top of the module will still be executed in both scenarios; this can be useful as it allows set up or initialisation behaviour to still be executed where appropriate.

A common pattern, or idiom is to place the code to be run when a file is being loaded directly (rather than as a module) in a function called `main()` and to call that function from within the `if` statement. This helps to clarify which behaviour is intended to run when, thus our module's final version is:

```python
"""This is a test module"""
print('Hello I am module 1')

def f1():
    print('f1[1]')

def f2():
    print('f2[1]')

def main():
    x = 1 + 2
    print('x is', x)
    f1()
    f2()

if __name__ == '__main__':
    main()
```

This version is what would now be called *idiomatic* Python or *Pythonic* in style.

25.9   Python Packages

25.9.1   Package Organisation

Python allows developers to organize modules together into packages, in a hierarchical structure based on directories.

A package is defined as

- a *directory* containing one or more Python source files and
- an *optional* source file named __init__.py. This file may also contain code that is executed when a module is imported from the package.

For example, the following picture illustrates a package `utils` containing two modules `classes` and `functions`.

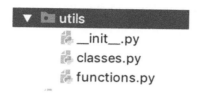

In this case the `__init__.py` file contains package level initialisation code:

```
print('utils package')
```

The contents of the `__init__.py` file will be run once, the first time either module within the package is referenced.

The `functions` module then contains several function definitions; while the `classes` module contains several class definitions.

We refer to elements of the package relative to the package name—as shown below:

```
from utils.functions import *
f1()
from utils.classes import *
p = Processor()
```

Here we are importing both the `functions` module and the `classes` module from the `utils` package. The function `f1()` is defined in the `functions` module while the `Processor` class is defined within the `classes` module.

You can use all the *from* and *import* styles we have already seen, for example you can import a function from a module in a package and give it an alias:

```
from util.functions import f1 as myfunc
myfunc()
```

It is possible to import all the modules from a package by simply importing the package name. If you wish to provide some control over what is imported from a package when this happens you can define a variable `all` in the `__init__.py` file that will indicate what will be imported in this situation.

25.9.2 Sub Packages

Packages can contain sub packages to any depth you require. For example, the
following diagram illustrates this idea:

    ▼ ◰ utils
        ▼ ◰ file_utils
            ◰ __init__.py
            ◰ file_support.py
        ▼ ◰ network_utils
            ◰ __init__.py
            ◰ network_monitoring.py
            ◰ network_support.py
        ◰ __init__.py
        ◰ classes.py
        ◰ functions.py

In the above diagram `utils` is the root package, this contains two sub packages
`file_utils` and `network_utils`. The `file_utils` package has an initialisation file and a `file_support` module. The `network_utils` package also has
a package initialisation file and two modules; `network_monitoring` and
`network_support`. Of course, the root package also has its own initialisation
file and its own modules `classes` and `functions`.

To import the sub package, we do the same as before but each package in the
path to the module is separate by a dot, for example:

    import utils.file_utils.file_support

or

    from utils.file_utils.file_support **import** file_logger

25.10 Online Resources

See the Python Standard Library documentation for:

- https://docs.python.org/3/tutorial/modules.html#standard-modules the standard
  modules.
- https://docs.python.org/3/tutorial/modules.html#packages packages.

- https://docs.python.org/3/tutorial/stdlib.html brief tour of the standard library part 1.
- https://docs.python.org/3/tutorial/stdlib2.html brief tour of the standard library part 2.
- https://pymotw.com/3/ the Python Module of the Week site listing very many modules and an extremely useful reference.

25.11   Exercise

The aim of this exercise is to create a module for the classes you have been developing.

You should move your `Account`, `CurrentAccount`, `DepositAccount` and `BalanceError` classes into a separate module (file) called `accounts`. Save this file into a new Python package called `fintech`.

Separate out the test application from this module so that you can import the classes from the package.

Your test application will now look like:

```python
import fintech.accounts as accounts

acc1 = accounts.CurrentAccount('123', 'John', 10.05, 100.0)
acc2 = accounts.DepositAccount('345', 'John', 23.55, 0.5)
acc3 = accounts.InvestmentAccount('567', 'Phoebe', 12.45, 'high
risk')

print(acc1)
print(acc2)
print(acc3)

acc1.deposit(23.45)
acc1.withdraw(12.33)
print('balance:', acc1.balance)

print('Number of Account instances created:',
accounts.Account.instance_count)

try:
    print('balance:', acc1.balance)
    acc1.withdraw(300.00)
    print('balance:', acc1.balance)
except accounts.BalanceError as e:
    print('Handling Exception')
    print(e)
```

You could of course also use `from accounts import *` to avoid prefixing the accounts related classes with accounts.

Chapter 26
Abstract Base Classes

26.1 Introduction

This chapter presents *Abstract Base Classes* (also known as ABCs) which were originally introduced in Python 2.6.

An Abstract Base Class is a class that you cannot instantiate and that is expected to be extended by one or more subclassed. These subclasses will then fill in any the gaps left the base class.

Abstract Base Classes are very useful for creating class hierarchies with a high level of reuse from the root class in the hierarchy.

26.2 Abstract Classes as a Concept

An abstract class is a class from which you cannot create an object. It is typically missing one or more elements required to create a fully functioning object.

In contrast a non-abstract (or concrete) class leaves nothing undefined and can be used to create a working object.

You may therefore wonder what use an abstract class is?

The answer is that you can group together elements which are to be shared amongst a number of classes, without providing a complete implementation. In addition, you can force subclasses to provide specific methods ensuring that implementers of a subclass at least supply appropriately named methods. You should therefore use abstract classes when:

- you wish to specify data or behaviour common to a set of classes, but insufficient for a single instance,
- you wish to force subclasses to provide specific behaviour.

© Springer Nature Switzerland AG 2019
J. Hunt, *A Beginners Guide to Python 3 Programming*,
Undergraduate Topics in Computer Science,
https://doi.org/10.1007/978-3-030-20290-3_26

In many cases, the two situations go together. Typically, the aspects of the class to be defined as abstract are specific to each class, while what has been implemented is common to all classes.

26.3   Abstract Base Classes in Python

Abstract Base Classes (or ABCs as they are sometimes referred to) cannot be instantiated themselves but can be extended by subclasses. These subclasses can be concrete classes or can themselves be Abstract Base Classes (that extend the concept defined in the root Abstract Base Class).

Abstract Base Classes can be used to define generic (potentially abstract) behaviour that can be mixed into other Python classes and act as an abstract root of a class hierarchy. They can also be used to provide a more formal way of specifying behaviour that must be provided by a concrete class.

Abstract Base Classes can have:

- Zero or more abstract methods or properties (but are not required to).
- Zero or more concrete methods and properties (but are not required to).
- Both *private* and *protected* attributes (following the single underscore and double underscore conventions).

ABCs can also be used to specify a specific interface or formal protocol. If an ABC defines any abstract methods or abstract properties, then the subclasses must provide implementations for all such abstract elements.

There are many built-in ABCs in Python including (but not limited to):

- data structures (`collection` module),
- `numbers` module,
- streams (`IO` module).

In fact, ABCs are widely used internally within Python itself and many developers use ABCs without ever knowing they exist or understanding how to define them.

Indeed, ABCs are not widely used by developers building systems with Python although this is in part because they are most appropriate to those building libraries, particularly those that are expected to be extended by developers themselves.

26.3.1   Subclassing an ABC

Typically, an Abstract Base Class will need to be imported from the module in which it is defined; of course, if the ABC is defined in the current module then this will not be necessary.

As an example, the `collections.MutableSequence` class is an ABC; this is an ABC for a sequence of elements that can be modified (mutable) and iterated over. We can use this as the base class for our own type of collection which we will call a Bag, for example:

```
from collections import MutableSequence

class Bag(MutableSequence):
    pass
```

In this example we are importing the `MutableSequence` from the `collections` module. We then define the class `Bag` as extending the `MutableSequence` Abstract Base Class. For the moment we are using the special Python keyword `pass` as a place holder for the body of the class.

However, this means that the `Bag` class is actually also an abstract class as it does not implement any of the abstract methods in the `MutableSequence` ABC.

Python, however, does not validate this at *import* time; instead it validates it at *runtime* when an instance of the type is to be created.

In this case, the `Bag` class does not implement the abstract methods in `MutableSequence` and thus if a program attempts to create an instance of `Bag`, then the following error would be raised:

```
Traceback (most recent call last):
  File "/pythonintro/abstract/Bag.py", line 10, in <module>
    main()
  File "/pythonintro/abstract/Bag.py", line 7, in main
    bag = Bag()
TypeError: Can't instantiate abstract class Bag with abstract
methods __delitem__, __getitem__, __len__, __setitem__,
insert
```

As can be seen this is a rather *formal* requirement; if you don't implement all the methods defined as abstract in the parent class then you can't create an instance of the class you are defining (because it is also abstract).

We can define a method for each of the abstract classes in the `Bag` class and then we will be able to create an instance of the class, for example:

```
from collections import MutableSequence

class Bag(MutableSequence):

    def __getitem__(self, index):
        pass

    def __delitem__(self, index):
        pass

    def __len__(self):
        pass

    def __setitem__(self, index, value):
        pass

    def insert(self, index, value):
        pass
```

This version of Bag meets all the requirements imposed on it by the ABC MutableSequence; that is, it implements each of the special methods listed and the insert method. The class Bag can now be considered to be a concrete class.

However, in this case the methods themselves don't do anything (they again use the Python keyword pass which acts as a placeholder for the code to implement each method). However, we can now write:

```
bag = Bag()
```

And the application will not generate an error message.

At this point we could now progress to implementing each method such that it provides an appropriate implementation of the Bag.

26.3.2 Defining an Abstract Base Class

An Abstract Base Class can be defined by specifying that the class has a metaclass; typically, ABCMeta. The ABCMeta metaclass is provided by the abc module.

The metaclass is specified using the metaclass attribute of the parent class list. This will create a class that can be used as an ABC. Alternatively you can extend the abc.ABC class that specified the ABCMeta as its metaclass.

This is exactly how the ABCs in the _collections_abc.py file are implemented.

The following code snippet illustrates this idea. The ABCMeta class is imported from the abc module. It is then used with the class Shape via the metaclass attribute of the class inheritance list:

```
from abc import ABCMeta

class Shape(metaclass=ABCMeta):

    def __init__(self, id):
        self.id = id
```

Note that at this point although Shape is an ABC, it does not define any abstract elements and so can actually be instantiated just like any other concrete class. However, we will next define some abstract methods for the Shape ABC.

To define an abstract method, we need to also import the abstractmethod decorator from the abc module, (if we want to define an abstract property then we need to add @property to an appropriate abstract method). Importing the abstractmethod decorator is illustrated below:

```
from abc import ABCMeta, abstractmethod
```

We can now expand the definition of our Shape class:

```
from abc import ABCMeta, abstractmethod

class Shape(metaclass=ABCMeta):
    def __init__(self, id):
        self._id = id

    @abstractmethod
    def display(self): pass

    @property
    @abstractmethod
    def id(self): pass
```

The class Shape is now an Abstract Base Class and requires that any subclass must provide an implementation of the method display() and the property id (otherwise the subclass will automatically become abstract).

The class Circle is a concrete subclass of the Shape ABC; it thus provides a __init__() initialisation method, a display method and an id property (the __init__() method is used to allow the _id attribute in the base class to be initialised).

```
class Circle(Shape):
    def __init__(self, id):
        super().__init__(id)

    def display(self):
        print('Circle: ', self._id)

    @property
    def id(self):
        """ the id property """
        return self._id
```

We can now use the class `Circle` in an application:

```
c = Circle("circle1")
print(c.id)
c.display()
```

We can instantiate the `Circle` class as it is concrete and we know we can call the method `display()` and access the property `id` on instances of `Circle`. The output from the above code is thus:

```
circle1
Circle:  circle1
```

26.4   Defining an Interface

Many languages such as Java and C# have the concept of an *interface* definition; this is a contract between the implementors of an interface and the user of the implementation guaranteeing that certain facilities will be provided.

Python does *not* explicitly have the concept of an interface contract (note here interface refers to the interface between a class and the code that utilizes that class).

However, it does have Abstract Base Classes.

Any Abstract Base Class that only has abstract methods or properties in it can be treated as a contract that must be implemented (it can of course also have concrete methods, properties and attributes; it is up to the developer). However, as we know that Python will guarantee that any instances can only be created from concrete classes, we can treat an ABC has behaving like a contract between a class and those using that class.

This is an approach that is adopted by numerous frameworks and libraries within Python.

26.5   Virtual Subclasses

In most object-oriented programming languages, for one class to be *treated* as a subclass of another class it is necessary for the subclass to *extend* the parent class. However, Python has a more relaxed approach to typing, as is illustrated by the idea of *Duck Typing* (discussed in the next chapter).

In some situations however, it is useful to be able to confirm that one type is a subclass of another or that an instance is an instance of a specific type (which may come from the object's class hierarchy) at runtime.

Indeed, in Python, it is not necessary to be an actual subclass of a parent class to be considered a subclass—instead *Virtual* subclasses allow one class to be treated as a subclass of another even though there is no direct inheritance relationship between them. The key here is that the *virtual* subclass must match the required *interface* presented by the virtual parent class.

This is done by registering one class as a Virtual Subclass of an Abstract Base Class. That is, the virtual parent class must be an ABC and then the subclass can be registered (at runtime) as a *virtual* subclass of the ABC. This is done using a method called `register()`.

Once a class is registered as a subclass of an ABC the `issubclass()` and `isintance()` methods will return `True` for that class with respect to the virtual parent class.

For example, given the following two currently independent classes:

```python
from abc import ABCMeta

class Person(metaclass=ABCMeta):
    def __init__(self, name, age):
        self.name = name
        self.age = age

    def birthday(self):
        print('Happy Birthday')

class Employee(object):
    def __init__(self, name, age, id):
        self.name = name
        self.age = age
        self.id = id

    def birthday(self):
        print('Its your birthday')
```

If we now check to see if `Employee` is a subclass of `Person` we will get the value `False` returned. We will of course also get `False` if we check to see an instance of `Employee` is actually an instance of the class `Person`:

```
print(issubclass(Employee, Person))
e = Employee('Megan', 21, 'MS123')
print(isinstance(e, Person))
```

This will generate the output:

```
False
False
```

However, if we now register the class Employee as a virtual subclass of the class Person, the two test methods will return True:

```
Person.register(Employee)
print(issubclass(Employee, Person))
e = Employee('Megan', 21, 'MS123')
print(isinstance(e, Person))
```

Which now generates the output:

```
True
True
```

This provides a very useful level of flexibility that can be exploited when using existing libraries and frameworks.

26.6   Mixins

A *mixin* is a class that represents some (typically concrete) functionality that has the potentially to be useful in multiple situations but on its own is not something that would be instantiated.

However, a *mixin* can be mixed into other classes and can extend the data and behavior of that type and can access data and methods provided by those classes.

Mixins are a common category of Abstract Base Classes; although they are implicit in their use (and naming) rather than being a concrete construct within the Python language itself.

For example, let us define a PrinterMixing class that provides a utility method to be used with other classes. It is not something that we want developers to instantiate itself so we will make it an ABC but it does not define any abstract methods or properties (so there is nothing for a subclass to have to implement).

```
from abc import ABCMeta

class PrinterMixin(metaclass=ABCMeta):
    def print_me(self):
        print(self)
```

We can now use this with a class `Employee` that extends the class `Person` and mixes in the `PrinterMixin` class:

```
class Person(object):
    def __init__(self, name):
        self.name = name

class Employee(Person, PrinterMixin):
    def __init__(self, name, age, id):
        super().__init__(name)
        self.age = age
        self.id = id

    def __str__(self):
        return 'Employee(' + self.id + ')' + self.name + '['
+ str(self.age) + ']'
```

This now means that when we instantiate the class `Employee` we can call the `print_me()` method on the `Employee` object:

```
e = Employee('Megan', 21, 'MS123')
e.print_me()
```

which will print out

```
Employee(MS123)Megan[21]
```

One point to note about the `PrinterMixin` is that it is completely independent of the class it is mixed into. However, mixins can also impose some *constraints* on the classes they will be mixed into. For example, the `IDPrinterMixin` shown below assumes that the class it will be mixed into has an attribute or property called `id`.

```
class IDPrinterMixin(metaclass=ABCMeta):
    def print_id(self):
        print(self.id)
```

This means that it cannot be mixed successfully into the class `Person`—if it was then when the `print_id()` method was called an error would be generated.

However, the class `Employee` does have an `id` attribute and thus the `IDPrinterMixin` can be mixed into the `Employee` class:

```
class Employee(Person, PrinterMixin, IDPrinterMixin):

    def __init__(self, name, age, id):
        super().__init__(name)
        self.age = age
        self.id = id

    def __str__(self):
        return 'Employee(' + self.id + ')' + self.name + '['
+ str(self.age) + ']'
```

Which means that we can now call write:

```
e = Employee('Megan', 21, 'MS123')
e.print_me()
e.print_id()
```

Which will generate:

```
Employee(MS123)Megan[21]
MS123
```

26.7   Online Resources

Some online references for Abstract Base Classes include:

- https://docs.python.org/3/library/abc.html The standard Library documentation on Abstract Base Classes.
- https://pymotw.com/3/abc/index.html The Python Module of the Week page for Abstract Base Classes.
- https://www.python.org/dev/peps/pep-3119/ Python PEP 3119 that introduced Abstract Base Classes.

26.8   Exercises

The aim of this exercise is to use an Abstract Base Class.

The Account class of the project you have been working on throughout the last few chapters is currently a concrete class and is indeed instantiated in our test application.

Modify the Account class so that it is an Abstract Base Class which will force all *concrete* examples to be a subclass of Account.

The account creation code element might now look like:

```
acc1 = accounts.CurrentAccount('123', 'John', 10.05, 100.0)
acc2 = accounts.DepositAccount('345', 'John', 23.55, 0.5)
acc3 = accounts.InvestmentAccount('567', 'Phoebe', 12.45,
'risky')
```

Chapter 27
Protocols, Polymorphism and Descriptors

27.1 Introduction

In this chapter we will explore the idea of an implicit contract between an object and the code that uses that object. As part of this discussion we will explore what is meant by Duck Typing. Following this we will introduce the Python concept called a *protocol*. We will explore its role within Python programming and look at two commonly occurring protocols; the *Context Manager Protocol* and the *Descriptor Protocol*.

27.2 Implicit Contracts

Some programming languages (most notable Java and C#) have the idea of an explicit contract between a class and the user of that class; this contract provides a guarantee of the methods that will be provided and the types that will be used for parameters and return values from these methods. In these languages it helps to guarantee that a method is only called with the appropriate type of values and only in appropriate situations. Slightly confusingly these contracts are referred to as *interfaces* in Java and C#; but are intended to describe the application programming *interface* presented by the class.

Python is a much more flexible and free flowing language than either Java or C# and so has no explicit concept of an *interface*. This can however make things more complex at times; for example, consider the very simple Calculator class given below:

```
class Calculator:
    def add(self, x, y):
        return x + y
```

© Springer Nature Switzerland AG 2019
J. Hunt, *A Beginners Guide to Python 3 Programming*,
Undergraduate Topics in Computer Science,
https://doi.org/10.1007/978-3-030-20290-3_27

What are the valid values that can be passed into the add method and used for the parameters x and y?

Initially it might seem that numeric values such as 1, 2 and 3.4, 5.77 etc. would be the only things that can be used with the add method:

```
calc = Calculator()

print('calc.add(3, 4):', calc.add(3, 4))
print('calc.add(3, 4.5):', calc.add(3, 4.5))
print('calc.add(4.5, 6.2):', calc.add(4.5, 6.2))
print('calc.add(2.3, 7):', calc.add(2.3, 7))
print('calc.add(-1, 4):', calc.add(-1, 4))
```

This generates the following output:

```
calc.add(3, 4): 7
calc.add(3, 4.5): 7.5
calc.add(4.5, 6.2): 10.7
calc.add(2.3, 7): 9.3
calc.add(-1, 4): 3
```

However, this actually represents a contract that the values passed into the Calculator.add() method will support the *plus* operator. In an earlier chapter we explored a class Quantity which implemented this operator (among others) and thus we can also use Quantity objects with the Calculator's add() method:

```
q1 = Quantity(5)
q2 = Quantity(10)
print(calc.add(q1, q2))
```

Which prints out:

```
Quantity[15]
```

This implied contract says that the Calculator.add() method will work with anything that supports the numeric add operator (or to put it another); anything that is numeric like.

This is also known as *Duck Typing*; this is described in the next section.

27.3 Duck Typing

This rather strange term comes from an old saying:

If it walks like a duck, swims like a duck and quacks like a duck then it's a Duck!

In Python *Duck Typing* (also known as shape typing or structural typing) implies that if a object can perform the required set of operations then it's a suitable thing to use for what you want. For example, if your type can be used with the add, multiply, divide and subtract operators than it can be treated as a Numeric type (even if it isn't).

This is a very powerful feature of Python and allows code originally written to work with a specific set of types, to also be used with a completely new set of types; as long as they meet the *implicit* contract defined within the code.

It is also interesting to note, that a particular set of methods may have a *super set* of requirements on a particular type, but you only need to implement as much as is required for the functionality you will actually use.

For example, let us modify the `Calculator` class a bit and add some more methods to it:

```python
class Calculator:
    """ Simple Calculator class"""
    def add(self, x, y):
        return x + y

    def subtract(self, x, y):
        return x - y

    def multiply(self, x, y):
        return x * y

    def divide(self, x, y):
        return x / y
```

At first sight this may indicate that anything being used with the `Calculator` must implement all four operators '+', '−', '/' and '*'. However, this is only true if you need to execute all four of the methods defined in the class.

For example, consider the type `Distance`:

```python
class Distance:
    def __init__(self, d):
        self.value = d
    def __add__(self, other):
        return Distance(self.value + other.value)
    def __sub__(self, other):
        return Distance(self.value - other.value)
    def __str__(self):
        return 'Distance[' + str(self.value) + ']'
```

This defines a class that implements only the __add__() and __sub__() methods and will thus only support the '+' and '−' operators.

Can instances of Distance be used with the Calculator class? The answer is that they can but only with the add and subtract methods (as they only meet part of the implied contract between the Calculator class and any types used with that class).

We can thus write:

```
d1 = Distance(6)
d2 = Distance(3)
print(calc.add(d1, d2))
print(calc.subtract(d1, d2))
```

And obtain the output:

```
Distance[9]
Distance[3]
```

However, if we try to use the multiply() or divide() methods, we will get an error, for example:

```
Traceback (most recent call last):
  File "Calculator.py", line 46, in <module>
    print(calc.divide(d1, d2))
  File "Calculator.py", line 15, in divide
    return x / y
TypeError: unsupported operand type(s) for /: 'Distance' and
'Distance'
```

Basically, it is telling you that the operator '/' is not supported when used with the Distance type.

27.4 Protocols

As mentioned above, Python does not have any formal mechanism for stating what is required between the supplier of some functionality and the user or consumer of that functionality. Instead the far less formal approach termed *Duck Typing* is adopted instead.

This however, raises the question; how do you know what is required? How do you know that you must provide the numeric operators for an object to be used with the `Calculator` class?

The answer is that a concept known as a *Protocol* is used.

A Protocol is an informal description of the programmer interface provided by something in Python (for example a class but it could also be a module or a set of stand-alone functions).

It is defined solely via documentation (and thus the `Calculator` class should have a class documentation string defining its protocol).

Based on the information provided by the protocol if a function or method requires an object to provide a specific operation (or method) then if it all works great; if not an error will be thrown, and the type is not compatible.

It is one of the key elements in Python which allows the Object-Oriented concept of *Polymorphism* to operate.

27.5   An Protocol Example

There are numerous commonly occurring Protocols that can be found in Python. For example, there is a protocol for defining Sequences, such as a container that can be accessed an item at a time.

This protocol requires that any type that will be held in the container must provide the __len__() and __getitem__() methods.

Thus any class that implements these two methods meets the requirements of the protocol.

However, because protocols are informal and unenforced in Python it is not actually necessary to implement all the methods in a protocol (as we saw in the previous section). For example, if it is known that a class will only be used with iteration then it may only be necessary to implement the __getitem__() method.

27.6   The Context Manager Protocol

Another concrete example is that of the *Context Manager Protocol*. This protocol was introduced in Python 2.5 so is very well established by now.

It is associated with the `'with as'` statement. This statement is typically used with classes which will need to allocate, and release so called *resources*.

These resources could be files, or database connections etc. In each of these cases a connection needs to be made (for example to a file or a database) before the associated object can be used.

However, the connection should then be closed and released before we finish using the object. This is because dangling connections to things such as files and databases can hang around and cause problems later on (for example typically only a limited number of concurrent connections are allowed to a file or a database at one time and if they are not closed properly a program can run out of available connections).

The 'with as' statement ensures that any set up steps are performed before an object is available for use and that any shut down behaviour is invoked when it is finished with.

The syntax for the use of the 'with as' statement is

```
with <managed object> as <localname>:
    Code to use managed object via <localname>
```

For example:

```
with ContextManagedClass() as cmc:
    print('In with block', cmc)
    print('Existing')
```

Note that in this case the object referenced by cmc is only in scope within the lines indented after the 'with as' statement; after this the cmc variable is no longer accessible.

How does this work? In fact what the 'with as' statement does is to call a special method when the 'with as' statement is entered (just after the ':' above); this method is the __enter__() method. It then also calls another special method just as the 'with as' statement is exited (just after the last indented statement). This second method is the __exit__() method.

- The __enter__() method is expected to do any setup/resource allocation/ making connections etc. It is expected to return an object that will be used within the block of statements that form that 'with as' statement. It is common to return self although it is not a requirement to do so (this flexibility allows the *managed object* to act as a factory for other objects if required).
- The __exit__() method is called on the *managed object* and is passed information about any exceptions that might have been generated during the body of the 'with as' statement. Note that the __exit__() method is called whether an exception has been thrown or not. The __exit__() method returns a bool, if it returns True then any exception that has been generated is swallowed (that is it is suppressed and not passed onto the calling code). If it returns False then if there is an exception it is also passed back to whatever code called the 'with as' statement.

An example class that can be used with the 'with as' statement (that meets the *Context Manager Protocol* requirements) is given below:

```python
class ContextManagedClass(object):
    def __init__(self):
        print('__init__')

    def __enter__(self):
        print('__enter__')
        return self

    # Args exception type, exception value and traceback
    def __exit__(self, *args):
        print('__exit__:', args)
        return True

    def __str__(self):
        return 'ContextManagedClass object'
```

The above class implements the Context Manager Protocol in that it defines both the __enter__() method and the __exit__() method.
We can now use this class with the with as statement:

```python
print('Starting')

with ContextManagedClass() as cmc:
    print('In with block', cmc)
    print('Exiting')

print('Done')
```

The output from this is:

```
Starting
__init__
__enter__
In with block ContextManagedClass object
Exiting
__exit__: (None, None, None)
Done
```

From this you can see that the __enter__() method is called before the code in the block and __exit__() is called after the code in the block.

27.7   Polymorphism

Polymorphism is the ability to send the same message (request to run a method) to different objects, each of which appear to perform the same function. However, the way in which the message is handled depends on the object's class.

Polymorphism is a strange sounding word, derived from Greek, for a relatively simple concept. It is essentially the ability to request that the same operation be

performed by a wide range of different types of things. How the request is processed depends on the thing that receives the request. The programmer need not
worry about how the request is handled, only that it is. This is illustrated below.

```
def night_out(p):
    p.eat()
    p.drink()
    p.sleep()
```

In this example, the parameter passed into the `night_out()` function expects
to be given something that will respond to the methods `eat()`, `drink()` and
`sleep()`. Any object that meets this requirement can be used with the function.

We can define multiple classes that meet this informal contract, for example we
can define a class hierarchy that provides these methods, or completely separate
classes that implement the methods. In the case of the class hierarchy the methods
may or may not override those from the parent class.

Effectively, this means that you can ask many different things to perform the same
action. For example, you might ask a range of objects to provide a printable string
describing themselves. In fact in Python this is exactly what happens. For exmaple, if
you ask an instance of a `Manager` class, a compiler object or a database object to
return such a string, you use the same method (`__str__()`, in Python).

The name polymorphism is unfortunate and often leads to confusion. It makes
the whole process sound rather grander than it actually is.

Note this is one of the most significant and flexible features of Python; it does
not tie a variable to a specific type; instead via Duck Typing as long as the object
provided meets the implied contract, then we are good.

The following classes all meet the contract implied by the `night_out()` function:

```
class Person:
    def eat(self): print('Person - Eat')
    def drink(self): print('Person - Drink')
    def sleep(self): print('Person - Sleep')

class Employee(Person):
    def eat(self): print('Employee - Eat')
    def drink(self): print('Employee - Drink')
    def sleep(self): print('Employee - Sleep')

class SalesPerson(Employee):
    def eat(self): print('SalesPerson - Eat')
    def drink(self): print('SalesPerson - Drink')

class Dog:
    def eat(self): print('Dog - Eat')
    def drink(self): print('Dog - Drink')
    def sleep(self): print('Dog - Sleep')
```

This means that instances of all of these classes can be used with the night_out() function.

Note that the SalesPerson class meets the implied contract partly via inheritance (the sleep() method is inherited from Employee).

27.8   The Descriptor Protocol

Another protocol is the *descriptor* protocol that was introduced back in Python 2.2.

Descriptors can be used to create what are known as *managed attributes*. A managed attribute is an object attributes that is managed (or protected) from direct access by external code via the descriptor. The descriptor can then take whatever action is appropriate such as validating the data, checking the format, logging the action, updating a related attribute etc.

The descriptor protocol defines four methods (as usual they are considered special methods and thus start with a double underbar '___'):

- __get__(self, instance, owner) This method is called when the value of an attribute is accessed. The instance is the instance being modified and the owner is the class defining the object. This method should return the (computed) attribute value or raise an AttributeError exception.
- __set__(self, instance, value) This is called when the value of an attribute is being set. The parameter value is the new value being set.
- __delete__(self, instance) Called to delete the attribute.
- __set_name__(self, owner, name) Called at the time the owning class owner is created. The descriptor has been assigned to name. This method was added to the protocol in Python 3.6.

The following class Logger implements the *Descriptor* protocol. It can therefore be used with other classes to log the creation, access and update of whatever attribute it is applied on.

```python
class Logger(object):
    """ Logger class implementing the descriptor protocol"""
    def __init__(self, name):
        self.name = name

    def __get__(self, inst, owner):
        print('__get__:', inst, 'owner', owner,
              ', value', self.name, '=',
              str(inst.__dict__[self.name]))
        return inst.__dict__[self.name]

    def __set__(self, inst, value):
        print('__set__:', inst, '-', self.name, '=', value)
        inst.__dict__[self.name] = value

    def __delete__(self, instance):
        print('__delete__', instance)

    def __set_name__(self, owner, name):
        print('__set_name__', 'owner', owner, 'setting', name)
```

Each of the methods defined for the protocol prints out a message so that access can be monitored.

The Logger class is used with the following Cursor class.

```python
class Cursor(object):
    # Set up the descriptors at the class level
    x = Logger('x')
    y = Logger('y')

    def __init__(self, x0, y0):
        # Initialise the attributes
        # Note use of __dict__ to avoid using self.x notation
        # which would invoke the descriptor behaviour
        self.__dict__['x'] = x0
        self.__dict__['y'] = y0

    def move_by(self, dx, dy):
        print('move_by', dx, ',', dy)
        self.x = self.x + dx
        self.y = self.y + dy

    def __str__(self):
        return 'Point[' + str(self.__dict__['x']) +
               ', ' + str(self.__dict__['y']) + ']'
```

There are several points to note about this class definition including:

The *Descriptors* must be defined at the class level not at the object/instance level. This the x and y attributes of Cursor object are defined as having Logger descriptors within the class (not within the __init__() method). If you try to define them using self.x and self.y the descriptors will not be registered.

The Cursor __init__() method uses the __dict__ dictionary to initialise the instance/object attributes x and y. This is an alternative approach to accessing an objects' attributes; it is used internally by an object to hold the actual attribute values. It by passes the normal attribute look up mechanism invoked when you use the *dot* notation (such as curser.x = 10). This means that it will not be intercepted by the Descriptor. This has been done because the logger uses the __str__() method to print out the instance holding the attribute which uses the current values of x and y. When the value of x is initially set there will be no value for y and thus an error would be generated by the __str__().

The __str__() method also uses the __dict__ dictionary to access the attributes as it is not necessary to log this access. It would also become recursive if the Logger also used the method to print out the instance.

We can now use instances of the Cursor object without knowing that the descriptor will intercept access to the attributes x and y:

```
cursor = Cursor(15, 25)
print('-' * 25)

print('p1:', cursor)
cursor.x = 20
cursor.y = 35
print('p1 updated:', cursor)
print('p1.x:', cursor.x)
print('-' * 25)

cursor.move_by(1, 1)
print('-' * 25)

del cursor.x
```

The output from this illustrates how the descriptors have intercepted access to the attributes. Note that the move_by() method accesses both the getter and the setter descriptor methods as this method reads the current value of the attributes and then updates them.

```
__set_name__ owner <class '__main__.Cursor'> setting x
__set_name__ owner <class '__main__.Cursor'> setting y
------------------------
p1: Point[15, 25]
__set__: Point[15, 25] - x = 20
__set__: Point[20, 25] - y = 35
p1 updated: Point[20, 35]
__get__: Point[20, 35] owner <class '__main__.Cursor'> , value
x = 20
p1.x: 20
------------------------
move_by 1 , 1
__get__: Point[20, 35] owner <class '__main__.Cursor'> , value
x = 20
__set__: Point[20, 35] - x = 21
__get__: Point[21, 35] owner <class '__main__.Cursor'> , value
y = 35
__set__: Point[21, 35] - y = 36
------------------------
__delete__ Point[21, 36]
```

27.9   Online Resources

The following online resources focussing on Python protocols are available:

- https://ref.readthedocs.io/en/latest/understanding_python/interfaces/existing_protocols.html Documentation on Pythons default (native) protocols including the comparison, hash, attribute access and sequence protocols.
- https://docs.python.org/3/library/stdtypes.html#context-manager-types for Context manager types.
- https://pymotw.com/3/contextlib/index.html The Python Module of the Week for Context Manager Utilities.
- https://en.wikipedia.org/wiki/Polymorphism_(computer_science)   Wikipedia page on Polymorphism.

27.10   Exercises

This exercise involves implementing the Context Manager Protocol.

Return to your `Account` related classes.

Modify the `Account` class such that it implements the *Context Manager* Protocol. This means that you will need to implement the __enter__() and __exit__() methods.

Place `print` messages within the methods so that you can see when they are run.

The new methods you have defined will be inherited by each of the subclasses you have created; namely CurrentAccount, DepositAccount and InvestmentAccount.

Now test out your modified calculator using:

```
with accounts.CurrentAccount ('891', 'Adam', 5.0, 50.0) as acc:
    acc.deposit(23.0)
    acc.withdraw(12.33)
    print(acc.balance)
```

Which should produce output similar to:

```
Creating new Account
__enter__
15.5
__exit__: (None, None, None)
```

Chapter 28
Monkey Patching and Attribute Lookup

28.1 Introduction

Monkey Patching is a term you might well come across when looking into the Python further or when searching the web for Python related concepts. It relates to the ability in Python to extend the functionality associated with a class/type at runtime.

Although not directly related to Monkey Patching; how Python looks up attributes and how this process can be managed is a useful aspect to understand. In particular, how to handle unknown attributes can be very useful in managing situations in which Monkey Patching might be used to solve an initial attribute incompatibility.

This chapter explores both Monkey Patching and Python Attribute lookup.

28.2 What Is Monkey Patching?

Monkey Patching is the idea that it is possible to add behaviour to an existing object, at runtime, to meet some requirement that originally the type did not meet. This can happen for example as there is no fixed requirement for a class to implement all of a protocol; in many cases a class may only implement as much of a protocol as is required to meet the current needs; if at a later stage, other elements of a protocol are required then they can be added.

Of course, if this is likely to be a common occurrence then the features can be added to the class for use by everyone; but if not, then those features can be added dynamically at runtime to an object itself. This avoids the public interface of the type becoming cluttered with rarely used features/functionality.

© Springer Nature Switzerland AG 2019
J. Hunt, *A Beginners Guide to Python 3 Programming*,
Undergraduate Topics in Computer Science,
https://doi.org/10.1007/978-3-030-20290-3_28

28.2.1   How Does Monkey Patching Work?

Python is a dynamic language which allows the definition of a type to change at runtime. As methods on objects are in essence just another attribute of a class, albeit one that can be executed, it is possible to add new functionality to a class by defining new attributes that will hold references to the new behaviour.

28.2.2   Monkey Patching Example

The following class, Bag, implements an initialisation method __init__(), __str__() and the __getitem__() method used to support indexed access to a container (or collection) type.

```python
class Bag():
    def __init__(self):
        self.data = ['a', 'b', 'c']

    def __getitem__(self, pos):
        return self.data[pos]

    def __str__(self):
        return 'Bag(' + str(self.data) + ')'

b = Bag()
print(b)
```

This creates a Bag object and prints out the contents of the Bag:

```
Bag(['a', 'b', 'c'])
```

However, if we try to run

```python
print(len(b))
```

We will get a runtime error:

```
Traceback (most recent call last):
  File "Bag.py", line 12, in <module>
    print(len(b))
TypeError: object of type 'Bag' has no len()
```

This is because the len() function expects the object passed to it will implement the __len__() method that is be used to obtain its length. In this case the class Bag does not implement this method.

However, we can define a stand-alone function that behaves in the way we would need the `Bag` to calculate its length, for example:

```
def get_length(self):
    return len(self.data)
```

This function takes a single parameter which we have called `self`. It then uses this parameter to reference an attribute called `data` which itself uses `len()` to return the length of the associated data items.

At present this function has no relationship to the `Bag` class other than the fact that it assumes that whatever is passed into it will have an attribute called `data`— which the `Bag` class does.

In fact, the `get_length()` function is compatible with any class that has an attribute `data` that can be used to determine its length.

We can now associate it with the `Bag` class; this can be done by assigning the function reference (in practice the function name) to an appropriate attribute on the `Bag` class. Since the `len()` function expects a class to implement the `__len__()` method we can assign the `get_length()` function to the `__len__()` attribute. This effectively adds a *new* method to the `Bag` class with the signature `__len__(self):`

```
# Monkey patching
Bag.__len__ = get_length
```

Now when we invoke

```
print(len(b))
```

We get the value 3 being printed out.

We have now *Monkey Patched* the class `Bag` so that the missing method becomes available.

28.2.3   The Self Parameter

One of the reasons that Monkey Patching works is because all methods receive the special first parameter (called `self` by convention) representing the object itself. This means that any function that treats the first parameter as being a reference to an object can potentially be used to define a method on a class.

If a function does not assume that the first parameter is a reference to an object (the one holding the method) then it cannot be used to add new functionality to a class.

28.2.4 Adding New Data to a Class

Monkey patching is not just limited to functionality; it is also possible to add new data attributes to a class. For example, if we wanted each Bag to have a *name* then we could add a new attribute to the class to hold its name:

```
Bag.name = 'My Bag'
print(b.name)
```

Which prints out the string 'My Bag' which now acts as a default value of the name of any Bag. Once the attribute is added we can then change the name of this particular instance of a Bag:

For example, if we extend the above example:

```
Bag.name = 'My Bag'
print(b.name)

b.name = 'Johns Bag'
print(b.name)

b2 = Bag()
print(b2.name)
```

We can now generate:

```
My Bag
Johns Bag
My Bag
```

28.3 Attribute Lookup

As shown above, Python is very dynamic and it is easy to add attributes and methods to a class, but how does this work. It is worth considering how Python manages attribute and method lookup for an object.

Python classes can have both *class* and *instance* oriented attributes, for example the following class Student has a *class* attribute count (that is associated with the class itself) and an *instance* or *object* attribute name. Thus each instance of the class Student will have its own name attribute.

```
class Student:
    count = 0

    def __init__(self, name):
        self.name = name
        Student.count += 1
```

Whenever an instance of the class `Student` is created the `Student.count` attribute will be incremented b y 1.

To manage these attributes Python maintains internal dictionaries; one for *class* attributes and one for *object* attributes. These dictionaries are called __dict__ and can be accessed either from the class `<class>.__dict__` (for class attributes) or from an instance of the class `<instance.>__dict__` (for object attributes). For example:

```
student = Student('John')

# Class attribute dictionary
print('Student.__dict__:', Student.__dict__)
# Instance / Object dictionary
print('student.__dict__:', student.__dict__)
```

Which produces the output shown below (note that the class dictionary holds more information than just the class attribute count):

```
Student.__dict__ : {'__module__': '__main__', 'count': 1,
                    '__init__': <function Student.__init__ at
                    0x10d515158>, '__dict__': <attribute
                    '__dict__' of 'Student' objects>,
                    '__weakref__': <attribute '__weakref__' of
                    'Student' objects>, '__doc__': None}
student.__dict__ : {'name': 'John'}
```

To look up an attribute, Python does the following for class attributes:

1. Search the class Dictionary for an attribute
2. If the attribute is *not* found in step 1 then search the parent class(es) dictionaries

For object attributes, Python first searches the instance dictionary and repeats the above steps, it thus performs these steps:

1. Search the object/instance dictionary
2. If the attribute was *not* found in step 1, then search the class Dictionary for an attribute
3. If the attribute is *not* found in step 2, then search the parent class(es) dictionaries

Thus given the following statements, different steps are taken each time:

```
student = Student('John')

print('Student.count:', Student.count)   # class lookup
print('student.name:', student.name)   # instance lookup
print('student.count:', student.count)   # lookup finds class
attribute
```

The output as expected is that either attempt to access the class attribute count will result in the value 1 where as the object attribute name returns 'John'.

```
Student.count: 1
student.name: John
student.count: 1
```

As the dictionaries used to hold the class and object attributes are just that dictionaries, they provide another way to access the attributes of a class such as Student. That is you can write code that will access an attribute value using the appropriate __dict__ rather than the more usual *dot* notation, for example the following are equivalent:

```
# class lookup
print('Student.count:', Student.count)
print("Student.__dict__['count']:", Student.__dict__['count'])

# Instance / Object Lookup
print('student.name:', student.name)
print("student.__dict__['name']:", student.__dict__['name'])
```

In both cases the end result is the same, either the class attribute count is accessed or the object/instance attribute name is accessed:

```
Student.count: 1
Student.__dict__['count']: 1
student.name: John
student.__dict__['name']: John
```

However, accessing attributes via the __dict__ does not trigger a search process; it is instead a direct lookup in the associated dictionary container. Thus if you try to access a class variable via the objects __dict__ then you will get an error. This is illustrated below where we attempt to access the count class variable via the *student* object:

```
# Attempt to look up class variable via object
print('student.name:', student.name)
print("student.__dict__['count']:", student.__dict__['count'])
```

This will generate a KeyError indicating that the object __dict__ does not hold a key called 'count':

```
Traceback (most recent call last):
  File "Student.py", line 60, in <module>
    print("student.__dict__['count']:",
student.__dict__['count'])
KeyError: 'count'
```

28.4 Handling Unknown Attribute Access

Monkey patching is of course very flexible and very useful when you know what you need to provide; however what happens when an attribute reference (or method invocation) occurs when it is not expected? By default an error is generated such as the AttributeError below:

```
student = Student('John')

res1 = student.dummy_attribute
print('p.dummy_attribute:', res1)
```

This generates an AttributeError for the dummy_attribute

```
Traceback (most recent call last):
  File "Student.py", line 51, in <module>
    res1 = student.dummy_attribute
AttributeError: 'Student' object has no attribute
'dummy_attribute'
```

You can of course catch the AttributeError if you want; but the means wrapping your code in a try block. An alternative approach is to define a method called __getattr__(); this method will be called when an attribute is not found in the objects (and classes) __dict__ dictionary. This method can then perform whatever action is appropriate such as logging a message or providing a default value etc.

For example, if we modify the definition of the Student class to include a __getattr__() method such that a default value is returned:

```
class Student:
    count = 0

    def __init__(self, name):
        self.name = name
        Student.count += 1

    # Method called if attribute is unknown

    def __getattr__(self, attribute):
        print('__getattr__: ', attribute)
        return 'default'
```

Now when we try and access the dummy_attribute on a student object we will get the string 'default' returned:

```
student = Student('John')

res1 = student.dummy_attribute
print('p.dummy_attribute:', res1)
```

Now generates:

```
__getattr__ :  dummy_attribute
p.dummy_attribute: default
```

Note that the __getattr__() method is only called for unknown attributes as Python first looks in __dict__ and thus if the attribute is found, no call is made to the __getattr__() method.

Also note that if an attribute is accessed directly from the __dict__ (for example student.__dict__['name']) then the __getattr__() method is never invoked.

28.5   Handling Unknown Method Invocations

The __getattr__() method is also invoked if an unknown method is called. For example, if we call the method dummy_method() on a Student object then an error is raised (in fact this is again an AttributeError). However, if we define a __getattr__() method we can return a reference to a method to use as a default. For example, if we modify the __getattr__() method to return a method reference (i.e. the name of a method in the Student class):

```
class Student:
    count = 0

    def __init__(self, name):
        self.name = name
        Student.count += 1

    # Method called if attribute is unknown
    def __getattr__(self, attribute):
        print('__getattr__: ', attribute)
        return self.my_default

    def my_default(self):
        return 'default'
```

Now when a undefined method is invoked (such as dummy-method()) __getattr__() will be called. This method will return a reference to the method my_default(). This will be run and the value returned as a side effect of the method invocation as indicated by the round baskets (the '()') after the call to the original method:

```
student = Student('John')

res2 = student.dummy_method()
print('student.dummy_method():', res2)
```

Which produces the following output: rather than an error message

```
__getattr__:   dummy_method
student.dummy_method(): default
```

28.6   Intercepting Attribute Lookup

It is also possible to always intercept attribute lookups using the *dot* nation (e.g. `student.name`) by implementing the `__getattribute__()` method. This method will always be called instead of looking the attribute up in the objects dictionary. The `__getattr__()` method will only be called if an `AttributeError` is raised or the `__getattribute__()` method explicitly calls the `__getattr__()` method.

The `__getattribute__()` method should therefore return an attribute value (which may be a default value) or raise an `AttributeError` if appropriate.

It is important to avoid implementing code that will recursively call itself (for example calling `self.name` within `__getattribute__()` will result in a recursive call back to `__getattribute__()`!). To avoid this the implementation of the method should either access the `__dict__` directory or call the base classes `__getattribute__()` method.

An example is given below of a simple `__getattribute__()` method that logs the call to a method and then passes the invocation onto the base class implementation:

```python
class Student:
    count = 0

    def __init__(self, name):
        self.name = name
        Student.count += 1

    # Method called if attribute is unknown
    def __getattr__(self, attribute):
        print('__getattr__: ', attribute)
        return 'default'

    # Method will always be called when an attribute
    # is accessed, will only called __getattr__ if it
    # does so explicitly or if an AttributeError is raised
    def __getattribute__(self, name):
        print('__getattribute__()', name)
        return object.__getattribute__(self, name)

    def my_default(self):
        return 'default'
```

We can use this version of the class with the following code snippet

```
student = Student('Katie')

print('student.name:', student.name)   # instance lookup

res1 = student.dummy_attribute # invoke missing attribute

print('student.dummy_attribute:', res1)
```

The output from this is now:

```
__getattribute__() name
student.name: Katie
__getattribute__() dummy_attribute
__getattr__:   dummy_attribute
student.dummy_attribute: default
```

As you can see from this the __getattribute__() method is called for both student.name and student.dummy_attribute. However the __getattr__() method is only called when the dummy_attribute is accessed.

Note that __getattribute__() is only invoked for attribute access and not for method invocation (unlike __getattr__()).

28.7   Intercepting Setting an Attribute

It is also possible to intercept object/instance attribute assignment when the *dot* notation (e.g. student.name = 'Bob') is being used. This can be done by implementing the __setattr__() method. This method is invoked instead of the assignment.

The __setattr() method can perform any action required including storing the value supplied. However, to do this it should either insert the value directly into the objects dictionary (e.g. student.__dict__['name'] = 'Bob') or preferably call the base class __setattr__() method, for example object.__setattr__(self, name, value) as shown below for the Student class:

```
class Student:
    count = 0

    def __init__(self, name):
        self.name = name
        Student.count += 1

    # Method will always be called when an attribute is set
    def __setattr__(self, name, value):
        print('__setattr__:', name, value)
        object.__setattr__(self, name, value)
```

If we now define the follow program that uses the Student class:

```
student = Student('John')

student.name = 'Bob'
print('student.name:', student.name)   # instance lookup
```

Running this could we generate the following output:

```
__setattr__ : name John
__setattr__ : name Bob
student.name: Bob
```

There are a few things to note about this output:

- Firstly the assignment of the Student's name within the __init__() method also invokes the __setattr__() method.
- Secondly, the assignment to the class variable count does not invoke the __setattr__() method.
- Thirdly the student.name assignment does of course invoke the __setattr__() method.

28.8 Online Resources

For further information on Monkey Patching the following resources may be of interest:

- https://en.wikipedia.org/wiki/Monkey_patch Wikipedia page on Monkey Patching.
- http://net-informations.com/python/iq/patching.htm A discussion on whether Monkey Patching should be considered good or bad practice.

28.9 Exercises

This exercises focusses on attribute look up.

You should add a method to the Account class that can be used to handle how accounts should behave when an attempt is made to access an undefined attribute.

In this case you should log the attempt to access the attribute (which means print out a warning message) then return a default value of −1.

For example, if you had the following line to your application:

```
print('acc1.branch:', acc1.branch)
```

Then this should invoke the __getattr__() method for the undefined attribute branch. Print a warning message and then return the value −1 which will be printed by the above statement.

The output of this statement should be something like:

```
__getattr__: unknown attribute accessed -  branch
acc1.branch: -1
```

Chapter 29
Decorators

29.1 Introduction

The idea behind Decorators comes from the *Gang of Four* Design Patterns book (so-called as there were four people involved in defining these design patterns). In this book numerous commonly occurring object oriented design patterns are presented. One of these design patterns is the Decorator design pattern.

The Decorator pattern addresses the situation where it is necessary to add additional behaviour to specific objects. One way to add such additional behaviour is to decorate the objects created with types that provide the extra functionality. These decorators wrap the original element but present exactly the same interface to the user of that element. Thus the Decorator Design pattern extends the behaviour of an object without using sub classing. This decoration of an object is transparent to the decorators' clients.

In Python Decorators are functions that take another function (or other callable object such as a method) and return a third function representing the decorated behaviour.

This chapter introduces decorators, how they are defined, how they are used and presents built-in decorators.

29.2 What Are Decorators?

A Decorator is a piece of code, that is used to mark a callable object (such as a function, method, class or object) typically to enhance or modify its behaviour (potentially replacing it). It thus *decorates* the original behaviour.

Decorators are in fact callable objects themselves and as such behave more like macros in other languages that can be applied to callable objects that then return a new callable object (typically a new function).

© Springer Nature Switzerland AG 2019
J. Hunt, *A Beginners Guide to Python 3 Programming*,
Undergraduate Topics in Computer Science,
https://doi.org/10.1007/978-3-030-20290-3_29

The basic idea is illustrated in the following diagram:

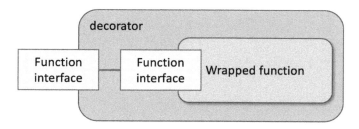

This diagram illustrates a decorator wrapping a callable object (in this case a function). Note that the decorator presents exactly the same interface to the user of the decorator as the original function would present; that is, it takes the same parameters and either returns nothing (None) or something.

It should also be noted that the decorator is also at liberty to completely replace a callable object rather than to wrap it; it's a design decision made by the implementor of the decorator.

29.3   Defining a Decorator

To define a decorator you need to define a callable object such as a function that takes another function as a parameter and returns a new function.

An example of the definition of a very simple logger decorator function is given below.

```
def logger(func):
    def inner():
        print('calling ', func.__name__)
        func()
        print('called ', func.__name__)

    return inner
```

In this case the logger decorator wraps the original function within a new function, here called inner. When this function is executed, a statement is logged before and after the original function is executed.

Every function has an attribute __name__ that provides the functions *name* and this is used in the inner() function above to printout the actual function about to be invoked.

Note that the function `inner()` is defined inside the `logger()` function (this is completely legal). A reference to the `inner()` function is then returned as the result of the `logger()` function. The `inner()` function is not executed at this point!

29.4   Using Decorators

To see what the effect of applying a decorator is; it is useful to explore the basic (explicit) approach to it use. This can be done by defining a function (we will call `target`) that prints out a simple message:

```
def target():
    print('In target function')
```

We can explicitly apply the `logger` decorator to this function by passing the reference to the `target` function (without invoking it), for example:

```
t1 = logger(target)
t1()
```

When we run this code, we actually execute the `inner()` function which was returned by the decorator. This function in turn prints out a message and then calls the function passed into the `logger`. Once this passed in function has executed, it prints another message. The effect of executing the `t1()` function is this to call the `inner()` function which calls the `target` function, thus printing out:

```
calling  target
In target function
called  target
```

This illustrates what happens when a decorator style function is *executed*.

Python provides some syntactic sugar that allows the definition of the function and the association with the decorator to be declared together using the '`@`' syntax, for example:

```
@logger
def target():
    print('In target function')

target()
```

This has the same effect as passing target into the logger function; but illustrates the role of the logger in a rather more Pythonic way. It is thus the more common use of Decorators.

The output of this function is the same as the previous version.

29.5   Functions with Parameters

Decorators can be applied to functions that take parameters; however the decorator function must also take these parameters as well.

For example, if you have a function such as

```
@logger
def my_func(x, y):
    print(x, y)

my_func(4, 5)
```

Then the function returned form the decorator must also take two parameters, for example:

```
def logger(func):
    def inner(x, y):
        print('calling ', func.__name__, 'with', x, 'and', y)
        func(x, y)
        print('returned from ', func.__name__)
    return inner
```

29.6   Stacked Decorators

Decorators can be stacked; that is more than one decorator can be applied to the same callable object. When this occurs, each function is wrapped inside another function; this idea is illustrated by the following code:

```python
# Define the decorator functions
def make_bold(fn):
    def makebold_wrapped():
        return "<b>" + fn() + "</b>"
    return makebold_wrapped

def make_italic(fn):
    def makeitalic_wrapped():
        return "<i>" + fn() + "</i>"
    return makeitalic_wrapped

# Apply decorators to function hello
@make_bold
@make_italic
def hello():
    return 'hello world'

# Call function hello
print(hello())
```

In this example, the function `hello()` is marked with two decorators, `@make_bold` and `@make_italic`.

This means that the function `hello()` is first passed into the `make_italic()` function and wrapped by the `makeitalic_wrapped` function. This function is then returned from the `make_italic` decorator.

The `makeitalic_wrapped` is then passed into the `make_bold()` function which then wraps it inside the `makebold_wrapped` function; which is returned by the `make_bold` decorator.

This means that the function invoked when `hello()` is called is the `makebold_wrapped` function which calls two further functions as shown below:

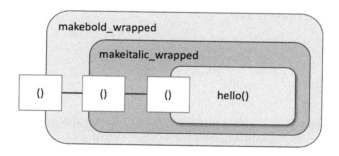

The end result is that the string returned by the function passed in is first wrapped by `<i>` and `</i>` (indicating italics) and then by `<b>` and `</b>` (indicating bold) in HTML.

Thus the output from `print(hello())` is:

```
<b><i>hello world</i></b>
```

29.7 Parameterised Decorators

Decorators can also take parameters however the syntax for such decorators is a little different; there is essentially an extra layer of indirection. The decorator function takes one or more parameters and returns a function that can use the parameter and takes the callable object that is being wrapped. For example:

```
def register(active=True):
    def wrap(func):
        def wrapper():
            print('Calling ', func.__name__, ' decorator param
', active)
            if active:
                func()
                print('Called ', func.__name__)
            else:
                print('Skipped ', func.__name__)
        return wrapper
    return wrap

@register()
def func1():
    print('func1')

@register(active=False)
def func2():
    print('func2')

func1()
print('-' * 10)
func2()
```

In this example, the wrapped function will only be called if the active parameter is `True`. This is the default and so for `func1()` it is not necessary to specify the parameter (although note that it is now necessary to provide the round brackets).

For `func2()` the `@register` decorator is defined with the active parameter set to False. This means that the wrapper function will not call the provided function.

Note that the usage of the decorator only differs in the need to include the round brackets even if no parameters are being specified; even though there are now two inner functions defined within the register decorator.

29.8   Method Decorators

29.8.1   Methods Without Parameters

It is also possible to decorate methods as well as functions (as they are also callable objects). However, it is important to remember that methods take the special parameter self as the first parameter which is used to reference the object that the method is being applied to. It is therefore necessary for the decorator to take this parameter into account; i.e. the *inner* wrapped function must take at least one parameter representing self:

```python
def pretty_print(method):
    def method_wrapper(self):
        return "<p>{0}</p>".format(method(self))

    return method_wrapper
```

The pretty_print decorator defines an inner function that takes as its first (and in this case only) parameter the reference to the object (which by convention uses the parameter self). This is then passed into the actual method when it is called.

The pretty_print decorator can now be used with any method that only takes the self parameter, for example:

```python
class Person:
    def __init__(self, name, surname, age):
        self.name = name
        self.surname = surname
        self.age = age

    def print_self(self):
        print('Person - ', self.name, ', ', self.age)

    @pretty_print
    def get_fullname(self):
        return self.name + " " + self.surname
```

In the above class the get_fullname() method is decorated with pretty_print. If we now call get_fullname() on an object, the resulting string will be wrapped in <p> and </p> (which is HTML markup for a paragraph):

```
print('Starting')
p = Person('John', 'Smith', 21)
p.print_self()
print(p.get_fullname())
print('Done')
```

This generates the output:

```
Starting
Person -  John ,   21
<p>John Smith</p>
Done
```

29.8.2   Methods with Parameters

As with functions, methods that take parameters in addition to `self` can also be decorated. In this case the function returned form the decorator must take not only the `self` parameter but also any parameters passed to the method. For example:

```
def trace(method):
    def method_wrapper(self, x, y):
        print('Calling', method, 'with', x, y)
        method(self, x, y)
        print('Called', method, 'with', x, y)
    return method_wrapper
```

Now this `trace` decorator defines an inner function that takes the parameter `self` and two additional parameters. It can be used with any method that also takes two parameters such as the method `move_to()` below:

```
class Point:
    def __init__(self, x, y):
        self.x = x
        self.y = y

    @trace
    def move_to(self, x, y):
        self.x = x
        self.y = y

    def __str__(self):
        return 'Point - ' + str(self.x) + ',' + str(self.y)
```

When a `Point` object is created below, we can call the `move_to()` method and see the result:

```
p = Point(1, 1)
print(p)
p.move_to(5, 5)
print(p)
```

The output from this is:

```
Point - 1,1
Calling <function Point.move_to at 0x110288b70> with 5 5
Called <function Point.move_to at 0x110288b70> with 5 5
Point - 5,5
```

29.9   Class Decorators

As well as being able to decorate functions and methods; it is possible to decorate classes.

A class can be decorated to add required functionality that may be external to that class.

As an example, a common class level operation is to want to indicate that a class should implement the singleton design pattern. The Singleton Design Pattern (again from the Gang of Four Design Patterns book) describes a type that can only have one object constructed for it. That is, unlike other objects it should not be possible to obtain more than one instance within the same program. Thus, the *Singleton* design pattern ensures that only one instance of a class is created. All objects that use an instance of that type use the same instance.

We can define a decorator that implements the singleton design pattern, for example:

```
def singleton(cls):
    print('In singleton for: ', cls)
    instance = None

    def get_instance():
        nonlocal instance
        if instance is None:
            instance = cls()
        return instance

    return get_instance
```

This decorator returns the `get_instance()` function. This function checks to see if the variable instance is set to `None` or not; if it is set to `None` it instantiates the class passed into the decorator and stores this in the instance variable. It then returns the instance. If the instance is already set it merely returns the instance.

We can apply this decorator to whole classes such as `Service` and `Foo` below:

```
@singleton
class Service(object):
    def print_it(self):
        print(self)

@singleton
class Foo(object):
    pass
```

We can now use the classes `Service` and `Foo` as normal; however only one instance of `Service` and one instance of `Foo` will ever be created in the same program:

```
print('Starting')
s1 = Service()
print(s1)
s2 = Service()
print(s2)
f1 = Foo()
print(f1)
f2 = Foo()
print(f2)
print('Done')
```

In the above code snippet, it looks as if we have created two new `Service` objects and two `Foo` objects; however, the `@singleton` decorator will restrict the number of instances created to one and will reuse that instance whenever a request is made to instantiate the given class. Thus when we run this example, we can see that the hexadecimal number representing the location of the object in memory is the same for the two `Service` objects and the same for the two `Foo` objects:

```
In singleton for:   <class '__main__.Service'>
In singleton for:   <class '__main__.Foo'>
Starting
<__main__.Service object at 0x10ac3f780>
<__main__.Service object at 0x10ac3f780>
<__main__.Foo object at 0x10ac3f7b8>
<__main__.Foo object at 0x10ac3f7b8>
Done
```

29.10   When Is a Decorator Executed?

An important feature of decorators is that they are executed right after the decorator function is defined. This is usually at *import time* (i.e. when a module is loaded by Python).

```python
def logger(func):
    print('In Logger')
    def inner():
        print('In inner calling ', func.__name__)
        func()
        print('In inner called ', func.__name__)
    print('Finishing Logger')
    return inner

@logger
def print_it():
    print('Print It')

print('Start')
print_it()
print('Done')
```

For example, the decorator `logger` shown above, prints out 'In Logger' and 'Finished Logger' when it is executed. If the output is examined, it can be seen that this output occurs before the program prints 'Start'.

```
In Logger
Finishing Logger
Start
In inner calling  print_it
Print It
In inner called  print_it
Done
```

Note that the decorated function and the wrapped function only execute when they are explicitly invoked.

This highlights the difference between what Pythonistas call *import time* and *runtime*.

29.11   Built-in Decorators

There are numerous built-in decorators in Python 3; some of which we have already seen such as @classmethod, @staticmethod and @property. We also saw some decorators when talking about abstract methods and properties. There are also decorators associated with unit testing and asynchronous operations.

29.12   FuncTools Wrap

One issue with decorated functions may become apparent when debugging or trying to trace what is happening. The problem is that by default the attributes associated with the function being called are actually those of the inner function returned by the decorator function. That is the name, doc and module of the function are those of the function returned by the decorator. The name and documentation of the original, decorated function, have been lost.

For example, returning to the original logger decorator we have:

```
def logger(func):
    def inner():
        print('calling ', func.__name__)
        func()
        print('called ', func.__name__)
    return inner


@logger
def get_text(name):
    """returns some text"""
    return "Hello "+name


print('name:', get_text.__name__)
print('doc: ', get_text.__doc__)
print('module; ', get_text.__module__)
```

When we run this code we get:

```
name: inner
doc:  None
module;  __main__
```

It appears that the `get_text` function is called inner and has no *docstring* associated with it. However, if we look at the function it should be called `get_text()` and does have a *docstring* of 'returns some text'!

Python (since version 2.5) has included the `functools` module which contains the `functools.wraps` decorator which can be used to overcome this problem.

Wraps is a decorator for updating the attributes of the wrapping function(inner) to those of the original function (in this case `get_text()`). This is as simple as decorating the 'inner' function with `@wraps(func)`.

```
from functools import wraps

def logger(func):
    @wraps(func)
    def inner():
        print('calling ', func.__name__)
        func()
        print('called ', func.__name__)
    return inner
```

The end result is that in the above example the name and doc are now updated to the name of the wrapped function and the documentation associated with that function.

If we now rerun the earlier example, we get:

```
name: get_text
doc:  returns some text
module;  __main__
```

29.13   Online Resources

For further information on decorators see:

* https://www.python-course.eu/python3_decorators.php a short introduction to Python decorators
* https://www.python.org/dev/peps/pep-0318/ PEP 318 considering decorators for functions and methods.
* https://www.python.org/dev/peps/pep-3129/ PEP 3129 introducing class decorators.
* https://docs.python.org/3.7/library/functools.html Python Standard Library documentation for `functoools`.
* https://pymotw.com/3/functools/index.html Python module of the Week for `functoools`.

- https://github.com/lord63/awesome-python-decorator A useful page that lists many Python decorators as well as third party contributions.
- https://wiki.python.org/moin/PythonDecoratorLibrary which provides a central repository for decorator examples.

29.14   Book Reference

For more information on the Decorator and Singleton design patterns see the "Patterns" book by the Gang of Four (E. Gamma, R. Helm, R. Johnson and J. Vlissades, *Design Patterns: Elements of Reusable Object-Oriented Software*, Addison-Wesley, 1995).

29.15   Exercises

The aim of this exercise its to develop your own decorator.

You will write a `timer` decorator to be used with methods in a class that take the first parameter `self`, followed by one other parameter.

The decorator should log how long a method takes to execute.

To do this you can use the `time` module and import the `default_timer`.

```
from timeit import default_timer
```

You can then obtain a `default_timer` object for the start and end of a function call and use these values to generate the time taken, for example:

```
start = default_timer()
func(self, value)
end = default_timer()
print('returned from ', func, 'it took', end - start,
'seconds')
```

You can then apply the decorator to the `deposit()` and `withdraw()` methods defined in the `Account` class. For example,

```
@timer
def deposit(self, amount):
    self._balance += amount

@timer
def withdraw(self, amount):
    self._balance -= amount
```

These methods will be inherited by the DepositAccount and InvestmentAccout classes. In the CurrentAccount class the withdraw method is over written so you will also need to decorate that method with @timer as well.

Now when you run your sample application you should get timing information printed out for the deposit and withdraw methods:

```
calling  deposit on Account[123] - John, current account =
10.05overdraft limit: -100.0 with 23.45
returned from  deposit it took 8.009999999999268e-07 seconds
calling  withdraw on Account[123] - John, current account =
33.5overdraft limit: -100.0 with 12.33
returned from  withdraw it took 1.141999999999116e-06 seconds
```

Chapter 30
Iterables, Iterators, Generators and Coroutines

30.1 Introduction

There are two protocols that you are very likely to use, or will possibly need to implement at some point or other; these are the *Iterable* protocol and the *Iterator* protocols.

These two closely related protocols are very widely used and supported by a large number of types.

One of the reasons that Iterators and Iterables are import is that they can be used with `for` statements in Python; this makes it very easy to integrate an iterable into code which needs to process a sequence of values in turn. Two further iteration like Python features are Generators and Coroutines which are discussed at the end of this chapter.

30.2 Iteration

30.2.1 Iterables

The *Iterable* protocol is used by types where it is possible to process their contents one at a time in turn. An Iterable is something that will supply an Iterator that can be used to perform this processing. As such it is not the iterator itself; but the provider of the iterator.

There are many iterable types in Python including Lists, Sets, Dictionaries, tuples etc. These are all iterable *containers* that will supply an iterator.

© Springer Nature Switzerland AG 2019
J. Hunt, *A Beginners Guide to Python 3 Programming*,
Undergraduate Topics in Computer Science,
https://doi.org/10.1007/978-3-030-20290-3_30

To be an *iterable* type; it is necessary to implement the __iter__() method (which is the only method in the Iterable protocol). This method must supply a reference to the iterator object. This reference could be to the data type itself or it could be to another type that implements the iterator protocol.

30.2.2 *Iterators*

An *iterator* is an object that will return a sequence of values. Iterators may be finite in length or infinite (although many container-oriented iterators provide a fixed set of values).

The iterator protocol specifies the __next__() method. This method is expected to return the next item in the sequence to return or to raise the StopIteration exception. This is used to indicate that the iterator has finished supplying values.

30.2.3 *The Iteration Related Methods*

To summarise then we have

- __iter__() from the *Iterable* protocol which is used to return the iterator object,
- __next__() from the *Iterator* protocol which is used to obtain the next value in a sequence of values.

Any data type can be both an Iterable and an Iterator; but that is not required. An Iterable could return a different object that will be used to implement the iterator or it can return itself as the iterator—it's the designers choice.

30.2.4 *The Iterable Evens Class*

To illustrate the ideas behind iterables and iterators we will implement a simple class; this class will be an Evens class that is used to supply a set of even values from 0 to some limit. This illustrates that it is not only data containers that can be iterable/iterators.

It also illustrates a type that is both an Iterable and an Iterator.

```python
class Evens(object):

    def __init__(self, limit):
        self.limit = limit
        self.val = 0

    # Makes this class iterable
    def __iter__(self):
        return self

    # Makes this class an iterator
    def __next__(self):
        if self.val > self.limit:
            raise StopIteration
        else:
            return_val = self.val
            self.val += 2
            return return_val
```

There are a few things to note about this class

- The __iter__() method returns self; this is a very common pattern and assumes that the class also implements the iterator protocol
- The __next__() method either returns the next value in the sequence or it raises the StopIteration exception to indicate that there are no more values available.

30.2.5   *Using the Evens Class with a for Loop*

Now that we have implemented both the *iterable* and *iterator* protocols for the class Evens we can use it with a for statement:

```python
print('Start')
for i in Evens(6):
    print(i, end=', ')

print('Done')
```

Which generates the output:

```
Start
0, 2, 4, 6, Done
```

This makes it look as if the Evens type is a built-in type as it can be used with an existing Python structure; however the for loop merely expects to be given an *iterable*; as such Evens is compatible with the for loop.

30.3   The Itertools Module

The itertools module provides a number of useful functions that return iterators constructed in various ways. It can be used to provide an iterator over a selection of values from a data type that is iterable; it can be used to combine iterables together etc.

30.4   Generators

In many cases it is not appropriate (or possible) to obtain all the data to be processed up front (for performance reasons, for memory reasons etc.). Instead lazily creating the data to be iterated over based on some underlying dataset, may be more appropriate.

Generators are a *special* function that can be used to *generate* a sequence of values to be iterated over on demand (that is when the values are needed) rather than produced up front.

The only thing that makes a generator a *generator function* is the use of the yield keyword (which was introduced in Python 2.3).

The yield keyword can only be used inside a function or a method. Upon its execution the function is suspended, and the value of the yield statement is returned as the current *cycle* value. If this is used with a for loop, then the loop runs once for this value. Execution of the generator function is then resumed after the loop has cycled once and the next cycle value is obtained.

The *generator* function will keep supplying values until it returns (which means that an infinite sequence of values can be generated).

30.4.1   Defining a Generator Function

A very simple example of a generator function is given below. This function is called the gen_numbers() function:

```
def gen_numbers():
    yield 1
    yield 2
    yield 3
```

This is a *generator* function as it has at least one `yield` statement (in fact it has three). Each time the `gen_numbers()` function is called within a `for` statement it will return one of the values associated with a `yield` statement; in this case the value 1, then the value 2 and finally the value 3 before it returns (terminates).

30.4.2   Using a Generator Function in a for Loop

We can use the `gen_numbers()` function with a `for` statement as shown below: Which produces 1, 2 and 3 as output.

```
for i in gen_numbers():
    print(i)
```

It is common for the body of a generator to have some form of loop itself. This loop is typically used to generate the values that will be *yielded*. However, as is shown above that is not necessary and here a `yield` statement is repeated three times.

Note that `gen_numbers()` is a function but it is a special function as it returns a generator *object*.

This is a generator function returns a generator object which wraps up the *generation* of the values required but this is hidden from the developer.

30.4.3   When Do the Yield Statements Execute?

It is interesting to consider what happens within the generator function; it is actually suspended each time a `yield` statement supplies a value and is only resumed when the next request for a value is received. This can be seen by adding some additional `print` statements to the `gen_numbers()` function:

```
def gen_numbers2():
    print('Start')
    yield 1
    print('Continue')
    yield 2
    print('Final')
    yield 3
    print('End')

for i in gen_numbers():
    print(i)
```

When we run this code snippet, we get

```
Start
1
Continue
2
Final
3
End
```

Thus the generator executes the `yield` statements on an as needed basis and not all at once.

30.4.4   An Even Number Generator

We could have used a generator to produce a set of even numbers up to a specific limit, as we did earlier with the `Evens` class, but without the need to create a class (and implement the two special methods `__iter__()` and `__next__()`). For example:

```
def evens_up_to(limit):
    value = 0
    while value <= limit:
        yield value
        value += 2

for i in evens_up_to(6):
    print(i, end=', ')
```

This produces

```
0, 2, 4, 6,
```

This illustrates the potential benefit of a generator over an iterator; the `evens_up_to()` function is a lot simpler and concise then the `Evens` iterable class.

30.4.5   Nesting Generator Functions

You can even nest generator functions as each call to the generator function is encapsulated in its own generator object which captures all the state information needed by that generator invocation. For example:

```
for i in evens_up_to(4):
    print('i:', i)

    for j in evens_up_to(6):
        print('j:', j, end=', ')

    print('')
```

Which generates:

```
i: 0
j: 0, j: 2, j: 4, j: 6,
i: 2
j: 0, j: 2, j: 4, j: 6,
i: 4
j: 0, j: 2, j: 4, j: 6,
```

As you can see from this the loop variable i is bound to the values produced by the first call to evens_up_to() (which produces a sequence up to 4) while the j loop variable is bound to the values produced by the second call to evens_up_to() (which produces a sequence of values up to 6).

30.4.6   *Using Generators Outside a for Loop*

You do not need a for loop to work with a generator function; the generator object actually returned by the generator function supports the next() function. This function takes a generator object (returned from the generator function) and returns the next value in sequence.

```
evens = evens_up_to(4)
print(next(evens), end=', ')
print(next(evens), end=', ')
print(next(evens))
```

This produces

```
0, 2, 4
```

Subsequent calls to next(evens) return no value; if required the generator can throw an error/exception.

30.5   Coroutines

Coroutines were introduced in Python 2.5 but are still widely misunderstood.

Much documentation introduces Coroutines by saying that they are similar to Generators, however there is a fundamental difference between Generators and Coroutines:

- generators are data producers,
- coroutines are data *consumers.*

That is coroutines *consume* data produced by something else; where as a generator produces a sequence of values that something else can process.

The send() function is used to send values to a coroutine. These data items are made available within the coroutine; which will wait for values to be supplied to it. When a value is supplied then some behaviour can be triggered. Thus, when a coroutine consumes a value it triggers some behaviour to be processed.

Part of the confusion between generators and coroutines is that the yield keyword is reused within a coroutine; it is used within a coroutine to cause the coroutine to wait until a value has been sent. It will then supply this value to the coroutine.

It is also necessary to *prime* a Coroutine using with next() or send(None) functions. This advances the Coroutine to the call to yield where it will then wait until a value is sent to it.

A coroutine may continue forever unless close() is sent to it. It is possible to pick up on the coroutine being closed by catching the GeneratorExit exception; you can then trigger some shut down behaviour if required.

An example of a coroutine is given by the grep() function below:

```python
def grep(pattern):
    print('Looking for', pattern)
    try:
        while True:
            line = (yield)
            if pattern in line:
                print(line)
    except GeneratorExit:
        print('Exiting the Co-routine')
```

This coroutine will wait for input data; when data is sent to the coroutine, then that data will be assigned to the line variable. It will then check to see if the pattern used to initialise the coroutine function is present in the line; if it is it will print the line; it will then loop and wait for the next data item to be sent to the coroutine. If while it is waiting the coroutine is closed, then it will catch the GeneratorExit exception and print out a suitable message.

The grep() coroutine is used below, notice that the coroutine function returns a coroutine object that can be used to submit data:

```
print('Starting')
# Initialise the coroutine
g = grep('Python')

# prime the coroutine
next(g)

# Send data to the coroutine
g.send('Java is cool')
g.send('C++ is cool')
g.send('Python is cool')

# now close the coroutine
g.close()
print('Done')
```

The output from this is:

```
Starting
Looking for Python
Python is cool
Exiting the Co-routine
Done
```

30.6 Online Resources

See the following for further information

* https://docs.python.org/3/library/stdtypes.html#iterator-types for iterator types.

30.7 Exercises

These exercises focusses on the creation of a generator.

Write a *prime number* generator; you can use the prime number program you wrote earlier in the book but convert it into a generator. The generator should take a *limit* to give the maximum size of the loop you use to generate the prime numbers. You could call this prime_number_generator().

You should be able to run the following code:

```
number = input('Please input the number:')
if number.isnumeric():
    num = int(number)
    if num <= 2:
        print('Number must be greater than 2')
    else:
        for prime in prime_number_generator(num):
            print(prime, end=', ')
else:
    print('Must be a positive integer')
```

If the user enters 27 then the output would be:

```
Please input the number:27
2, 3, 5, 7, 11, 13, 17, 19, 23,
```

Now create the `infinite_prime_number_generator()`; this generator does not have a limit and will keep generating prime numbers until it is no longer used. You should be able to use this prime number generator as follows:

```
prime = infinite_prime_number_generator()
print(next(prime))
print(next(prime))
print(next(prime))
print(next(prime))
print(next(prime))
```

Chapter 31
Collections, Tuples and Lists

31.1 Introduction

Earlier in this book we looked at some Python built-in types such as `string`, `int` and `float` as well as `bools`. These are not the only built-in types in Python; another group of built-in types are collectively known as collection types. This is because they represent a collection of other types (such as a collection of strings, or integers).

A collection is a single object representing a group of objects (such as a list or dictionary). Collections may also be referred to as *containers* (as they contain other objects). These collection classes are often used as the basis for more complex or application specific data structures and data types.

These collection types support various types of data structures (such as lists and maps) and ways to process elements within those structures. This chapter introduces the Python Collection types.

31.2 Python Collection Types

There are four classes in Python that provide container like behaviour; that is data types for holding collections of other objects, these are

- **Tuples** A Tuple represents a collection of objects that are ordered and immutable (cannot be modified). Tuples allow duplicate members and are indexed.
- **Lists** Lists hold a collection of objects that are ordered and mutable (changeable), they are indexed and allow duplicate members.
- **Sets** Sets are a collection that is unordered and unindexed. They are mutable (changeable) but do not allow duplicate values to be held.
- **Dictionary** A dictionary is an unordered collection that is indexed by a *key* which references a *value*. The value is returned when the *key* is provided. No

© Springer Nature Switzerland AG 2019
J. Hunt, *A Beginners Guide to Python 3 Programming*,
Undergraduate Topics in Computer Science,
https://doi.org/10.1007/978-3-030-20290-3_31

duplicate keys are allowed. Duplicate values are allowed. Dictionaries are mutable containers.

Remember that everything in Python is actually a type of object, integers are instances/objects of the type `int`, strings are instances of the type `string` etc. Thus, container types such as `Set` can hold collections of any type of thing in Python.

31.3   Tuples

Tuples, along with Lists, are probably one of Pythons most used container types. They will be present in almost any non-trivial Python program.

Tuples are an immutable ordered collection of objects; that is each element in a tuple has a specific position (its index) and that position does not change over time. Indeed, it is not possible to add or remove elements from the tuple once it has been created.

31.3.1   Creating Tuples

Tuples are defined using parentheses (i.e. round brackets '`()`') around the elements that make up the tuple, for example:

```
tup1 = (1, 3, 5, 7)
```

This defines a new `Tuple` which is referenced by the variable `tup1`. The `Tuple` contains exactly 4 elements (in this case integers) with the first element in the tuple (the integer 1) having the index 0 and the last element in the `Tuple` (the integer 7) having the index 3. This is illustrated below:

31.3.2   The tuple() Constructor Function

The `tuple()` function can also be used to create a new tuple from an iterable. An iterable is something that implements the iterable protocol (see the last chapter).

This means that a new tuple can be created from a Set, a List, a Dictionary (as these are all *iterable* types) or any type that implements the iterable protocol.

The syntax of the tuple() function is:

```
tuple(iterable)
```

For example:

```
list1 = [1, 2, 3]
t1 = tuple(list1)
print(t1)
```

which generates the output:

```
(1, 2, 3)
```

Note that in the above the square brackets are used to represent a *list* of things (the List container type is described in more detail later in this chapter).

31.3.3 Accessing Elements of a Tuple

The elements of a Tuple can be accessed using an *index* in square brackets. The index returns the object at that position, for example:

```
print('tup1[0]:\t', tup1[0])
print('tup1[1]:\t', tup1[1])
print('tup1[2]:\t', tup1[2])
print('tup1[3]:\t', tup1[3])
```

which generates the output

```
tup1[0]:    1
tup1[1]:    3
tup1[2]:    5
tup1[3]:    7
```

31.3.4 Creating New Tuples from Existing Tuples

It is also possible to return what is known as a slice from a Tuple. This is a new Tuple which is comprised of a subset of the original Tuple. This is done by providing the start and end indexes for the slice, separated by a colon, within the index square brackets. For example:

```
print('tup1[1:3]:\t', tup1[1:3])
```

Which returns a new `Tuple` of two elements containing the elements from index 1 up to (but not including) element 3. Note that the original `Tuple` is not affected in any way (remember its immutable so cannot be modified). The output of the above is thus:

```
tup1[1:3]:      (3, 5)
```

There are in fact numerous variations on the use of the slicing indices. For example, if the first index is omitted it indicates that the slice should start from the beginning of the tuple, while omitting the last index indicates it should go to the end of the Tuple.

```
print('tup1[:3]:\t', tup1[:3])
print('tup1[1:]:\t', tup1[1:])
```

which generates:

```
tup1[:3]:      (1, 3, 5)
tup1[1:]:      (3, 5, 7)
```

You can reverse a `Tuple` using the `:: − 1` notation (again this returns a new `Tuple` and has no effect on the original `Tuple`):

```
print('tup1[::-1]:\t', tup1[::-1])
```

This thus produces:

```
tup1[::-1]:    (7, 5, 3, 1)
```

31.3.5 *Tuples Can Hold Different Types*

Tuples can also contain a mixture of different types; that is they are not restricted to holding elements all of the same type. You can therefore write a `Tuple` such as:

```
tup2 = (1, 'John', Person('Phoebe', 21), True, -23.45)
print(tup2)
```

Which produces the output:

```
(1, 'John', <__main__.Person object at 0x105785080>, True,
-23.45)
```

31.3.6   Iterating Over Tuples

You can iterate over the contents of a Tuple (that is process each element in the Tuple in turn). This is done using the for loop that we have already seen; however, it is the Tuple that is used for the value to which the loop variable will be applied:

```
tup3 = ('apple', 'pear', 'orange', 'plum', 'apple')
for x in tup3:
    print(x)
```

This prints out each of the elements in the Tuple tup3 in turn:

```
apple
pear
orange
plum
apple
```

Note that again the order of the elements in the Tuple is persevered.

31.3.7   Tuple Related Functions

You can also find out the length of a Tuple

```
print('len(tup3):\t', len(tup3))
```

You can count how many times a specified value appears in a Tuple (remember Tuples allow duplicates);

```
print(tup3.count('apple')) # returns 2
```

You can also find out the (first) index of a value in a Tuple:

```
print(tup3.index('pear')) # returns 1
```

Note that both index() and count() are methods defined on the class Tuple where as len() is a function that the tuple is passed into. This is because len() is a generic function and can be used with other types as well such as strings.

31.3.8   Checking if an Element Exists

You can check to see if a specific element exists in a Tuple using the in operator, for example:

```
if 'orange' in tup3:
    print('orange is in the Tuple')
```

31.3.9   Nested Tuples

Tuples can be nested within Tuples; that is a Tuple can contain, as one of its elements, another Tuple. For example, the following diagram illustrates the nesting of a tree of Tuples:

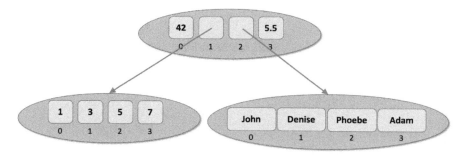

In code we could define this structure as:

```
tuple1 = (1, 3, 5, 7)
tuple2 = ('John', 'Denise', 'Phoebe', 'Adam')
tuple3 = (42, tuple1, tuple2, 5.5)
print(tuple3)
```

The output from this is:

```
(42, (1, 3, 5, 7), ('John', 'Denise', 'Phoebe', 'Adam'), 5.5)
```

Note the *nesting* of round brackets in the printout illustrating where one Tuple is contained within another.

This feature of Tuples (and other containers) allows for arbitrarily complex data structures to be constructed as required by an application.

In fact, a `Tuple` can have nested within it not just other Tuples but any type of container, and thus it can contain Lists, Sets, Dictionaries etc. This provides for a huge level of flexibility when constructing data structures for use in Python programs.

31.3.10   Things You Can't Do with Tuples

It is not possible to add or remove elements from a `Tuple`; they are *immutable*. It should be particularly noted that none of the functions or methods presented above actual change the original tuple they are applied to; even those that return a subset of the original Tuple actually return a new instance of the class `Tuple` and have no effect on the original Tuple.

31.4   Lists

Lists are mutable ordered containers of other objects. They support all the features of the `Tuple` but as they are mutable it is also possible to add elements to a `List`, remove elements and modify elements. The elements in the list maintain their order (until modified).

31.4.1   Creating Lists

Lists are created using square brackets positioned around the elements that make up the `List`. For example:

```
list1 = ['John', 'Paul', 'George', 'Ringo']
```

In this case we have created a list of four elements with the first element being indexed from Zero, we thus have:

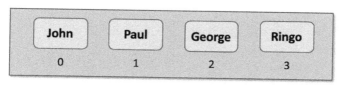

As with Tuples we can have nested lists and lists containing different types of elements.

We can thus create the following structure of nested Lists:

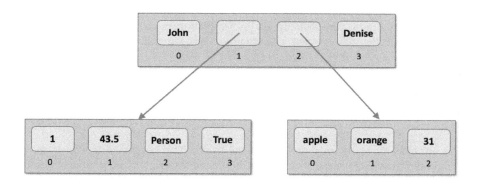

In code this can be defined as:

```
l1 = [1, 43.5, Person('Phoebe', 21), True]
l2 = ['apple', 'orange', 31]
root_list = ['John', l1, l2, 'Denise']
print(root_list)
```

When the root_list is printed we get

```
['John', [1, 43.5, <tuples.Person object at 0x1042ba4a8>,
True], ['apple', 'orange', 31], 'Denise']
```

Note the square brackets inside the outer square brackets indicating nested lists.

We can of course also nest Tuples in lists and lists in Tuples. For example, the following structure shows Tuples (the ovals) hold references to Lists (the rectangles) and vice versa:

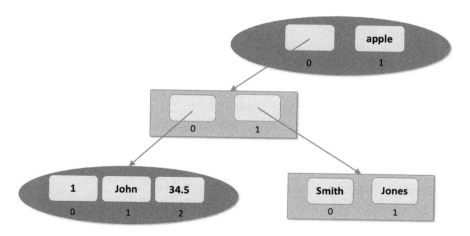

In code this would look like:

```
t1 = (1, 'John', 34.5)
l1 = ['Smith', 'Jones']
l2 = [t1, l1]
t2 = (l2, 'apple')
print(t2)
```

which produces

```
([(1, 'John', 34.5), ['Smith', 'Jones']], 'apple')
```

31.4.2 *List Constructor Function*

The list() function can be used to construct a list from an iterable; this means that it can construct a list from a Tuple, a Dictionary or a Set. It can also construct a list from anything that implements the iterable protocol.

The signature of the list() function is

```
list(iterable)
```

For example:

```
vowelTuple = ('a', 'e', 'i', 'o', 'u')
print(list(vowelTuple))
```

produces

```
['a', 'e', 'i', 'o', 'u']
```

31.4.3   Accessing Elements from a List

You can access elements from a list using an index (within square brackets). The index returns the object at that position, for example:

```
list1 = ['John', 'Paul', 'George', 'Ringo']
print(list1[1])
```

This will print out the element at index 1 which is Paul (lists are indexed from Zero so the first element is the zeroth element).

If you use a negative index such as −1 then the index is reversed so an index of −1 starts from the end of the list (−1 returns the last element, −2 the second to last etc.).

It is also possible to extract a slice (or sublist) from a list. This is done by providing a starting and end index to within the square brackets separated by a colon. For example [1:4] indicates a slice starting at the *oneth* element and extending up to (but not including) the fourth element. If either of the indexes is missed for a slice then that indicates the start or end of the list respective.

The following illustrates some of these ideas:

```
list1 = ['John', 'Paul', 'George', 'Ringo']
print('list1[1]:', list1[1])
print('list1[-1]:', list1[-1])
print('list1[1:3]:', list1[1:3])
print('list[:3]:', list1[:3])
print('list[1:]:', list1[1:])
```

Which produces:

```
list1[1]: Paul
list1[-1]: Ringo
list1[1:3]: ['Paul', 'George']
list[:3]: ['John', 'Paul', 'George']
list[1:]: ['Paul', 'George', 'Ringo']
```

31.4.4 Adding to a List

You can add an item to a list using the `append()` method of the `List` class (this changes the actual list; it does not create a copy of the list). The syntax of this method is:

```
<alist>.append(<object>)
```

As an example, consider the following list of strings, to which we append a fifth string:

```
list1 = ['John', 'Paul', 'George', 'Ringo']
list1.append('Pete')
print(list1)
```

this will generate the output:

```
['John', 'Paul', 'George', 'Ringo', 'Pete']
```

You can also add all the items in a list to another list. There are several options here, we can use the `extend()` method which will add the items passed to it to the end of the list or we can use the `+=` operator which does the same thing:

```
list1 = ['John', 'Paul', 'George', 'Ringo', 'Pete']
print(list1)
list1.extend(['Albert', 'Bob'])
print(list1)
list1 += ['Ginger', 'Sporty']
print(list1)
```

The output from this code snippet is:

```
['John', 'Paul', 'George', 'Ringo', 'Pete']
['John', 'Paul', 'George', 'Ringo', 'Pete', 'Albert', 'Bob']
['John', 'Paul', 'George', 'Ringo', 'Pete', 'Albert', 'Bob',
'Ginger', 'Sporty']
```

Which approach you prefer to use is up to you.

Note that strictly speaking both `extend()` and `+=` take an *iterable*.

31.4.5   Inserting into a List

You can also insert elements into an existing list. This is done using the `insert()` method of the `List` class. The syntax of this method is:

```
<list>.insert(<index>, <object>)
```

The `insert()` method takes an index indicating where to insert the element and an object to be inserted.

For example, we can insert the string 'Paloma' in between the *Zeroth* and *oneth* item in the following list of names:

```
a_list = ['Adele', 'Madonna', 'Cher']
print(a_list)
a_list.insert(1, 'Paloma')
print(a_list)
```

The result is:

```
['Adele', 'Madonna', 'Cher']
['Adele', 'Paloma', 'Madonna', 'Cher']
```

In other words, we have inserted the string 'Paloma' into the index position 1 pushing 'Madonna' and 'Cher' up one in the index within the `List`.

31.4.6   List Concatenation

It is possible to concatenate two lists together using the concatenation operator `'+'`:

```
list1 = [3, 2, 1]
list2 = [6, 5, 4]
list3 = list1 + list2
print(list3)
```

generates

```
[3, 2, 1, 6, 5, 4]
```

31.4.7   *Removing from a List*

We can remove an element from a List using the remove() method. The syntax for this method is:

```
<list>.remove(<object>)
```

This will remove the object from the list; if the object is not in the list then an error will be generated by Python.

```
another_list = ['Gary', 'Mark', 'Robbie', 'Jason', 'Howard']
print(another_list)
another_list.remove('Robbie')
print(another_list)
```

The output from this is:

```
['Gary', 'Mark', 'Robbie', 'Jason', 'Howard']
['Gary', 'Mark', 'Jason', 'Howard']
```

31.4.8   *The pop() Method*

The syntax of the pop() method is:

```
a.pop(index=-1)
```

It removes an element from the List; however, it differs from the remove() method in two ways:

- It takes an index which is the index of the item to remove from the list rather than the object itself.
- The method returns the item that was removed as its result.

An example of using the pop() method is given below:

```
list6 = ['Once', 'Upon', 'a', 'Time']
print(list6)
print(list6.pop(2))
print(list6)
```

Which generates:

```
['Once', 'Upon', 'a', 'Time']
a
['Once', 'Upon', 'Time']
```

An overload of this method is just

```
<list>.pop()
```

Which removes the last item in the list. For example:

```
list6 = ['Once', 'Upon', 'a', 'Time']
print(list6)
print(list6.pop())
print(list6)
```

with the output:

```
['Once', 'Upon', 'a', 'Time']
Time
['Once', 'Upon', 'a']
```

31.4.9   Deleting from a List

It is also possible to use the del keyword to delete elements from a list.
    The del keyword can be used to delete a single element or a slice from a list.
    To delete an individual element from a list use del and access the element via
its index:

```
my_list = ['A', 'B', 'C', 'D', 'E']
print(my_list)
del my_list[2]
print(my_list)
```

which outputs:

```
['A', 'B', 'C', 'D', 'E']
['A', 'B', 'D', 'E']
```

To delete a slice from within a list use the del keyword and the slice returned
from the list.

```
my_list = ['A', 'B', 'C', 'D', 'E']
print(my_list)
del my_list[1:3]
print(my_list)
```

which deletes the slice from index 1 up to (but not including) index 3:

```
['A', 'B', 'C', 'D', 'E']
['A', 'D', 'E']
```

31.4.10 List Methods

Python has a set of built-in methods that you can use on lists.

Method	Description
append()	Adds an element at the end of the list
clear()	Removes all the elements from the list
copy()	Returns a copy of the list
count()	Returns the number of elements with the specified value
extend()	Add the elements of a list (or any iterable), to the end of the current list
index()	Returns the index of the first element with the specified value
insert()	Adds an element at the specified position
pop()	Removes the element at the specified position
remove()	Removes the item with the specified value
reverse()	Reverses the order of the list
sort()	Sorts the list

31.5 Online Resources

See the Python Standard Library documentation for:

- https://docs.python.org/3/tutorial/datastructures.html Python Tutorial on data structures.
- https://docs.python.org/3/library/stdtypes.html#sequence-types-list-tuple-range for lists and tuples.
- https://docs.python.org/3/tutorial/datastructures.html#tuples-and-sequences the online tuples tutorial.
- https://docs.python.org/3/tutorial/datastructures.html#lists the online List tutorial.

31.6 Exercises

The aim of this exercise is to work with a collection/container such as a list.

To do this we will return to your `Account` related classes.

You should modify your `Account` class such that it is able to keep a history of transactions.

A *Transaction* is a record of a deposit or withdrawal along with an amount.

Note that the initial amount in an account can be treated as an initial deposit.

The history could be implemented as a *list* containing an ordered sequence to transactions. A Transaction itself could be defined by a class with an action (deposit or withdrawal) and an amount.

Each time a withdrawal or a deposit is made a new transaction record should be added to a transaction history list.

Now provide support for iterating through the transaction history of the account such that each deposit or withdrawal can be reviewed. You can do this by implementing the Iterable protocol—refer to the last chapter if you need to check how to do this. Note that it is the transaction history that we want to be able to iterate through—so you can use the history list as the basis of your iterable.

You should be able to run this following code at the end of your Accounts application:

```
for transaction in acc1:
    print(transaction)
```

Depending upon the exact set of transactions you have performed (deposits and withdrawals) you should get a list of those transactions being printed out:

```
Transaction[deposit: 10.05]
Transaction[deposit: 23.45]
Transaction[withdraw: 12.33]
```

Chapter 32
Sets

32.1 Introduction

In the last chapter we looked at Tuples and Lists; in this chapter we will look at a further container (or collection) types; the Set type. A Set is an unordered (un indexed) collection of *immutable* objects that does not allow duplicates.

32.2 Creating a Set

A Set is defined using curly brackets (e.g. '{ }'). For example,

```
basket = {'apple', 'orange', 'apple', 'pear',
          'orange', 'banana'}
print(basket)
```

When run this code will show that *apple* is only added once to the set:

```
{'banana', 'orange', 'pear', 'apple'}
```

Note that because a Set is unordered it is not possible to refer to elements of the set using an index.

© Springer Nature Switzerland AG 2019
J. Hunt, *A Beginners Guide to Python 3 Programming*,
Undergraduate Topics in Computer Science,
https://doi.org/10.1007/978-3-030-20290-3_32

32.3   The Set() Constructor Function

As with tuples and lists Python provides a predefined function that can convert any iterable type into a Set. The function signature is:

```
set(iterable)
```

Given an iterable object, this function returns a new Set based on the values obtained from the iterable. This means that a Set can be easily created from a List, Tuple or Dictionary as well as any other data type that implements the iterable protocol. For example, the following code snippet converts a Tuple into a Set:

```
set1 = set((1, 2, 3)
print(set1)
```

which prints out

```
{1, 2, 3}
```

32.4   Accessing Elements in a Set

Unlike Lists it is not possible to access elements from a Set via an index; this is because they are unordered containers and thus there are no indexes available. However, they are Iterable containers.

Elements of a Set can be iterated over using the for statement:

```
for item in basket:
    print(item)
```

This applies the print function to each item in the list in turn.

32.5   Working with Sets

32.5.1   Checking for Presence of an Element

You can check for the presence of an element in a set using the in keyword, for example:

```
print('apple' in basket)
```

This will print True if 'apple' is a member of the set basket.

32.5.2   Adding Items to a Set

It is possible to add items to a set using the add() method:

```
basket = {'apple', 'orange', 'banana'}
basket.add('apricot')
print(basket)
```

This generates:

```
{'orange', 'apple', 'banana', 'apricot', 'pear'}
```

If you want to add more than one item to a Set you can use the update() method:

```
basket = {'apple', 'orange', 'banana'}
basket.update(['apricot', 'mango', 'grapefruit'])
print(basket)
```

Generating

```
{'orange', 'apple', 'mango', 'banana', 'apricot', 'grapefruit'}
```

The argument to update can be a set, a list, a tuple or a dictionary. The method automatically converts the parameter into a set if it is not a set already and then adds the value to the original set.

32.5.3   Changing Items in a Set

It is not possible to change the items already in a Set.

32.5.4 Obtaining the Length of a Set

As with other collection/container classes; you can find out the length of a Set using the len() function.

```
basket = {'apple', 'orange', 'apple', 'pear', 'orange',
'banana'}
print(len(basket)) # generates 4
```

32.5.5 Obtaining the Max and Min Values in a Set

You can also obtain the maximum or minimum values in a set using the max() and min() functions:

```
print(max(a_set))
print(min(a_set))
```

32.5.6 Removing an Item

To remove an item from a set, use the remove() or discard() functions. The remove() function removes a single item from a Set but generates an error if that item was not initialling the set. The remove() function also removes a single item from a set but does not throw an error if it was not initially present in the set.

```
basket = {'apple', 'orange', 'apple', 'pear', 'orange',
'banana'}
print(basket)
basket.remove('apple')
basket.discard('apricot')
print(basket)
```

This generates:

```
{'pear', 'banana', 'orange', 'apple'}
{'pear', 'banana', 'orange'}
```

There is also a method pop() that can be used to remove an item (and return that item as a result of running the method); however it removes the last item in the Set (although as a set is unordered you will not know which item that will be).

The method clear() is used to remove all elements from a Set:

```
basket = {'apple', 'orange', 'banana'}
basket.clear()
print(basket)
```

which prints out

```
set()
```

Which is used to represent an empty set.

32.5.7   *Nesting Sets*

It is possible to hold any *immutable* object within a set. This means that a set can contain a reference to a `Tuple` (as that is immutable). We can thus write:

```
s1 = { (1, 2, 3)}
print(s1)
```

This prints out:

```
{(1, 2, 3)}
```

However, we cannot nest Lists or other Sets within a `Set` as these are not immutable types. The following would both generate a runtime error in Python:

```
# Can't have the following
s2 = { {1, 2, 3} }
print(s2)

s3 = { [1, 2, 3] }
print(s3)
```

However we can use `Frozensets` and nest these within sets. A `Frozenset` is exactly like a `Set` except that it is immutable (it cannot be modified) and thus it can be nested within a `Set`. For example:

```
# Need to convert sets and lists into frozensets
s2 = { frozenset({1, 2, 3}) }
print(s2)

s3 = { frozenset([1, 2, 3]) }
print(s3)
```

This generates:

```
{frozenset({1, 2, 3})}
{frozenset({1, 2, 3})}
```

32.6 Set Operations

The Set container also supports *set like* operations such as (|), intersection (&), difference (−) and symmetric difference (^). These are based on simple Set theory.
Given the two sets:

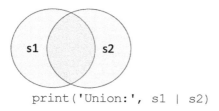

```
print('Union:', s1 | s2)
```

For example, the Union of two sets represents the combination of all the values in the two sets:

```
s1 = {'apple', 'orange', 'banana'}
s2 = {'grapefruit', 'lime', 'banana'}
```

This would print out:

```
Union: {'apple', 'lime', 'banana', 'grapefruit', 'orange'}
```

The intersection of two sets represents the common values between two sets:

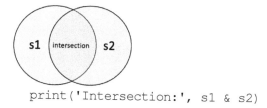

```
print('Intersection:', s1 & s2)
```

This generates

```
Intersection: {'banana'}
```

The difference between two sets is the set of values in the first set that are not in the second set:

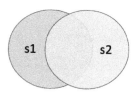

```
print('Difference:', s1 - s2)
```

which produces the output

```
Difference: {'apple', 'orange'}
```

The symmetric difference represents all the unique values in the two sets (that is it is the inverse of the intersection:

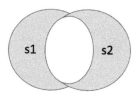

```
print('Symmetric Difference:', s1 ^ s2)
```

The output from this final operation is

```
Symmetric Difference: {'orange', 'apple', 'lime', 'grapefruit'}
```

In addition to the operators there are also method versions:

- `s1.union(s2)` is the equivalent of `s1 | s2`
- `s1.interaction(s2)` is the equivalent of `s1 & s2`
- `s1.difference(s2)` is the equivalent of `s1 - s2`
- `s1.symmetric_difference(s2)` is the equivalent of `s1 ^ s2`

32.7   Set Methods

Python has a set of built-in methods that you can use on sets.

Method	Description
add()	Adds an element to the set
clear()	Removes all the elements from the set
copy()	Returns a copy of the set
difference()	Returns a set containing the difference between two or more sets
difference_update()	Removes the items in this set that are also included in another, specified set
discard()	Remove the specified item
intersection()	Returns a set, that is the intersection of two other sets
intersection_update()	Removes the items in this set that are not present in other, specified set(s)
isdisjoint()	Returns whether two sets have a intersection or not
issubset()	Returns whether another set contains this set or not
issuperset()	Returns whether this set contains another set or not
pop()	Removes an element from the set
remove()	Removes the specified element
symmetric_difference()	Returns a set with the symmetric differences of two sets
symmetric_difference_update()	inserts the symmetric differences from this set and another
union()	Return a set containing the union of sets
update()	Update the set with the union of this set and others

32.8   Online Resources

Online resources on sets are listed below:

- https://docs.python.org/3/tutorial/datastructures.html Python Tutorial on data structures.
- https://docs.python.org/3/tutorial/datastructures.html#sets the online Set tutorial.

- https://www.python-course.eu/python3_sets_frozensets.php A tutorial on sets and frozen sets.
- https://docs.python.org/3/library/stdtypes.html#set-types-set-frozenset for sets

32.9 Exercises

The aim of this exercise is to use a Set.

Create two sets of students, one for those who took an exam and one for those that submitted a project. You can use simple strings to represent the students, for example:

```
# Set up sets
exam = {'Andrew', 'Kirsty', 'Beth', 'Emily', 'Sue'}
project = {'Kirsty', 'Emily', 'Ian', 'Stuart'}

# Output the basic sets
print('exam:', exam)
print('project:', project)
```

Using these sets answer the following questions:

- Which students took both the exam and submitted a project?
- Which students only took the exam?
- Which students only submitted the project?
- List all students who took either (or both) of the exam and the project.
- List all students who took either (but *not* both) of the exam and the project.

Chapter 33
Dictionaries

33.1 Introduction

A `Dictionary` is a set of associations between a key and a value that is unordered, changeable (mutable) and indexed. Pictorially we might view a Dictionary as shown below for a set of countries and their capital cities. Note that in a Dictionary the keys must be unique but the values do not need to be unique.

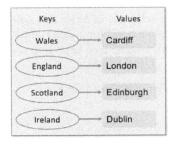

33.2 Creating a Dictionary

A `Dictionary` is created using curly brackets (`'{}'`) where each entry in the dictionary is a key:value pair:

```
cities = {'Wales': 'Cardiff',
          'England': 'London',
          'Scotland': 'Edinburgh',
          'Northern Ireland': 'Belfast',
          'Ireland': 'Dublin'}
print(cities)
```

© Springer Nature Switzerland AG 2019
J. Hunt, *A Beginners Guide to Python 3 Programming*,
Undergraduate Topics in Computer Science,
https://doi.org/10.1007/978-3-030-20290-3_33

This creates a dictionary referenced by the variable `cities` which holds a set of key:value pairs for the Capital cities of the UK and Ireland. When this code is run we see:

```
{'Wales': 'Cardiff', 'England': 'London', 'Scotland':
'Edinburgh', 'Northern Ireland': 'Belfast', 'Ireland':
'Dublin'}
```

33.2.1 The dict() Constructor Function

The `dict()` function can be used to create a new dictionary object from an iterable or a sequence of key:value pairs. The signature of this function is:

```
dict(**kwarg)
dict(mapping, **kwarg)
dict(iterable, **kwarg)
```

This is an overloaded function with three version that can take different types of arguments:

- The first option takes a sequence of key:value pairs.
- The second takes a mapping and (optionally) a sequence of key:value pairs.
- The third version takes an iterable of key:value pairs and an optional sequence of key:value pairs.

Some examples are given below for reference:

```
# note keys are not strings
dict1 = dict(uk='London', ireland='Dublin', france='Paris')
print('dict1:', dict1)
# key value pairs are tuples
dict2 = dict([('uk', 'London'), ('ireland', 'Dublin'),
('france', 'Paris')])
print('dict2:', dict2)
# key value pairs are lists
dict3 = dict((['uk', 'London'], ['ireland', 'Dublin'],
['france', 'Paris']))
print('dict3:', dict3)
```

The output printed by these examples is:

```
dict1: {'uk': 'London', 'ireland': 'Dublin', 'france': 'Paris'}
dict2: {'uk': 'London', 'ireland': 'Dublin', 'france': 'Paris'}
dict3: {'uk': 'London', 'ireland': 'Dublin', 'france': 'Paris'}
```

33.3   **Working with Dictionaries**

33.3.1   *Accessing Items via Keys*

You can access the values held in a Dictionary using their associated key. This is specified using either the square bracket ('[ ]') notation (where the key is within the brackets) or the get() method:

```
print('cities[Wales]:', cities['Wales'])
print('cities.get(Ireland):', cities.get('Ireland'))
```

The output of this is:

```
cities[Wales]: Cardiff
cities.get(Ireland): Dublin
```

33.3.2   *Adding a New Entry*

A new entry can be added to a dictionary by providing the key in square brackets and the new value to be assigned to that key:

```
cities['France'] = 'Paris'
```

33.3.3   *Changing a Keys Value*

The value associated with a key can be changed by reassigning a new value using the square bracket notation, for example:

```
cities['Wales'] = 'Swansea'
print(cities)
```

which would now show 'Swansea' as the capital of wales:

```
{'Wales': 'Swansea', 'England': 'London', 'Scotland':
'Edinburgh', 'Northern Ireland': 'Belfast', 'Ireland':
'Dublin'}
```

33.3.4 Removing an Entry

An entry into the dictionary can be removed using one of the methods pop() or
popitem() method or the del keyword.

- The pop(<key>) method removes the *entry* with the specified *key*. This
  method returns the value of the key being deleted. If the key is not present then a
  default value (if it has been set using setdefault()) will be returned. If no
  default value has been set an error will be generated.
- The popitem() method removes the last inserted item in the dictionary
  (although prior to Python 3.7 a random item in the dictionary was deleted
  instead!). The *key:value* pair being deleted is returned from the method.
- The del keyword removes the entry with the specified key from the dictionary.
  This keyword just deletes the item; it does not return the associated value. It is
  potentially more efficient than pop(<key>).

Examples of each of these are given below:

```
cities = {'Wales': 'Cardiff',
          'England': 'London',
          'Scotland': 'Edinburgh',
          'Northern Ireland': 'Belfast',
          'Ireland': 'Dublin'}
print(cities)
cities.popitem() # Deletes 'Ireland' entry
print(cities)
cities.pop('Northern Ireland')
print(cities)
del cities['Scotland']
print(cities)
```

The output from this code snippet is thus:

```
{'Wales': 'Cardiff', 'England': 'London', 'Scotland':
'Edinburgh', 'Northern Ireland': 'Belfast', 'Ireland':
'Dublin'}
{'Wales': 'Cardiff', 'England': 'London', 'Scotland':
'Edinburgh', 'Northern Ireland': 'Belfast'}
{'Wales': 'Cardiff', 'England': 'London', 'Scotland':
'Edinburgh'}
{'Wales': 'Cardiff', 'England': 'London'}
```

In addition the clear() method empties the dictionary of all entries:

```
cities = {'Wales': 'Cardiff',
          'England': 'London',
          'Scotland': 'Edinburgh',
          'Northern Ireland': 'Belfast',
          'Ireland': 'Dublin'}
print(cities)
cities.clear()
print(cities)
```

Which generates the following output:

```
{'Wales': 'Cardiff', 'England': 'London', 'Scotland':
'Edinburgh', 'Northern Ireland': 'Belfast', 'Ireland':
'Dublin'}
{}
```

Note that the empty dictionary is represented by the '{}' above which as the empty set was represented as set().

33.3.5 *Iterating over Keys*

You can loop through a dictionary using the for loop statement. The for loop processes each of the *keys* in the dictionary in turn. This can be used to access each of the values associated with the keys, for example:

```
for country in cities:
    print(country, end=', ')
    print(cities[country])
```

Which generates the output:

```
Wales, Cardiff
England, London
Scotland, Edinburgh
Northern Ireland, Belfast
Ireland, Dublin
```

If you want to iterate over all the values directly, you can do so using the values() method. This returns a collection of all the values, which of course you can then iterate over:

```
for e in d.values():
    print(e)
```

33.3.6   Values, Keys and Items

There are three methods that allow you to obtain a view onto the contents of a
dictionary, these are values(), keys() and items().

- The values() method returns a view onto the dictionary's values.
- The keys() method returns a view onto a dictionary's keys.
- The items() method returns a view onto the dictionary's items
  ((key, value) pairs).

A view provides a dynamic window onto the dictionary's entries, which means
that when the dictionary changes, the view reflects these changes.

The following code iuses the cities dictionaries with these three methods:

```
print(cities.values())
print(cities.keys())
print(cities.items())
```

The output makes it clear that these are all related to a dictionary by indicating
that the type is dict_values, dict_keys or dict_items etc:

```
dict_values(['Cardiff', 'London', 'Edinburgh', 'Belfast',
'Dublin'])
dict_keys(['Wales', 'England', 'Scotland', 'Northern Ireland',
'Ireland'])
dict_items([('Wales', 'Cardiff'), ('England', 'London'),
('Scotland', 'Edinburgh'), ('Northern Ireland', 'Belfast'),
('Ireland', 'Dublin')])
```

33.3.7   Checking Key Membership

You can check to see if a key is a member of a dictionary using the in syntax (and
that it is not in a dictionary using the not in syntax), for example:

```
print('Wales' in cities)
print('France' not in cities)
```

Which both print out True for the cities dictionary.

33.3.8 Obtaining the Length of a Dictionary

Once again, as with other collection classes; you can find out the length of a Dictionary (in terms of its key:value pairs) using the len() function.

```
cities = {'Wales': 'Cardiff',
          'England': 'London',
          'Scotland': 'Edinburgh',
          'Northern Ireland': 'Belfast',
          'Ireland': 'Dublin'}
print(len(cities)) # prints 5
```

33.3.9 Nesting Dictionaries

The *key* and *value* in a dictionary must be an object; however, everything in Python is an object and thus anything can be used as a key or a value.

One common pattern is where the *value* in a dictionary is itself a container such as a List, Tuple, Set or even another Dictionary.

The following example uses Tuples to represent the months that make up the seasons:

```
seasons = {'Spring': ('Mar', 'Apr', 'May'),
           'Summer': ('June', 'July', 'August'),
           'Autumn': ('September', 'October', 'November'),
           'Winter': ('December', 'January', 'February')}
print(seasons['Spring'])
print(seasons['Spring'][1])
```

The output is:

```
('Mar', 'Apr', 'May')
Apr
```

Each season has a Tuple for the value element of the entry. When this Tuple is returned using the key it can be treated just like any other Tuple.

Note in this case we could easily have used a List or indeed a Set instead of a Tuple.

33.4   A Note on Dictionary Key Objects

A class whose objects are to be used as the key within a dictionary should consider implementing two special methods, these are __hash__() and __eq__(). The hash method is used to generate a hash number that can be used by the dictionary container and the equals method is used to test if two objects are equal. For example:

```
print('key.__hash__():', key.__hash__())
print("key.__eq__('England'):", key.__eq__('England'))
```

The output from these two lines for an example run is:

```
key.__hash__(): 8507681174485233653
key.__eq__('England'): True
```

Python has two rules associated with these methods:

- If two objects are equal, then their hashes should be equal.
- In order for an object to be hashable, it must be immutable.

It also has two properties associated with the hashcodes of an object that should be adhered to:

- If two objects have the same hash, then they are likely to be the same object.
- The hash of an object should be cheap to compute.

Why do you need to care about these methods?

For built in type you do not need to worry; however for user defined c lasses/ types then if these types are to be used as keys within a dictionary then you should consider implementing these methods.

This is because a Dictionary uses

- the *hashing* method to manage how values are organised and
- the *equals* method to check to see if a key is already present in the dictionary.

As an aside if you want to make a class something that cannot be used as a key in a dictionary, that is it is not hashable, then you can define this by setting the __hash__() method to None.

```
class NotHashableThing(object):
    __hash__ = None
```

33.5   Dictionary Methods

Python has a set of built-in methods that you can use on dictionaries.

Method	Description
clear()	Removes all the elements from the dictionary
copy()	Returns a copy of the dictionary
fromkeys()	Returns a dictionary with the specified keys and values
get()	Returns the value of the specified key
items()	Returns a list containing the tuple for each key value pair
keys()	Returns a list containing the dictionary's keys
pop()	Removes the element with the specified key
popitem()	Removes the last inserted key-value pair
setdefault()	Returns the value of the specified key. If the key does not exist: insert the key, with the specified value
update()	Updates the dictionary with the specified key-value pairs
values()	Returns a list of all the values in the dictionary

33.6   Online Resources

Online resources on dictionaries are listed below:

- https://docs.python.org/3/tutorial/datastructures.html Python Tutorial on data structures.
- https://www.python-course.eu/python3_dictionaries.php A tutorial on dictionaries in Python.
- https://docs.python.org/3/library/stdtypes.html#mapping-types-dict for Dictionaries.
- https://docs.python.org/3/tutorial/datastructures.html#dictionaries the online dictionary tutorial.
- https://en.wikipedia.org/wiki/Hash_table For more information on defining hash functions and how they are used in containers such as Dictionary.

33.7 Exercises

The aim of this exercise is to use a Dictionary as a simple form of data cache.
    Calculating the factorial for a very large number can take some time. For
example calculating the factorial of 150,000 can take several seconds. We can
verify this using a timer decorator similar to that we created back in chapter on
Decorators.
    The following program runs several factorial calculations on large numbers and
prints out the time taken for each:

```
from timeit import default_timer

def timer(func):
    def inner(value):
        print('calling ', func.__name__, 'with', value)
        start = default_timer()
        func(value)
        end = default_timer()
        print('returned from ', func.__name__, 'it took',
int(end - start), 'seconds')

    return inner

@timer
def factorial(num):
    if num == 0:
        return 1
    else:
        Factorial_value = 1
        for i in range(1, num + 1):
            Factorial_value = factorial_value * i
        return factorial_value

print(factorial(150000))
print(factorial(80000))
print(factorial(120000))
print(factorial(150000))
print(factorial(120000))
print(factorial(80000))
```

An example of the output generated by this program is given below:

```
calling   factorial with 150000
returned from   factorial it took 5 seconds
None
calling   factorial with 80000
returned from   factorial it took 1 seconds
None
calling   factorial with 120000
returned from   factorial it took 3 seconds
None
calling   factorial with 150000
returned from   factorial it took 5 seconds
None
calling   factorial with 120000
returned from   factorial it took 3 seconds
None
calling   factorial with 80000
returned from   factorial it took 1 seconds
None
```

As can be seen from this, in this particular run, calculating the factorial of 150,000 took 5 s, while the factorial of 80,000 took just over 1 1/4 s etc.

In this particular case we have decided to re run these calculations so that we have actually calculated the factorial of 150,000, 80,000 and 120,000 at least twice.

The idea of a *cache* is that it can be used to save previous calculations and reuse those if appropriate rather than have to perform the same calculation multiple times. The use of a cache can greatly improve the performance of systems in which these repeat calculations occur.

There are many commercial caching libraries available for a wide variety of languages including Python. However, at their core they are all somewhat dictionary like; that is there is a *key* which is usually some combination of the operation invoked and the parameter values used. In turn the *value* element is the result of the calculation.

These caches usually also have eviction policies so that they do not become overly large; these eviction policies can usually be specified so that they match the way in which the cache is used. One common eviction policy is the Least Recently Used (or LRU) policy. When using this policy once the size of the cache reaches a predetermined limit the Least Recently Used value is evicted etc.

For this exercise you should implement a simple caching mechanism using a dictionary (but without an eviction policy).

The cache should use the parameter passed into the factorial() function as the key and return the stored value if one is present.

The logic for this is usually:

1. Look in the cache to see if the key is present
2. If it is return the value
3. If not perform the calculation
4. Store the calculated result for future use
5. Return the value

Note as the factorial() function is exactly that a function; you will need to think about using a global variable to hold the cache.

Once the cache is used with the factorial() function, then each subsequent invocation of the function using a previous value should return almost immediately. This is shown in the sample output before where subsequent method calls return in less than a second.

```
calling   factorial with 150000
returned from   factorial it took 5 seconds
None
calling   factorial with 80000
returned from   factorial it took 1 seconds
None
calling   factorial with 120000
returned from   factorial it took 3 seconds
None
calling   factorial with 150000
returned from   factorial it took 0 seconds
None
calling   factorial with 120000
returned from   factorial it took 0 seconds
None
calling   factorial with 80000
returned from   factorial it took 0 seconds
None
```

Chapter 34
Collection Related Modules

34.1 Introduction

The chapter introduces a feature known as a *list comprehension* in Python.
It then introduces the `collections` and `itertools` modules.

34.2 List Comprehension

This is a very powerful mechanism that can be used to generate new lists.
The syntax of the List Comprehension is:

```
[ <expression> for item in iterable <if optional_condition> ]
```

The new list is formed of the results from the expression. Note that the whole `for` statement and expression is surrounded by the square brackets normally used to create a `List`.

When a List Comprehension is executed it generates a new list by applying the expression to the items in another collection.

For example, given one list of integers, another (new) list can be created using the List Comprehension format:

```
list1 = [1, 2, 3, 4, 5,6]
print('list1:', list1)

list2 = [item + 1 for item in list1]
print('list2:', list2)
```

© Springer Nature Switzerland AG 2019
J. Hunt, *A Beginners Guide to Python 3 Programming*,
Undergraduate Topics in Computer Science,
https://doi.org/10.1007/978-3-030-20290-3_34

which produces the output:

```
list1: [1, 2, 3, 4, 5, 6]
list2: [2, 3, 4, 5, 6, 7]
```

Here the new list is generated by adding 1 to each element in the initial list list1. Essentially, we iterate (loop) over all the elements in the initial list and bind each element in the list to the item variable in turn. The result of the expression item + 1 is then captured, in order, in the new list.

This feature is not limited to processing values in a list; any iterable collection can be used such as Tuples or Sets as the source of the values to process.

Another feature of the List Comprehension is the ability to filter the values passed to the expression using the optional if condition.

For example, if we wish to only consider even numbers for the expression then we can use the optional if statement to filter out all odd numbers:

```
list3 = [item + 1 for item in list1 if item % 2 == 0]
print('list3:', list3)
```

The output from these two lines of code is:

```
list3: [3, 5, 7]
```

Thus only the even numbers were passed to the expression item + 1 resulting in only the values 3, 5 and 7 being generated for the new list.

34.3   The Collections Module

The collections module extends that basic features of the collection-oriented data types within Python with high performance container data types. It provides many useful containers such as:

Name	Purpose
namedtuple()	Factory function for creating tuple subclasses with named fields
deque	List-like container with fast appends and pops on either end
ChainMap	Dict-like class for creating a single view of multiple mappings
Counter	Dict subclass for counting hashable objects
OrderedDict	Dict subclass that remembers the order entries were added
Defaultdict	Dict subclass that calls a factory function to supply missing values
UserDict	Wrapper around dictionary objects for easier dict subclassing
UserList	Wrapper around list objects for easier list subclassing
UserString	Wrapper around string objects for easier string subclassing

As this is not one of the default modules that are automatically loaded for you by Python; you will need to `import` the collection.

As an example, we will use the `Counter` type to efficiently hold multiple copies of the same element. It is efficient because it only holds one copy of each element but keeps a count of the number of times that element has been added to the collection:

```python
import collections

fruit = collections.Counter(['apple', 'orange', 'pear',
'apple', 'orange', 'apple'])
print(fruit)
print(fruit['orange'])
```

The output of this is:

```
Counter({'apple': 3, 'orange': 2, 'pear': 1})
2
```

Which makes the counting behaviour associated with the `Counter` class quite clear.

There are many uses of such a class, for example, it can be used to find out the most frequently used word in an essay; all you have to do is add each word in an essay to the `Counter` and then retrieve the word with the highest count. This can be done using the `Counter` class's `most_common()` method. This method takes a parameter n that indicates how many of the *most common* elements should be returned. If n is ommitted (or `None`) then the method returns an ordered list of elements. Thus to obtain the most common fruit from the above `Counter` collection we can use:

```python
print('fruit.most_common(1):', fruit.most_common(1))
```

Which generates:

```
fruit.most_common(1): [('apple', 3)]
```

You can also perform some mathematical operations with multiple `Counter` objects. For example, you can add and subtract `Counter` objects. You can also obtain a combination of Counters that combines the maximum values from two `Counter` objects. You can also generate an intersection of two Counters. These are all illustrated below:

```
fruit1 = collections.Counter(['apple', 'orange', 'pear',
'orange'])
fruit2 = collections.Counter(['banana', 'apple', 'apple'])

print('fruit1:', fruit1)
print('fruit2:', fruit2)

print('fruit1 + fruit2:', fruit1 + fruit2)
print('fruit1 - fruit2:', fruit1 - fruit2)
# Union (max(fruit1[n], fruit2[n])
print('fruit1 | fruit2:', fruit1 | fruit2)
# Intersection (min(fruit1[n], fruit2[n])
print('fruit1 & fruit2:', fruit1 & fruit2)
```

Which produces:

```
fruit1: Counter({'orange': 2, 'apple': 1, 'pear': 1})
fruit2: Counter({'apple': 2, 'banana': 1})
fruit1 + fruit2: Counter({'apple': 3, 'orange': 2, 'pear': 1,
'banana': 1})
fruit1 - fruit2: Counter({'orange': 2, 'pear': 1})
fruit1 | fruit2: Counter({'apple': 2, 'orange': 2, 'pear': 1,
'banana': 1})
fruit1 & fruit2: Counter({'apple': 1})
```

Once a `Counter` object has been created you can test it to see if an item is present using the `in` keyword, for example:

```
print('apple' in fruit)
```

You can also add items to a `Counter` object by accessing the value using the item as the key, for example:

```
fruit['apple'] = 1 # initialises the number of apples
fruit['apple'] =+ 1 # Adds one to the number of apples
fruit['apple'] =- 1 # Subtracts 1 from the number of apples
```

34.4   The Itertools Module

The `itertools` module is another module that it is worth being familiar with. This module provides a number of useful functions that return iterators constructed in various ways. As there are many different options available it is worth looking at the documentation for a complete list of available functions.

To give you a flavour of some of the facilities available look at the following listing:

```
import itertools

# Connect two iterators together
r1 = list(itertools.chain([1, 2, 3], [2, 3, 4]))
print(r1)

# Create iterator with element repeated specified number of
#   times (possibly infinite)
r2 = list(itertools.repeat('hello', 5))
print(r2)

# Create iterator with elements from first iterator starting
#   where predicate function fails
values = [1, 3, 5, 7, 9, 3, 1]
r3 = list(itertools.dropwhile(lambda x: x < 5, values))
print(r3)

# Create iterator with elements from supplied iterator between
#   the two indexes (use 'None' for second index to go to end)
r4 = list(itertools.islice(values, 3, 6))
print(r4)
```

The output from this code is:

```
[1, 2, 3, 2, 3, 4]
['hello', 'hello', 'hello', 'hello', 'hello']
[5, 7, 9, 3, 1]
[7, 9, 3]
```

34.5   Online Resources

Online resources on the itertools library are listed below:

- https://docs.python.org/3.7/library/itertools.html The standard library documentation on the itertools module.
- https://pymotw.com/3/itertools/index.html The Python module of the week page for itertools.

34.6   Exercises

The aim of this exercise is to create a concordance program in Python using the collections.Counter class.

For the purposes of this exercise a concordance is an alphabetical list of the words present in a text or texts with a count of the number of times that the word occurs.

Your concordance program should include the following steps:

- Ask the user to input a sentence.

- Slit the sentence into individual words (you can use the split() method of the string class for this.

- Use the Counter class to generate a list of all the words in the sentence and the number of times they occur.

- Produce an alphabetic list of the words with their counts. You can obtain a sorted list of the keys using the sorted() function. You can then use a collection.OrderedDict to generate a dictionary that maintains the order in which keys were added.

- Print out the alphabetically ordered list.

An example of how the program might operate is given below:

```
Please enter text to be analysed: cat sat mat hat cat hat cat
Unordered Counter
Counter({'cat': 3, 'hat': 2, 'sat': 1, 'mat': 1})
Ordered Word Count
OrderedDict([('cat', 3), ('hat', 2), ('mat', 1), ('sat', 1)])
```

Chapter 35
ADTs, Queues and Stacks

35.1   Introduction

There are a number of common data structures that are used within computer programs that you might expect to see within Python's list of collection or container classes; these include Queues and Stacks. However, in the basic collection classes these are missing. However, we can either create our own implementations or use one of the extension libraries that provide such collections. In this chapter we will explore implementing our own versions.

35.2   Abstract Data Types

The Queue and Stack are concrete examples of what are known as Abstract Data Types (or ADTs).

An Abstract Data Type (or ADT) is a model for a particular type of data, where a data type is defined by its behaviour (or semantics) from the point of view of the *user* of that data type. This behaviour is typically defined in terms of possible values, possible operations on the data of this type and behaviour of the operations provided by the data type.

An ADT is used to define a common concept that can be implemented by one or more concrete data structures. These implementations may use different internal representations of the data or different algorithms to provide the behaviour; by semantically they meet the descriptions provided by the ADT.

For example, a List ADT may be defined that defines the operations and behaviour that a List like data structure must provide. Concrete implementations may meet the semantics of a List using an underlying array of elements, or by linking elements together with pointers or using some form of hash table (all of which are different internal representations that could be used to implement a list).

© Springer Nature Switzerland AG 2019
J. Hunt, *A Beginners Guide to Python 3 Programming*,
Undergraduate Topics in Computer Science,
https://doi.org/10.1007/978-3-030-20290-3_35

35.3 Data Structures

We will look at how the Python collection types can be used as both a Queue and a Stack but first we need to define both these ADTs:

- **Queue** is an ADT that defines how a collection of entities are managed and maintained. Queues have what is known as a First-In-First-Out (or FIFO) behaviour that is the first entity added to a queue is the first thing removed from the queue. Within the queue the order in which the entities were added is maintained.
- **Stack** is another ADT but this time it has a Last-In-First-Out (or LIFO) behaviour. That is the most recently added entity to the Stack will be the next entity to be removed. Within the stack the order that the entities were added in is maintained.

35.4 Queues

Queues are very widely used within Computer Science and in Software Engineering. They allow data to be held for processing purposes where the guarantee is that the earlier elements added will be processed before later ones.

There are numerous variations on the basic queue operations but in essence all queues provide the following features:

- Queue creation.
- Add an element to the back of the queue (known as enqueuing).
- Remove an element from the front of the queue (known as dequeuing).
- Find out the length of the queue.
- Check to see if the queue is empty.
- Queues can be of fixed size or variable (growable) in size.

The basic behaviour of a queue is illustrated by:

In the above diagram there are five elements in the queue, one element has already been removed from the front and another is being added at the back. Note that when one element is removed from the front of the queue all other element move forward one position. Thus, the element that was the second to the front of the queue becomes the front of the queue when the first element is dequeued.

Many queues also allow features such as:

- *Peek* at the element at the front of the queue (that is see what the element is but do not remove it from the queue).
- Provide *priorities* so that elements with a higher priority are not added to the back of the queue but to a point in the middle of the queue related to their priority.

35.4.1 Python List as a Queue

The Python List container can be used as a queue using the existing operations such as append() and pop(), for example:

```
queue = [] # Create an empty queue
queue.append('task1')
print('initial queue:', queue)
queue.append('task2')
queue.append('task3')
print('queue after additions:', queue)
element1 = queue.pop(0)
print('element retrieved from queue:', element1)
print('queue after removal', queue)
```

The output of which is

```
initial queue: ['task1']
queue after additions: ['task1', 'task2', 'task3']
element retrieved from queue: task1
queue after removal ['task2', 'task3']
```

Note that each *task* was added to the end of the queue, but the first task obtained from the queue was task 1.

35.4.2 Defining a Queue Class

In the last section we used the List class as a way of providing a queue; this approach does work but it is not obvious that we are using the list as a queue (with the exception of the name of the variable that we are holding the List in). For example we have used pop(0) to dequeue an element from the queue and we have used append() to enqueue an element. In addition there is nothing to stop a programmer forgetting to use pop(0) and instead using pop() which is an easy mistake to make and which will remove the most recently added item from the queue.

It would be better to create a new data type and ensure that this data provides the queue like behaviour and hide the list inside this data type.

We can do this by defining our own Queue class in Python.

```python
class Queue:
    def __init__(self):
        self._list = [] # initial internal data

    def enqueue(self, element):
        self._list.append(element)

    def dequeue(self):
        return self._list.pop(0)

    def __len__(self):
        """ Supports the len protocol """
        return len(self._list)

    def is_empty(self):
        return self.__len__() == 0

    def peek(self):
        return self._list[0]

    def __str__(self):
        return 'Queue: ' + str(self._list)
```

This Queue class internally holds a list. Note we are using the convention that the internal list instance variable name is preceded by an underbar ('_') thereby indicating that no one should access it directly.

We have also defined methods for dequeuing and enqueuing elements to the queue. To complete the definition, we have also defined methods for checking the current length of the queue, whether the queue is empty or not, allowing the element at the front of the queue to be peeked at and of course proving a string version of the queue for printing.

Note that the is_empty() method uses the __len__() method when determining if the queue is empty; this is an example of an important idea; only define something once. As we want to use the length of the queue to help determine if the queue is empty, we reuse the __len__() method rather than the code implementing the length method; thus, if the internal representation changes we will not affect the is_empty() method.

The following short program illustrate show the Queue class can be used:

```python
queue = Queue()
print('queue.is_empty():', queue.is_empty())
queue.enqueue('task1')
print('len(queue):', len(queue))
queue.enqueue('task2')
queue.enqueue('task3')
print('queue:', queue)
```

```
print('queue.peek():', queue.peek())
print('queue.dequeue():', queue.dequeue())
print('queue:', queue)
```

The output from this is:

```
initial queue: ['task1']
queue after additions: ['task1', 'task2', 'task3']
element retrieved from queue: task1
queue after removal ['task2', 'task3']
queue.is_empty(): True
len(queue): 1
queue: Queue: ['task1', 'task2', 'task3']
queue.peek(): task1
queue.dequeue(): task1
queue: Queue: ['task2', 'task3']
```

This provides a far more explicit and semantically more meaningful implementation of a Queue than the use of the raw List data structure.

Of course, Python understands this and provides a queue container class in the collections module called deque. This implementation is optimised to be more efficient than the basic List which is not very efficient when it comes to popping elements from the front of the list.

35.5   Stacks

Stacks are another very widely used ADT within computer science and in software applications. They are often used for evaluating mathematical expressions, parsing syntax, for managing intermediate results etc.

The basic facilities provided by a Stack include:

- Stack creation.
- Add an element to the top of the stack (known as pushing onto the stack).
- Remove an element from the top of the stack (known as popping from the stack).
- Find out the length of the stack.
- Check to see if the stack is empty.
- Stacks can be of fixed size or a variable (growable) stack.

The basic behaviour of a stack is illustrated by:

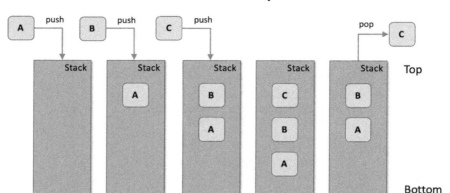

This diagram illustrates the behaviour of a Stack. Each time a new element is pushed onto the Stack, it forces any existing elements further down the stack. Thus the most recent element is at the *top* of the stack and the oldest element is at the *bottom* of the stack. To get to older elements you must first pop newer elements off the top etc.

Many stacks also allow features such as

- *Top* which is often an operation that allows you to peek at the element at the top of the stack (that is see what the element is but do not remove it from the queue).

35.5.1 *Python List as a Stack*

A List may initially appear particularly well suited to being used as a Stack as the basic append() and pop() methods can be used to emulate the stack behaviour. Whatever was most recently appended to the list is the element that will be next returned from the pop() method, for example:

```python
stack = [] # create an empty stack
stack.append('task1')
stack.append('task2')
stack.append('task3')
print('stack:', stack)
top_element = stack.pop()
print('top_element:', top_element)
print('stack:', stack)
```

Which produces the output:

```
stack: ['task1', 'task2', 'task3']
top_element: task3
stack: ['task1', 'task2']
```

This certainly works although when we print out the stack it does not make it clear that 'task3' is at the front of the stack.

In addition, as when using the `List` as a queue ADT it is still possible to apply any of the other methods defined on a `List` to this *stack* and thus we can still write `stack.pop(0)` which would remove the very first element added to the stack.

We could therefore implement a `Stack` class to wrap the list and provide suitable stack like behaviour as we did for the `Queue` class.

35.6   Online Resources

For more information on ADTs, Queues and Stacks see:

- https://en.wikipedia.org/wiki/Abstract_data_type Wikipedia page on ADTs (Abstract Data Types).
- https://en.wikipedia.org/wiki/Queue_(abstract_data_type) Wikipedia page on the Queue data structure.
- https://en.wikipedia.org/wiki/Stack_(abstract_data_type) Wikipedia page on Stacks.
- https://en.wikibooks.org/wiki/Data_Structures/Stacks_and_Queues Wikibooks tutorial on Stack and Queue data structures.

35.7   Exercises

Implement your own `Stack` class following the pattern used for the `Queue` class. The `Stack` class should provide

- A `push(element)` method used to add an element to the `Stack`.
- A `pop()` method to retrieve the top element of the `Stack` (this method removes that element from the stack).
- A `top()` method that allows you to peek at the top element on the stack (it does not remove the element from the stack).
- A `__len__()` method to return the size of the stack. This method also meets the `len` protocol requirements.
- An `is_empty()` method that checks to see if the stack is empty.
- A `__str__()` method used to convert the stack into a string.

Once completed you should be able to run the following test application:

```
stack = Stack()
stack.push('T1')
stack.push('T2')
stack.push('T3')
print('stack:', stack)
print('stack.is_empty():', stack.is_empty())
print('stack.length():', stack.length())
print('stack.top():', stack.top())
print('stack.pop():', stack.pop())
print('stack:', stack)
```

An example of the type of output this might produce is

```
stack: ['task1', 'task2', 'task3']
top_element: task3
stack: ['task1', 'task2']
stack: Stack: ['T1', 'T2', 'T3']
stack.is_empty(): False
stack.length(): 3
stack.top(): T3
stack.pop(): T3
stack: Stack: ['T1', 'T2']
```

Chapter 36
Map, Filter and Reduce

36.1 Introduction

Python provides three functions that are widely used to implement functional programming style solutions in combination with collection container types.

These functions are what are known as higher-order functions that take both a collection and a function that will be applied in various ways to that collection.

This chapter introduces three functions filter(), map() and reduce().

36.2 Filter

The filter() function is a higher order function that takes a function to be used to filter out elements from a collection. The result of the filter() function is a new iterable containing only those elements selected by the test function.

That is, the function passed into filter() is used to test all the elements in the collection that is also passed into filter. Those where the test filter returns True are included in the list of values returned. The result returned is a new iterable consisting of all elements of this list that satisfy the given test function. Note that the order of the elements is preserved.

The syntax of the filter() function is

```
filter(function, iterable)
```

Note that the second argument to the filter function is anything that implements the iterable protocol which includes all Lists, Tuples, Sets and dictionaries or and many other types etc.

The function passed in as the first argument is the test function; it can be a lambda (a function defined in line) or the name of an existing function. The result returned will be an iterable that can be used to create an appropriate collection.

© Springer Nature Switzerland AG 2019
J. Hunt, *A Beginners Guide to Python 3 Programming*,
Undergraduate Topics in Computer Science,
https://doi.org/10.1007/978-3-030-20290-3_36

Here are some examples of using filter with a simple list of integers:

```
data = [1, 3, 5, 2, 7, 4, 10]
print('data:', data)

# Filter for even numbers using a lambda function
d1 = list(filter(lambda i: i % 2 == 0, data))
print('d1:', d1)

def is_even(i):
    return i % 2 == 0

# Filter for even numbers using a named function
d2 = list(filter(is_even, data))
print('d2:', d2)
```

The output from this is:

```
Data: [1, 3, 5, 2, 7, 4, 10]
d1: [2, 4, 10]
d2: [2, 4, 10]
```

One difference between the two examples is that it is more obvious what the role is of the test function in the second example as it is explicitly named (i.e. is_even()), that is the function is testing the integer to see whether it is even or not. The in-line lambda function does exactly the same, but it is necessary to understand the test function itself to work out what it is doing.

It is also worth pointing out that defining a named function such as is_even() may actually pollute the namespace of the module as there is now a function that others might decide to use even though the original designer of this code never expected anyone else to use the is_even() function. This is why lambda functions are often used with filter() (and indeed map() and reduce()).

Of course, you are not just limited to fundamental built in types such as integers, or real numbers or indeed strings; any type can be used. For example, if we have a class Person such as:

```
class Person:

    def __init__(self, name, age):
        self.name = name
        self.age = age

    def __str__(self):
        return 'Person(' + self.name +
                        ', ' + str(self.age) + ')'
```

Then we can create a list of instances of the class Person and then filter out all those over 21:

```
data = [Person('Alun', 54), Person('Niki', 21), Person('Megan',
19)]
for p in data:
    print(p, end=', ')

print('\n-----')

# Use a lambda to filter out People over 21
d3 = list(filter(lambda p: p.age <= 21, data))
for p in d3:
    print(p, end=', ')
```

The output from this is:

```
Person(Alun, 54), Person(Niki, 21), Person(Megan, 19),
-----
Person(Niki, 21), Person(Megan, 19),
```

36.3 Map

Map is another higher order function available in Python. Map applies the supplied function to all items in the iterable(s) passed to it. It returns a new iterable of the results generated by the applied function.

It is the functional equivalent of a for loop applied to an iterable where the results of each iteration round the for loop are gathered up.

The map function is very widely used within the functional programming world and it is certainly worth becoming familiar with it.

The function signature of map is

```
map(function, iterable, ...)
```

Note that the second argument to the map function is anything that implements the iterable protocol.

The function passed into the map function is applied to each item in the iterable passed as the second argument. The result returned from the function is then gathered up into the iterable object returned from map.

The following example applies a function that adds one to a number, to a list of integers:

```
data = [1, 3, 5, 2, 7, 4, 10]
print('data:', data)

# Apply the lambda function to each element in the list
# using the map function
d1 = list(map(lambda i: i + 1, data))
print('d1', d1)

def add_one(i):
    return i + 1

# Apply the add_one function to each element in the
# list using the map function
d2 = list(map(add_one, data))
print('d2:', d2)
```

The output of the above example is:

```
data: [1, 3, 5, 2, 7, 4, 10]
d1 [2, 4, 6, 3, 8, 5, 11]
d2: [2, 4, 6, 3, 8, 5, 11]
```

As with the filter() function, the function to be applied can either be defined in line as a lambda or it can be named function as in add_one(). Either can be used, the advantage of the add_one() named function is that it makes the intent of the function explicit; however, it does pollute the namespace of functions defined.

Note that more than one iterable can be passed to the map function. If multiple iterables are passed to map, then the function passed in must take as many parameters as there are iterables. This feature is useful if you want to merge data held in two or more collections into a single collection.

For example, let us assume that we want to add the numbers in one list to the numbers in another list, we can write a function that takes two parameters and returns the result of adding these two numbers together:

```
data1 = [1, 3, 5, 7]
data2 = [2, 4, 6, 8]

result = list(map(lambda x, y: x + y, data1, data2))
print(result)
```

The output printed by this is:

```
[3, 7, 11, 15]
```

As with the filter function, it is not only built-in types such as numbers that can be processed by the function supplied to map; we can also use user defined types such as the class Person. For example, if we wanted to collect all the ages for a list of Person we could write:

```
data = [Person('John', 54), Person('Phoebe', 21),
Person('Adam', 19)]
ages = list(map(lambda p: p.age, data))
print(ages)
```

Which creates a list of the ages of the three people:

```
[54, 21, 19]
```

36.4 Reduce

The reduce() function is the last higher order function that can be used with collections of data that we will look at.

The reduce() function applies a function to an iterable and combines the result returned for each element together into a single result.

This function was part of the core Python 2 language but was not included into the core of Python 3. This is partly because Guido van Rossum believed (probably correctly) that the applicability of reduce is quite limited, but where it is useful it is very useful. Although it has to be said that some developers try and shoe horn reduce() into situations that just make the implementation very hard to understand—remember always aim to keep it simple.

To use reduce() in Python 3 you need to import it from the functools module. One point that is sometimes misunderstood with reduce() is that the function passed into reduce takes two parameters, which are the previous result and the next value in the sequence; it then returns the result of applying some operation to these parameters.

The signature of the functools.reduce function is:

```
functools.reduce(function, iterable[, initializer])
```

Note that optionally you can provide an initialiser that is used to provide an initial value for the result.

One obvious use of reduce() is to sum all the values in a list:

```
from functools import reduce

data = [1, 3, 5, 2, 7, 4, 10]
result = reduce(lambda total, value: total + value, data)
print(result)
```

The result printed out for this is 32.

Although it might appear that reduce() is only useful for numbers such as integers; it can be used with other types as well. For example, let us assume that we want to calculate the average age for a list of people, we could use reduce to add together all the ages and then divide by the length of the data list we are processing:

```
data = [Person('John', 54), Person('Phoebe', 21),
        Person('Adam', 19)]

total_age = reduce(lambda running_total, person: running_total
+ person.age, data, 0)

average_age = total_age // len(data)
print('Average age:', average_age)
```

In this code example, we have a data list of three people. We then use the `reduce`
function to apply a lambda to the data list. The lambda takes a `running_total`
and adds a person's age to that total. The value zero is used to initialise this running
total. When the lambda is applied to the data list, we will add 54, 21 and 19 together.
We then divide the final result returned by the length of the data list (3) using the
`//` operator which will use `floor()` division to return a whole integer (rather than a
real number such as 3.11). Finally, we print out the average age:

```
Average age: 31
```

36.5   Online Resources

More information on *map*, *filter* and *reduce* can be found using the following online
resources:

- http://book.pythontips.com/en/latest/map_filter.html Summary of map, filter and
  reduce.
- https://www.w3schools.com/python/ref_func_map.asp The W3C schools map()
  function tutorial.
- https://www.w3schools.com/python/ref_func_filter.asp The W3 schools filter()
  function tutorial.
- https://pymotw.com/3/functools/index.html The Python Module of the Week
  page including reduce().
- https://docs.python.org/3.7/library/functools.html The Python Standard Library
  documentation for functors including `reduce()`.

36.6   Exercises

This exercise aims to allow you to use map and filter with your `Stack` class.
    Take the `Stack` that you developed in the last chapter and make it iterable. This
can be done by implementing the `__iter__()` method from the iterable protocol.
As a list is held internally to the `Stack` this could be implemented by returning an
iterable wrapper around the list, for example:

```
def __iter__(self):
    return iter(self._list)
```

Now define a function that will check to see if a string passed to it starts with 'Job'; if it does return `True` if not return `False`. Call this function `is_job()`.

Also define a function that will prepend the string 'item': to the string passed in and will then return this as the result of the function. Call this function `add_item()`.

You should now be able to use the `filter()` and `map()` functions with the `Stack` class as shown below:

```
stack = Stack()
stack.push('Task1')
stack.push('Task2')
stack.push('Job1')
stack.push('Task3')
stack.push('Job2')
print('stack contents:', stack)

# Apply functions to stack contents using map and filter
new_list = list(map(add_item, stack))
print('new_list:', new_list)

filtered_list = list(filter(is_job, stack))
print('filtered_list: ', filtered_list)
```

Chapter 37
TicTacToe Game

37.1 Introduction

In this chapter we will explore the creation of a simple TicTacToe (or Noughts and Crosses) game using an Object Oriented approach. This example utilises:

- Python classes, methods and instance variables/attributes.
- Abstract Base Classes and an abstract method.
- Python Properties.
- Python lists.
- A simple piece of game playing logic.
- While loops, for loops and if statements for flow of control behaviour.

The aim of the game is to make a line of 3 counters (either X or O) across a 3 by 3 grid. Each player takes a turn to place a counter. The first player to achieve a line of three (horizontal, vertically or diagonally) wins.

37.2 Classes in the Game

We will begin by identifying the key classes in the game. Note that there is not necessarily a right or wrong answer here; although one set of classes may be more obvious or easier to understand than another.

In our case we will start with what data we will need to represent for our TicTacToe game as recommended back in the 'Introduction to Object Orientation' chapter.

Our key data elements include:

- the tic-tac-toe board itself,
- the players involved in the game (both computer and human),
- the state of the game, i.e. whose go it is and whether someone has won,

© Springer Nature Switzerland AG 2019
J. Hunt, *A Beginners Guide to Python 3 Programming*,
Undergraduate Topics in Computer Science,
https://doi.org/10.1007/978-3-030-20290-3_37

- the moves being made by the players etc.
- the counters used which are traditionally O and X (hence the alternative name 'Noughts and Crosses').

Based on an analysis of the data one possible set of classes is shown below:

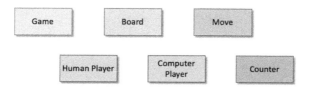

In this diagram we have

- Game the class that will hold the board, players and the core game playing logic,
- Board this is a class that represents the current state of the TicTacToe board or grid within the game,
- Human Player this class represents the human player involved in the game,
- Computer Player this class represents the computer playing the game,
- Move this class represents a particular move made by a player,
- Counter which can be used to represent the counters to play with; this will be either X or Y.

We can refine this a little further. For example, much of what constituents a player will be common for both the human and the computer player. We can therefore introduce a new class Player, with both Computer Player and Human Player inheriting from this class, for example:

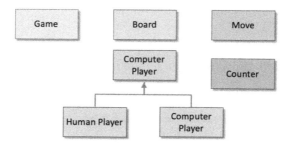

In terms of the data held by the classes we can say:

- Game has a board, a human and a computer player. It also has links to the current player and an attribute indicating whether a player has won.
- Board holds a 3 by 3 grid of cells. Each cell can be empty or contains a counter.
- Player Each player has a current counter and can see the board.

- `Move` represent a players selected move; it therefore holds the counter being played and the location to put the counter in.
- `Counter` holds a label indicating either X or O.

We can now update the class diagram with data and links between the classes:

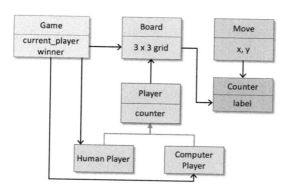

At this point it looks as though the `HumanPlayer` and `ComputerPlayer` classes are unnecessary as they do not hold any data of there own. However, in this case the behaviour for the `HumanPlayer` and the `ComputerPlayer` are quite different.

The `HumanPlayer` class will prompt the human user to select the next move. In contrast the `ComputerPlayer` class must implement an algorithm which will allow the next move to be generated within the program.

Other behavioural aspects of the classes are:

- `Game` this must hold the overall logic of the game. It must also be able to select which player will go first. We will also allow the human player to select which counter they will play with (X or O). This logic will also be placed within the `Game` class.
- `Board` The Board class must allow a move to be made but it must also be able to verify that a move is legal (as cell is empty) and whether a game has been won or whether there is a draw. This latter logic could be located within the game instead; however the `Board` holds the data necessary to determine a win or a draw and thus we are locating the logic with the data.

We can now add the behavioural aspects of the classes to the diagram. Note we have followed the convention here for separating the data and behaviour into different areas within a class box:

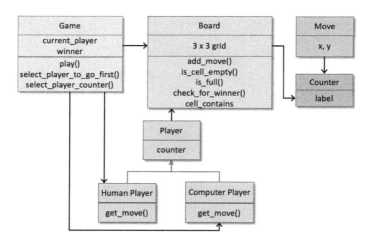

We are now ready to look at the Python implementation of our class design.

37.3   Counter Class

The Counter class is given below; it is a data oriented class, sometimes referred to as a *value* type. This is because it holds *values* but does not include any behaviour.

```python
class Counter:
    """ Represents a Counter used on the board """

    def __init__(self, string):
        self.label = string

    def __str__(self):
        return self.label
# Set up Counter Globals
X = Counter('X')
O = Counter('O')
```

We have also defined two constants X and Y to represent the X and O counters used in the game.

37.4   Move Class

The Move class is given below; it is another a data oriented class or *value* type.

```
class Move:
    """ Represents a move made by a player """

    def __init__(self, counter, x, y):
        self.x = x
        self.y = y
        self.counter = counter
```

37.5   The Player Class

The root of the Player class hierarchy is presented below. This class is an *abstract* class in which the get_move() method is marked as being *abstract*. The class maintains a reference to the board and to a counter.

```
class Player(metaclass=ABCMeta):
    """ Abstract class representing a Player
        and their counter """

    def __init__(self, board):
        self.board = board
        self._counter = None

    @property
    def counter(self):
        """ Represents Players Counter - may be X or Y"""
        return self._counter

    @counter.setter
    def counter(self, value):
        self._counter = value

    @abstractmethod
    def get_move(self): pass

    def __str__(self):
        return self.__class__.__name__ + '[' +
    str(self.counter) + ']'
```

Note that counter is defined as a Python property.

The class Player is extended by the classes HumanPlayer and ComputerPlayer.

37.6   The HumanPlayer Class

This class extends the abstract `Player` class and defines the `get_move()` method. This method returns a `Move` object representing the counter to be placed and the location in the 3×3 grid in which to place the counter. Note that the `get_move()` method relies on a reference being maintained by the player to the board so that it can check that the selected location is empty.

To support the `get_move()` method a `_get_user_input()` method has been defined. This method could have been defined as a stand alone function as it is really independent of the `HumanPlayer`; however it has been defined within this class to keep the related behaviour together. It also follows the Python convention by starting the method name with an underbar (_) which indicates that the method is private and should not be accessed from outside of the class.

```python
class HumanPlayer(Player):
    """ Represents a Human Player and their behaviour """

    def __init__(self, board):
        super().__init__(board)

    def _get_user_input(self, prompt):
        invalid_input = True
        while invalid_input:
            print(prompt)
            user_input = input()
            if not user_input.isdigit():
                print('Input must be a number')
            else:
                user_input_int = int(user_input)
                if user_input_int < 1 or user_input_int > 3:
                    print('input must be a number in the range 1 to 3')
                else:
                    invalid_input = False
        return user_input_int - 1

    def get_move(self):
        """ Allow the human player to enter their move """
        while True:
            row = self._get_user_input('Please input the row: ')
            column = self._get_user_input('Please input the column: ')

            if self.board.is_empty_cell(row, column):
                return Move(self.counter, row, column)
            else:
                print('That position is not free')
                print('Please try again')
```

37.7 The ComputerPlayer Class

This class provides an algorithmic implementation of the get_move() method.
This algorithm tries to find the best empty grid location in which to place the
counter. If it cannot find one of these locations free then it randomly finds an empty
cell to fill. The get_move() method could be replaced with whatever game
playing logic you want.

```python
class ComputerPlayer(Player):
    """ Implements algorithms for playing game """

    def __init__(self, board):
        super().__init__(board)

    def randomly_select_cell(self):
        """ Use a simplistic random selection approach
        to find a cell to fill. """
        while True:
            # Randomly select the cell
            row = random.randint(0, 2)
            column = random.randint(0, 2)
            # Check to see if the cell is empty
            if self.board.is_empty_cell(row, column):
                return Move(self.counter, row, column)

    def get_move(self):
        """ Provide a very simple algorithm for selecting a
move"""
        if self.board.is_empty_cell(1, 1):
            # Choose the center
            return Move(self.counter, 1, 1)
        elif self.board.is_empty_cell(0, 0):
            # Choose the top left
            return Move(self.counter, 0, 0)
        elif self.board.is_empty_cell(2, 2):
            # Choose the bottom right
            return Move(self.counter, 2, 2)
        elif self.board.is_empty_cell(0, 2):
            # Choose the top right
            return Move(self.counter, 0, 2)
        elif self.board.is_empty_cell(0, 2):
            # Choose the top right
            return Move(self.counter, 2, 0)
        else:
            return self.randomly_select_cell()
```

37.8   The Board Class

The Board class holds a 3 by 3 grid of cells in the form of a list of lists. It also defines the methods used to verify or make a move on the board. The check_for_winner() method determines if there is a winner given the current board positions.

```python
class Board:
    """ The ticTacToe board"""

    def __init__(self):
        # Set up the 3 by 3 grid of cells
        self.cells = [[' ', ' ', ' '], [' ', ' ', ' '], [' ',
' ', ' ']]
        self.separator = '\n' + ('-' * 11) + '\n'

    def __str__(self):
        row1 = ' ' + str(self.cells[0][0]) + ' | ' +
str(self.cells[0][1]) + ' | ' + str(self.cells[0][2])
        row2 = ' ' + str(self.cells[1][0]) + ' | ' +
str(self.cells[1][1]) + ' | ' + str(self.cells[1][2])
        row3 = ' ' + str(self.cells[2][0]) + ' | ' +
str(self.cells[2][1]) + ' | ' + str(self.cells[2][2])
        return row1 + self.separator + row2 + self.separator +
row3

    def add_move(self, move):
        """ A a move to the board """
        row = self.cells[move.x]
        row[move.y] = move.counter

    def is_empty_cell(self, row, column):
        """ Check to see if a cell is empty or not"""
        return self.cells[row][column] == ' '

    def cell_contains(self, counter, row, column):
        """ Check to see if a cell contains the provided
counter """
        return self.cells[row][column] == counter

    def is_full(self):
        """ Check to see if the board is full or not """
        for row in range(0, 3):
            for column in range(0, 3):
                if self.is_empty_cell(row, column):
                    return False
        return True

    def check_for_winner(self, player):
        """ Check to see if a player has won or not """
        c = player.counter
        return (# across the top
                (self.cell_contains(c, 0, 0) and
```

```
self.cell_contains(c, 0, 1) and self.cell_contains(c, 0, 2)) or
                    # across the middle
                    (self.cell_contains(c, 1, 0) and
self.cell_contains(c, 1, 1) and self.cell_contains(c, 1, 2)) or
                    # across the bottom
                    (self.cell_contains(c, 2, 0) and
self.cell_contains(c, 2, 1) and self.cell_contains(c, 2, 2)) or
                    # down the left side
                    (self.cell_contains(c, 0, 0) and
self.cell_contains(c, 1, 0) and self.cell_contains(c, 2, 0)) or
                    # down the middle
                    (self.cell_contains(c, 0, 1) and
self.cell_contains(c, 1, 1) and self.cell_contains(c, 2, 1)) or
                    # down the right side
                    (self.cell_contains(c, 0, 2) and
self.cell_contains(c, 1, 2) and self.cell_contains(c, 2, 2)) or
                    # diagonal
                    (self.cell_contains(c, 0, 0) and
self.cell_contains(c, 1, 1) and self.cell_contains(c, 2, 2)) or
                    # other diagonal
                    (self.cell_contains(c, 0, 2) and
self.cell_contains(c, 1, 1) and self.cell_contains(c, 2, 0)))
```

37.9   The Game Class

The Game class implements the main game playing loop. The play() method will
loop until a winner is found. Each time round the loop one of the players takes a
turn and makes a move. A check is then made to see if the game has been won.

```
class Game:
    """ Contains the Game Playing Logic """

    def __init__(self):
        self.board = Board()
        self.human = HumanPlayer(self.board)
        self.computer = ComputerPlayer(self.board)
        self.next_player = None
        self.winner = None

    def select_player_counter(self):
        """ Let the player select their counter """
        counter = ''
        while not (counter == 'X' or counter == 'O'):
            print('Do you want to be X or O?')
            counter = input().upper()
            if counter != 'X' and counter != 'O':
                print('Input must be X or O')
        if counter == 'X':
            self.human.counter = X
            self.computer.counter = O
```

```
        else:
            self.human.counter = O
            self.computer.counter = X

    def select_player_to_go_first(self):
        """ Randomly selects who will play first -
        the human or the computer."""
        if random.randint(0, 1) == 0:
            self.next_player = self.human
        else:
            self.next_player = self.computer

    def play(self):
        """ Main game playing loop """
        print('Welcome to TicTacToe')
        self.select_player_counter()
        self.select_player_to_go_first()
        print(self.next_player, 'will play first first')
        while self.winner is None:
            # Human players move
            if self.next_player == self.human:
                print(self.board)
                print('Your move')
                move = self.human.get_move()
                self.board.add_move(move)
                if self.board.check_for_winner(self.human):
                    self.winner = self.human
                else:
                    self.next_player = self.computer
            # Computers move
            else:
                print('Computers move')
                move = self.computer.get_move()
                self.board.add_move(move)
                if self.board.check_for_winner(self.computer):
                    self.winner = self.computer
                else:
                    self.next_player = self.human
            # Check for a winner or a draw
            if self.winner is not None:
                print('The Winner is the ' + str(self.winner))
            elif self.board.is_full():
                print('Game is a Tie')
                break
        print(self.board)
```

37.10   Running the Game

To run the game we need to instantiate the Game class and then call the play()
method on the object obtained. For example:

```
def main():
    game = Game()
    game.play()

if __name__ == '__main__':
    main()
```

A sample output from running the game is given below in which the human users goes first.

```
Welcome to TicTacToe
Do you want to be X or O? X
ComputerPlayer[Y] will play first first
Computers move
   |   |
-----------
   | Y |
-----------
   |   |
Your move
Please input the row: 1
Please input the column: 1
Computers move
 X |   |
-----------
   | Y |
-----------
   |   | Y
Your move
Please input the row: 2
Please input the column: 1
Computers move
 X |   | Y
-----------
 X | Y |
-----------
   |   | Y
Your move
Please input the row: 3
Please input the column: 1
The Winner is the HumanPlayer[X]
 X |   | Y
-----------
 X | Y |
-----------
 X |   | Y
```

Correction to: Functions in Python

Correction to:
Chapter 11 in: J. Hunt,
A Beginners Guide to Python 3 Programming,
Undergraduate Topics in Computer Science,
https://doi.org/10.1007/978-3-030-20290-3_11

In the original version of the book, the text "Rugby" has been replaced with "Python" in Chapter 11 page 126. The corrections have been carried out in the chapter. The erratum chapter and the book have been updated with the change.

The updated version of this chapter can be found at
https://doi.org/10.1007/978-3-030-20290-3_11

CPSIA information can be obtained
at www.ICGtesting.com
Printed in the USA
LVHW081418160222
711289LV00007B/175